Follow On:
50 Years of Rangers in Europe

Follow On:
50 Years of Rangers in Europe

Iain Duff

Fort Publishing Ltd

First published in 2006 by Fort Publishing Ltd, Old Belmont House,
12 Robsland Avenue, Ayr, KA7 2RW

Cover photographs courtesy of Newsquest

Graphics by Mark Blackadder

Typeset by Senga Fairgrieve

Printed by Bell and Bain Ltd, Glasgow

ISBN 10: 1-905769-03-2
ISBN 13: 978-1-905769-03-2

This book is dedicated to my dad John, who introduced me to European football when I was seven, and to my son Callum, who has all this to look forward to.

Contents

Preface

This is the story of Rangers in Europe. Fifty years ago Scotland's dominant football club took to the international stage for the first time, putting their domestic superiority to the test against the elite of European football. The club's debut in the fledgling European Cup began with hope and expectation but ended in controversy and disappointment – setting in motion a roller-coaster ride of emotion that has continued for five decades.

Almost three hundred games have passed since that first fiery culture clash against French champions Nice. Through it all, there has been plenty of joy and lots of despair, not to mention political intrigue, international incidents and even allegations of corruption. From the highs of the 1972 European Cup Winners Cup triumph in Barcelona to the lows of humiliating defeats at the hands of minnows like Gornik Zabrze, Levski Sofia and Viktoria Zizkov, there has rarely been a dull moment over the last fifty years.

This book relives the all the triumphs and the disasters and, through the recollections of players and fans, tells the story of Rangers' quest for glory in Europe. It's not a sanitised version of events, nor does it focus only on the positive achievements. As miserable as they are for the Rangers fans to endure, every early exit, every embarrassing defeat, is as much a part of the rich tapestry that is Rangers in Europe as every triumph over Juventus, Parma, Leeds United or Bayern Munich.

The story is told chronologically, looking in detail at every match played. It also features the off-field stories that in many cases were as dramatic as the events on the park. I hope that the first-hand accounts from players and supporters add colour to the match reports and reflect in some way what it is like to play and follow Rangers in Europe.

I was born a few months before Rangers won their only European trophy, so my memories of the victory over Dynamo Moscow are somewhat vague.

My first experience of European football came seven years later, when I sat in the old Centenary Stand at Ibrox and watched Rangers grind out a drab 1–0 win over Lillestrom of Norway. I have since checked the records to discover that Gordon Smith scored the only goal and I was one of 25,000 hardy souls inside the partially redeveloped stadium. I don't remember much about the match at all to be honest, other than the fact that all the foreigners seemed to have beards or droopy moustaches and were incredibly tall. But my match programme provided me with a fascinating list of odd names that looked nothing like anything I had ever seen before and for several years Lillestrom was the only place in Norway I could name. In fact, watching European football for more than twenty-five years has taught me just about everything I know about geography.

That game may not have been a classic but it was enough to get me hooked. It's difficult to put your finger on why it should be more enjoyable to watch a team of Scandinavian part-timers attempt to kill the game by putting ten players in defence than watching a team of Scottish part-timers do the same. But it is. And that is why, despite the desperate disappointments that are always around the corner, thousands pack out Ibrox for every European game and why many of them use up all their work holidays and spend all their savings on following Rangers around the Continent.

Many people have helped me put this book together. My thanks go especially to Eric Caldow, Harold Davis, Jimmy Millar, Sandy Jardine, Alex MacDonald, Kai Johansen, Gordon Smith, Bobby Russell, Robert Prytz, Dave McPherson, Sergei Baltacha, Bill Martin, Michel Oreggia, Mark Dingwall, Jim Hannah, Gillian Dorricott, Nick Peel and Ronnie Esplin. Thanks also to the many Rangers supporters who assisted me and who gave up their time to share their stories. Some are named in the book, while others preferred to keep their contributions anonymous.

I have read hundreds of newspaper, magazine and football-programme articles from around Europe in compiling the book. I am grateful for the help provided to me by the staff at the Central Library in Edinburgh for helping me trawl through the archives. Also, *merci beaucoup* and *viel dank* to those who have helped me translate articles from various European languages.

I've read many other books as part of my research, and while it would be impossible to list all of them, some are worthy of mention: *We Will Follow Rangers* by Hugh Taylor (1962); *Playing For Rangers* edited by Ken Gallagher (1964); *Rebirth of The Blues* by Chick Young (1987); *Rangers in Europe* by Alan Fairley (1991); *Blue Heaven: The Ibrox Trophy Room* by Willie Thornton (1991); *Blue And True: Unforgettable Rangers Days* by Roddy Forsyth (1996); *Glasgow Rangers: Player By Player* by Bob Ferrier and Robert McElroy (1999); *Rangers: The Waddell Years* by Stephen Halliday (1999); *The Rough Guide To European Football* (1999); *Rangers: The Managers* by David Mason (2000); *The European Cup: An Illustrated History* by Rab McWilliam (2000); *Barcelona Here We Come* by Ronnie Esplin (2002); *L.A. Confidential* by Lorenzo Amoruso (2002); *Tor! The Story of German Football* by Ulrich Hesse-Lichtenberger (2003); *And Smith Did Score . . .* by Gordon Smith (2005); *My Story* by John Greig (2005); and *Engineering Archie* by Simon Inglis (2005).

Finally, to my wife: thank you for your unstinting support and assistance and for giving up so many weekends and evenings for the cause. I couldn't have done it without you.

Iain Duff
July 2006

1

In the Beginning

When French journalist Gabriel Hanot dreamt up the idea of a competition to determine the best football team in Europe, he probably harboured lofty notions that the tournament would be a Corinthian festival of sport, bringing the Continent together in a post-war spirit of cross-border friendship and understanding. If he managed to get along to any of the three matches between Rangers and his fellow countrymen OGC Nice in 1956 he would surely have wondered just what had gone wrong.

To describe the contest as eventful would be a serious understatement. The tie featured the full gamut of controversies: crowd trouble, foul play, brawling players, sendings-off, a questionable penalty, bizarre refereeing decisions, travel chaos and even dreadful weather. For Rangers, the end result in their European debut, a 3–1 play-off defeat, was all too typical of what was to follow in later years. Glorious failure, defeat snatched from the jaws of victory, call it what you will, it was a feeling Rangers supporters would soon become accustomed to on their annual jaunts to foreign lands.

But all that was in the future when the European Cup came into being in 1955. With its midweek floodlit matches between opponents from distant corners of the Continent, it quickly became a favourite among fans.

Hanot, editor of the sports magazine *L'Équipe*, proposed the creation of a competition in a bid to settle arguments over who was the best team in Europe. English newspapers had declared Wolverhampton Wanderers the best in the world after they defeated highly-rated Hungarian side Honved in December 1954. Unhappy at this somewhat presumptuous claim, Hanot decided to come up with a contest to prove once and for all who the top team was. The magazine drew up proposals for a knockout competition and a list of possible participants. Surprisingly, more than half the teams – including Hibernian of Scotland – were not even the current champions in their domestic leagues.

The football establishment was wary of the proposals, with Europe's governing body, UEFA, initially refusing to organize the contest. They preferred a rather bizarre competition, which had been proposed by the civic leaders of European cities that held annual trade fairs; it became the Inter-Cities Fairs Cup. Fearing a damaging split FIFA stepped in and, following a meeting, brokered an agreement that three competitions should be given official approval: *L'Équipe*'s tournament (to be called the European Champion Clubs' Cup); the Inter-Cities Fairs Cup; and the Mitropa Cup, proposed by Central European countries.

Finally, in September 1955, the first European Champion Clubs' Cup match took place between Portugal's Sporting Lisbon and Partizan, from Yugoslavia. English champions Chelsea were due to take part and were actually drawn against Djurgarden of Sweden. But under pressure from the Football League, the Londoners withdrew and their place went to Gwardia Warsaw.

Hibernian, with their 'Famous Five' forward line, and not champions Aberdeen, were invited to represent Scotland in the inaugural competition and the Edinburgh club acquitted themselves surprisingly well, reaching the semi-final stage. The following year, UEFA insisted that domestic-league winners would qualify for the tournament, and so Rangers, who had just won their twenty-ninth league title, became the first Scottish champions to take part.

At the start of season 1956/57 the Ibrox club, under manager Scot Symon, was going through a transitional period that would eventually blossom into an era of domestic supremacy that was to last until the mid-sixties. Symon – full name James Scotland Symon – was a former Rangers player, and had taken the reins in 1954 as the chosen successor of legendary manager William Struth. Struth had been manager of Rangers for thirty-four years, cementing the club's position as the biggest and best in the country, and controlling virtually every facet of life at Ibrox. But in the last few years of his tenure, Rangers had begun to slip from their position of dominance. By the mid-fifties, Struth's influence was on the wane, along with his health, and his team was growing old together. After being rushed to hospital after a fall at Ibrox on New Year's Day 1954, Struth realised that his time as manager had come to an end. Four months later he tendered his resignation, having already identified Scot Symon as his successor.

Symon had signed for Rangers as a player in 1938, and was a key figure in the club's domination of Scottish football for the next nine years. He also played in the Rangers team that defeated Celtic 8–1 in 1943, at the height of the second world war. On his retirement he moved into management with East Fife, leading that unfashionable side to promotion in his first season and then, to everyone's surprise, to a League Cup win in his second.

When Symon got the call to take over at Ibrox in 1954 he knew he faced a mammoth task. Rangers were in turmoil, having endured one of their worst-ever seasons. The squad needed to be rebuilt and by 1955 a new team was taking shape. Great names from the days of Struth rubbed shoulders with some of the younger players introduced by Symon. Defensive stalwarts George Young and Ian McColl, South African penalty king Johnny Hubbard, goalkeeper George Niven and Ulsterman Billy Simpson were all Struth players while youngsters like Bobby Shearer, Eric Caldow and Alex Scott were brought in by Symon and would feature heavily in the years to come. The mixture of old and new was to prove successful, with Rangers claiming the 1955/56 title after going on a lengthy unbeaten run. That league win granted the Light Blues the right to compete in the European Cup for the first time, and Symon's men were handed a trip to the south of France in the draw for the first round.

Nice – or Olympique Gymnaste Club de Nice Cote d'Azur to give them their full title – were in the midst of the most successful spell in their history when they were drawn against Rangers. Their 1956 triumph in the league championship was the third of four achieved in that decade, along with two wins in the French Cup. It was certainly a golden era for their followers; since 1959 the club has won nothing, apart from a solitary cup final secured in a penalty shoot-out against Guingamp in 1997.

Having comfortably disposed of Danish champions Aarhus 6–2 over two legs in the preliminary round of the 1956/57 European Cup, it was a bewildered and bedraggled-looking bunch of Frenchmen who arrived for a training session at Ibrox on the eve of the first-round proper. International travel was still in its infancy in the 1950s and Nice were beset with problems as they tried to get to Scotland. The players were grounded by fog in Paris, finally touching down in London at 7.15 p.m., four hours after they should have been in Glasgow. The party was then informed there were no seats available on any flights north that night, while accommodation in the capital was impossible to find because the motor show was taking place. The only option was to take the 10.15 night train from King's Cross to Dundee, changing at Edinburgh at six in the morning, before catching another train to Glasgow.

It was hardly the ideal preparation for a top-class football match, but Nice manager Lucien Lapayre was unconcerned. As his players, resplendent in black-and-red club tracksuits, posed for photos on the platform at King's Cross, he declared, 'I think there will be only one goal between us when we meet. Naturally I hope that we will have the one extra goal.'

His confidence seemed well placed as the Frenchmen held a training session the next day, only a few hours after their gruelling trip. After a short period of exercise, the players turned to ball practice, putting on a ninety-minute exhibition of passing, dribbling and body swerving that left observers as breathless as the players. It was an eye-opener for the Rangers officials and assorted journalists, who had never seen anything like it before, and they were suitably impressed. Yet the prevailing opinion was that while the Nice players would be clever with the ball and would possess all the usual Continental artistry, Rangers would prove too strong over the two legs.

On 24 October 1956, a torrid night of rain and hailstones, 65,000 brave souls turned out to witness the first foray by Rangers into European football and, according to the *Glasgow Herald*, were treated to 'a disgraceful exhibition of fouling and other misbehaviour'. English referee Arthur Ellis, one of the top officials in the game at the time, was at the centre of much of the drama as the game descended into chaos.

With Argentinians and Spaniards in the Nice team, as well as Frenchmen, Ellis struggled to cope with the language barriers as well as the roughhouse tactics the foreign players employed. Nice were guilty of persistent fouling, pushing, elbowing, obstruction and dissent, with defenders Nani and Gonzalez the prime offenders. Rangers were by no means innocent; a clash shortly after the start of the match between Bobby Shearer and Nurenberg set the tone for the game, and Logie and Baird were lucky not to be sent off, according to newspaper reports.

When football sporadically broke out between the hostilities, the French, as predicted, adopted a rhythmic passing game, which initially had little impact. Rangers dominated the opening quarter of the game, and went close with a powerful twenty-yard shot from Baird that was saved by Colonna. However, the French opened the scoring in the twenty-third minute with a solo effort from outside left Faivre and took a grip of the game. Five minutes before the break, though, Max Murray scored the first-ever Rangers goal in European football, equalizing after taking a pass from Baird. Rangers could even have gone in at the interval ahead had Colonna not been able to pull off a good save from a free kick.

Shortly after half-time, as the game threatened to descend into a free-for-all, an increasingly vexed Ellis called a conference of the two teams on the pitch and warned Nice in particular that he would 'stand no more nonsense'. The message, relayed through a hurriedly summoned interpreter, seemed to do the trick and proceedings resumed, albeit in a more tense atmosphere. Rangers were well in control and could have scored at least three more goals in the second half, but had to make do with a Billy Simpson header after sixty-one minutes following a Murray cross.

At 2–1 to the Ibrox men, the scoring may have been over but the drama was not, with the match ending in shambolic scenes as the referee inexplicably blew for full-time a full five minutes early. The players and officials disappeared from view, leaving the crowd bemused and less than happy. When the mistake was eventually discovered the players had to be recalled to the pitch, with Eric Caldow having to be retrieved from the bath. The Rangers full back was first in the water as he had an important engagement the following day. He recalled: 'I was in a rush to get away for my brother's wedding in Cumnock where I was to be best man. The whistle was blown and naturally when the whistle goes you get off as quick as you can – but the man had made a mistake.'

After the match, Ellis – who later officiated in the farcical television series *It's A Knockout* – offered no explanation for his actions, but put forward a theory for the bad behaviour of the Nice players. He declared, 'I feel that one of the reasons for the French team indulging in the tackling they did was the high bonus they were on to make sure of victory. If the figures I hear are paid as bonuses in Continental club football games are correct, it is not to be wondered at that so many of their matches are played out on a basis of victory at any price.'

While the Scottish papers laid the blame for the trouble squarely at Nice's door, unsurprisingly their French press counterparts didn't see it quite the same way, with one Nice-based journal chastising Ellis for tolerating the 'far too hard' play of the Scots. The indiscipline of the foreign teams was a surprise to the Scots players, particularly some of the off-the-ball antics. Caldow recalled, 'We saw a lot of that, especially after a few years in Europe. It was just stupidity on the players' part. But the referees weren't as bright in Europe as they were over here either, and that's how they seemed to get away with it.'

Fellow defender Harold Davis was convinced that match officials contributed to the on-field trouble that seemed to occur in almost every game in the early days. 'The reason there were so many punch-ups and so much bad feeling, was the referees,' he argued. 'In those days, 90 per cent of the referees were homers, and I suppose you can understand why. There were crowds of eighty, ninety or one hundred thousand and they were all standing, and were pretty volatile. Most referees in those days tended to go the home way and that led to bad feeling.'

The second leg was due to take place on 1 November 1956 and Rangers flew in to the Côte d'Azure in high spirits. During the BEA flight the captain came through from the cockpit to chat with the players, and was met with some mild ribbing about the fact that Rangers had been given an Elizabethan-class airliner, rather than the more luxurious Viscount.

The captain's good-humoured response was that the Elizabethan was an easier plane to fly. Just over a year later, the very same plane that had taken Rangers to Nice crashed trying to take-off in snowy conditions at Munich airport, killing eight members of the Manchester United team that was on its way back from a European Cup game in Belgrade. Thankfully the Glasgow to Nice flight was uneventful and the Scottish party touched down expecting sunshine and warm temperatures. Instead, they were met with a deluge of rain and, as they relaxed at L'Hotel Cavallero before spending a quiet night at the cinema watching a rock-and-roll film, the incessant downpour meant that the game was postponed the next morning.

Two weeks later, Rangers returned to the south of France, for the rearranged fixture. After the fireworks of the first leg, it was always likely that the return match at the Leo Lagrange stadium would be a fiery affair, and so it proved. In front of a small but tempestuous crowd of 8,439 there was little evidence of the famed Auld Alliance between Scotland and France. The afternoon match was described as 'ninety minutes of insane animation' by the French daily newspaper Le Patriote and it seems as good a way to describe the events as any. On a waterlogged pitch, Rangers took the lead from the penalty spot in the fortieth minute through the ever-dependable Johnny Hubbard. The award, given after Murray was fouled by Martinez, sparked vociferous protests from the Nice players, several of whom were lucky not to be booked.

Five minutes later, though, the French players had plenty reason to be thankful to the Italian referee, Signor Pieri, as he ruled out what appeared to be a perfectly legitimate Rangers goal, and almost certainly denied the Scots victory in the match. Hubbard and Murray had combined again as the winger's corner was headed home by the Rangers centre forward. But the celebrations were short-lived as Pieri made it known he had already blown for half-time as Murray met the ball with his head.

In the second half, encouraged by this lucky escape, Nice gained the upper hand, with Rangers custodian George Niven performing heroics to keep out the French team's forwards, particularly the skilful Hungarian, Ujlaki. However, Nice eventually managed to find a way through and scored twice inside three minutes to gain the advantage in the match, and draw level on aggregate.

From that point on Rangers defender Ian McColl was outstanding as Nice bombarded the Rangers goal and his efforts combined with Niven's agility prevented Rangers going further behind. Then, with just six minutes remaining, all hell broke loose. With Nice going for a late winner the atmosphere in the ground was electric, and the crowd erupted when young

Gers left half Billy Logie collided with Muro. The Frenchman limped away from the challenge, screaming in apparent agony, but not in so much pain that he could not aim a sly blow at Logie. His teammate Bravo then entered the fray, punching the Scot square in the face. Unsurprisingly, Logie attempted to retaliate but the pair were dragged apart, before the referee stepped in to order off Logie and Bravo. Pieri's decision was met with howls of derision from the terraces and inevitable protests from the players, but despite the efforts to make him change his mind, the referee was adamant that neither player would play any further part.

As Logie disappeared to the changing rooms, Bravo refused to depart the arena, huffily throwing a raincoat over his shoulders and sitting on the bench for the last few minutes of the match. As the game restarted trouble flared behind the Rangers goal and armed police had to step in to prevent a pitch invasion. At the final whistle, nine gendarmes escorted Pieri to the dressing room, protecting him from the increasingly hysterical crowd. A further fifty armed officers had to be drafted in to prevent hotheads on the terracing from scaling the wire fencing to get to the Italian. Later he had to be smuggled out of the stadium through a side door.

Nowadays, had a referee been treated to such hostility, a heavy fine or ban would almost certainly result for the home club, but Signor Pieri was in a forgiving mood, despite his obvious fright. He said afterwards, 'I am convinced I only did my duty in ordering-off both men. The football field is not the place for fighting. I admit I was alarmed, but I am certain after the excitement has died down, the same people who wanted my blood will be in agreement with the action I took.'

Rangers manager Scot Symon felt the decision was tough on Logie. But he went on, 'He is an inexperienced youngster and it was perhaps only natural that he should try to retaliate.' Director John Lawrence, a man whose pronouncements on later European occasions would cause huge controversy, declared drily, 'And we look upon the French as allies . . . '

And so to Paris, for a third attempt to settle the tie at the famous Parc des Princes, home of French rugby. It was another night of drama, marred by trouble on and off the field. Rangers suffered a major injury blow on the morning of the match when veteran captain and centre half George Young pulled up during a late fitness test. Harold Davis was called in as a late replacement, and while he could not be blamed for Rangers' eventual 3–1 defeat, Young's dominating presence was sorely missed. Davis, now living in the north of Scotland, vividly recalls his European debut. 'I was just a boy and getting thrown in to that, especially on foreign soil, was quite an experience. We had a hard time of it in that game.'

In truth, the skilful French, who took the lead through Foix shortly before half-time, outplayed Rangers on the night. Nice then conceded an own goal, which briefly gave the Scots hope before the French sealed it, scoring twice in the closing stages of the game to book their place in the second round.

The controversy was not over though. With ten minutes to go, and the game all but lost for the Scottish champions, Rangers right back Bobby Shearer went in hard on the French inside left, Muro. His tackle sent his opponent spinning onto the track, and Muro was knocked unconscious for a few moments. Nice coach Carniglia raced onto the pitch and made to attack Shearer who was pulled away by captain for the night Ian McColl. A bemused McColl was then booked, as some of the incensed crowd of 12,000 invaded the park. Muro was stretchered off but recovered minutes after being taken to the dressing room and suffered only mild concussion.

For all that had gone before, and perhaps somewhat surprisingly, the opposing teams were the best of friends after the match. Players and officials from both sides joined together in a Paris hotel for a dinner party at which the Rangers group gave their unreserved congratulations to the Nice team. Typically of Rangers, there was none of the petty sniping that others may have resorted to in similar circumstances.

But there was no doubt that everyone at the club was sorely disappointed at the outcome. It was widely felt that Rangers did not have the guile or the craft to exploit potential weaknesses in the opposing team and that a solid defence would not be enough to compete with the Continental elite. The failure to take advantage of good scoring chances was a problem that Rangers would encounter time and again in Europe.

Eric Caldow, who at one point held the British record for the number of appearances in Europe, believed the Scottish players felt they had a point to prove. He said:

We heard a lot of stories about the teams in Europe: that they were supposed to be better than the British players, but it was good to play against them. That first game against Nice was a really big game for us and it was an honour to be part of the first Rangers team to play in the European Cup. In those days, every team had wingers, including in Europe, so as a full back I had a job to do and that was to look after my winger. There was none of the constant passing back that you get nowadays, especially in Europe. We had ten attackers and ten defenders – it was more entertaining in my opinion. You get some games now that the goalkeeper doesn't make a save for the whole game.

At the age of seventy-two, Caldow was still working in the Ibrox hospitality suites on match days, and in that role he still enjoyed the big European nights at the stadium. The spine-tingling atmosphere brings back happy memories. 'I enjoyed every minute of my experience in Europe,' he said. 'The atmosphere now for the big games is special but that's with crowds of 50,000. When I was playing in front of 80,000 the noise was out of this world. Playing in Europe for that first time was unforgettable. It was all about the thrill and excitement of such a new venture.'

Scot Symon had his own concerns about the new challenge of European football. Although Rangers went out in the first round, the team had made three trips to France and had taken part in three highly physical matches. Symon was particularly worried about the effects of travelling and the potential injuries that rough play might inflict on his players. However, the Rangers players had enjoyed their experience, despite the defeat, and were looking forward to pitting their skills against Continental opponents again.

2

Frankfurt 1960: A Humbling Experience

It was hoped that the defeat to Nice would be a valuable, if painful, lesson for the Ibrox club, and so it seemed when they re-entered the European Cup the following season, 1957/58, after winning a second successive championship.

In the preliminary round, Rangers again faced French opposition, this time in the shape of St Etienne, known as *Les Verts* (The Greens). In the first leg at Ibrox, before a crowd of 90,000 (that paid gate receipts of £15,000) Rangers, in white rather than the usual blue, secured a 3–1 lead with goals from burly South African signing Don Kichenbrand, Alex Scott and Billy Simpson. Again there were concerns that the Rangers forward play had not provided as many goals as would have been desired, and the concession of a goal to the visitors made the second leg a tricky prospect.

An early home goal and soaring temperatures in St Etienne made life even more difficult for the Scots, but European debutant Davie Wilson, who was in for the injured Hubbard, settled nerves with a vital equaliser and, although St Etienne scored again, Rangers held on. At the end of the tie, the visiting players had to flee to the safety of the tunnel as hundreds of French supporters in the 35,000 crowd shook the perimeter fences and hurled coins at those on the field.

In the first round Rangers were taught a football lesson by the Italian giants AC Milan as the *Rossoneri* destroyed the Scots in a classic European performance at Ibrox. Rangers – wearing dazzling white strips under the Ibrox floodlights – were a goal up with fifteen minutes to go following Max Murray's deserved first-half strike but the Italian champions extinguished any prospect of a famous victory. Rangers collapsed spectacularly as Milan scored four goals though Grillo (2), Baruffi and Bean, in a stunning eleven-minute spell, making the second leg a formality. The shell-shocked Rangers supporters generously applauded the Italians off the field at the end, but the match demonstrated there was a huge gulf between Scottish football and the Continental game.

As defender Ian McColl recollected:

> Scot never had the players in to form an approach to AC Milan. He'd never gone to see them anyway. That was before the days of coaches going to see the opponents or even sending someone to see them. So we had no preparation for them. It was just a matter of going and saying 'we are us and we are going to win'. We started off well at Ibrox – and went one-up. But they thought 'this lot are not as good as they think they are' and they set about us and scored four.

The return was played in dreadful weather. Rangers had been forced to land at Turin because of fog and made a 120-mile late-night dash to Milan in a blacked-out bus, with opera music blaring from the radio adding to the drama. In torrential rain, and on a quagmire of a pitch, Galli and Baruffi scored without reply to give Milan a comprehensive 6–1 aggregate victory. The weather and the first leg result ensured that the match was not much of a draw for the locals; just three thousand turned up, one of the smallest crowds Rangers had played in front of since the turn of the century. To add insult to injury, the match was moved away from the famous San Siro to an alternative arena on the outskirts of Milan. The ground, also used for showjumping, was almost entirely open to the elements, offering no protection to the supporters and club officials on the sidelines.

Milan went on to reach the final, losing narrowly to Real Madrid at the Heysel stadium in Brussels, and of course were a team packed with quality players. But the ease with which they disposed of the Rangers challenge showed just how far the Scots had fallen behind Europe's big names.

Following the embarrassment of 1957, it was almost a relief the next season when Rangers relinquished their title and were spared the trauma of another European venture. But in 1959/60, as the great Rangers team of the early sixties began to take shape, the Light Blues were back in the competition, having won the league ahead of Hearts. It was a campaign that started with some promise, only to end in further humiliation.

Rangers were drawn to take part in the tournament's preliminary round and came out of the hat against Belgian champions Anderlecht. Hearts had been thrashed in the previous season's first round by Belgian opposition, losing 6–3 on aggregate to Standard Liege, but in Anderlecht's two previous ties in the European Cup they had conceded an astonishing twenty-two goals, an average of more than five per match.

Rangers were two up in the first three minutes of the first leg at Ibrox, through goals from Jimmy Millar and Alex Scott. Determined not to go down without a fight, and presumably keen to avoid a repeat of their 10–0 defeat to Manchester United a couple of seasons earlier, the Belgians proceeded to use every means at their disposal to prevent further goals. Before the match, Anderlecht's English coach Bill Gormlie had warned ominously, 'We've heard that Rangers are a rugged team, so we are preparing accordingly. We are no team of softies. We can take care of ourselves.'

After half an hour of being obstructed, kicked and tripped, the Rangers players decided it was time to give Anderlecht a taste of their own medicine. The result was a bad-tempered, at times brutal, encounter and, despite the goals, a poor spectacle for the huge crowd of 80,000.

The game was perhaps best remembered for a brief comical interlude. Harold Davis, frustrated at the repeated fouls by the Belgians, lost patience and decided to take matters into his own hands. Having been bundled to the ground once too often, he leapt to his feet and made for his adversary, the forward Jurion, who promptly took to his heels. To howls of derision from the crowd, the Belgian hared across the pitch with Davis in hot pursuit, before the Scot realised how farcical it must have looked and stopped in his tracks. Jurion, taking no chances, continued to flee for safety.

Almost fifty years on, Davis plays the incident down. 'It just happened,' he said. 'There had been a bit of needle during the game and I was actually lying on the ground when it happened and he took a kick at me in the passing. I got up and chased him, but he had a head start on me. I had only taken a few paces when I thought "What am I doing?" But it was right in front of the main stand, so I think that's why everyone cottoned on to it.'

Rangers scored their third goal three minutes into the second half through Andy Matthew, who headed home after keeper Meert saved his penalty kick. The Ibrox crowd was given a shock when Anderlecht pulled back two goals, but Rangers powered ahead again through a double from Sammy Baird and left the pitch having recorded a 5–2 scoreline.

Television viewers in Scotland were treated to coverage of the return leg in Brussels, and while the football on offer was not of the highest quality, Rangers fans watching on the small screen would have been happy with the two-goal victory, thanks to strikes by Matthew and the 'Wee Prime Minister', Ian McMillan.

In the first-round proper, Rangers were drawn against a team from behind the Iron Curtain for the first time. Czechoslovakian champions Red

Star Bratislava came to Ibrox with little fanfare, but they performed superbly on a misty night in Govan, recovering from an early McMillan goal to go 2–1 up. But they suffered a triple blow in the minutes before half-time. First, Rangers equalized through Scott in the fortieth minute. Goalkeeper Hlavaty was injured in the process and moments later Matlak was ordered-off for a kick at Sammy Baird.

But, despite starting the second half with ten men, including a heavily bandaged keeper, Bratislava defied the Rangers attacks and in their first attempt at goal of the half, took the lead themselves. Five minutes later Eric Caldow missed a penalty but Davie Wilson eventually got the equaliser and in the closing seconds Jimmy Millar made the final score 4–3 to Rangers as the ten men wilted under pressure.

A controlled performance in the second leg, on a bitterly cold but sunny November afternoon in Bratislava, suggested Rangers had finally started to get to grips with the requirements of European football. For once it was the Scots who relied on stout defensive work to keep the home team at bay and silence the crowd, before breaking away to score a decisive goal. It was the first time in three attempts at the competition that Rangers had used the more subtle tactics needed in Europe. The back line performed admirably, frustrating Red Star and nullifying the threat of their most dangerous players Scherer and Dolinsky. In classic European fashion, after soaking up pressure for seventy minutes, the Light Blues swept upfield to score through Scott, his fourth goal in the European Cup.

Of course it wouldn't be Rangers without drama. With the game winding down, first-leg hero Jimmy Millar decided to deliver some summary justice after being mercilessly battered for the whole of the match. Teammate Harold Davis recalled, 'The centre half had kicked him up and down the park the whole game, so he walked straight up to him and punched him right in the middle of the pitch, then turned and walked off. He had had enough of it and just said, "Oh to hell with this." He had taken a real beating that day, punched and kicked.' Millar was of course sent off, and there was a late scare when Red Star scored with two minutes to go. But overall it was a mature Rangers performance, in a hostile environment, and they gave the distinct impression that, finally, lessons were being learned.

The part-timers of Sparta, from the Dutch port of Rotterdam, were the next opponents, and provided far tougher resistance than many expected. Surprise winners of their national league in 1958, Sparta were led by wily English coach Denis Neville, who had made his name as a player with Fulham. His team adopted a British approach, which, despite being considered old fashioned by many, certainly achieved results. Their passage to the last eight of the European Cup was not too arduous, though; they were given a bye in the qualifying round and beat the Swedes IFK Gothenburg after a play-off in the first-round proper.

Rangers travelled to Rotterdam to face a team made up of dockers, labourers, clerks and salesmen, with every expectation of a comfortable win. The several hundred Rangers fans in the 45,000 crowd in the stadium of city rivals Feyenoord shared that optimism and made themselves heard throughout the game with lusty renditions of 'I Belong To Glasgow' and the club anthem 'Follow, Follow'. Neville had done his homework on Rangers and identified speedy winger Alex Scott as their biggest threat. The Dutchmen failed to heed their manager's warnings and Scott lived up to his billing, causing the Sparta defence untold trouble. He inspired Rangers to a 3–1 lead, with Wilson, Baird and Murray getting on the score sheet.

The 20-year-old Sparta inside-left Peter de Vries, who was on military service at the time, scored his second of the night close to the end to give the Dutch team some hope for the second leg. But most observers believed Rangers had done the hard part by gaining the away win in Holland. Indeed even the *Glasgow Herald*'s football correspondent Cyril Horne – a man who seemed to have a pathological dislike for Rangers and an unstinting ability to look on the negative side – declared dismissively, 'Sparta are hardly likely to overcome the tremendous advantage Rangers will have in their huge fanatical support.'

Well, Rangers did have a huge support for the second leg, but not for the first, or last, time Mr Horne was wide of the mark with his scathing assessment of Sparta's abilities. This time they snuffed out the threat of Scott by detailing four men to stop him and, without his contribution, Rangers were toothless. Sparta still needed a goal to at least save the tie, but coach Neville had no intention of sending his team out to score early. In fact, his tactics were quite the opposite; fearing that if his team found the net early, Rangers would be spurred into action and would punish them with a barrowload of goals.

Instead Sparta set out their stall to keep Rangers at bay and, inspired by 21-year-old centre back Jan Villerius, they did just that for eighty minutes, before breaking away to steal a late winner from Tony van Ede to make the aggregate score 3–3. Although Rangers would have qualified under today's away-goals rule, there was no such provision in place in those days and the tie was to be decided by a play-off in London. The Rangers fans booed the home team off the park at the end as the Sparta players triumphantly carried defensive hero Villerius from the field.

A crowd of around 35,000, mostly made up of Scots, turned up at

Arsenal's Highbury stadium for the decider and their southern hosts were determined to make an occasion of it. The Metropolitan Police band treated the spectators to a selection of pre-match ditties including 'The Swing Of The Kilt' and 'The Little Dutch Doll', presumably chosen for their national flavour rather than on musical merit. Once the real action got underway, Rangers put in a much-improved performance to secure a 3–2 win. McMillan and Scott tormented the Sparta defence, which struggled to cope with the heavy pitch. Baird's goal in the fifty-seventh minute was sandwiched between two own goals, which were enough to put the Light Blues into the semi-final.

Rangers went into the last four knowing that the final was to be played at Hampden Park, against either Barcelona or four-times cup-winners Real Madrid. But the dream of taking on one of the Spanish giants in their home city was quickly extinguished as Rangers suffered one of their worst-ever defeats – to West German champions Eintracht Frankfurt. Eintracht were undoubtedly a good team, but there have to be question marks over how well prepared Rangers were under Scot Symon. In *Tor!* – his excellent history of German football – Ulrich Hesse-Lichtenberger tells how, on landing in Germany, ahead of the first leg, Symon was asked his views on the local favourites. His reply was surprisingly dismissive. 'Eintracht? Who are they?' Later, asked if he would like to inspect the pitch, Symon answered: 'Why? One pitch is like the next. We'll have time to inspect the pitch during the match.'

It was an astonishing attitude to take. In the previous round, Sparta coach Denis Neville had shown what could be achieved with thorough preparation. A team of undoubtedly inferior players had gone close to knocking Rangers out, almost entirely because their manager had identified the threats they would face and had calculated the most effective way of nullifying them.

Symon's dismissive comments suggested he paid little attention to his opponents, displaying an arrogance that was suicidal in football terms. Not only did it leave his team woefully unprepared but also inspired the opposition to greater effort. Such an attitude was nothing unusual as far as Eric Caldow was concerned. He agreed that Rangers were naïve when it came to competing in Europe in the fifties and sixties. 'Scot Symon hadn't a clue as far as tactics were concerned,' he said. 'He hardly ever told us anything about the team in front of us. He just told us to go out and play our own game. It's a far more tactical game now.'

It would perhaps be unfair to single out Symon for criticism. His approach was hardly unusual at the time, particularly in Britain, and subsequent Rangers managers undoubtedly took the same attitude, particularly when taking on 'lesser' teams. As Jim Baxter put it, 'We would play against Inter Milan the way we played against Partick Thistle and Third Lanark. We didn't change anything but you can't do that in Europe.'

Harold Davis also questioned the approach taken in the early days of European competition:

> I think Rangers did pretty well considering, in these European ties, but I don't think we were up to the standard we should have been. Our tactics were a bit behind the times; we were plodding a wee bit. Scot Symon was a great manager, but, like the rest of Scottish football, he was slow in catching up with the times. His attitude was: get it up the wing, get it over and head it in the net. But times were changing and Scot didn't. He was the old school. I am not saying anything against Scot Symon, because I thought he was a great guy and I got on well with him, but he was slow in catching up. The Europeans cottoned on to the fact that there was more to the game than brute force and fitness. I think we were late in picking that up and we probably battled against that for the next number of years.

In Frankfurt, things initially looked good for Rangers as they held the Germans to one apiece in the first half. Stinka's goal in the twenty-seventh minute was quickly cancelled out by a Caldow penalty, given after McMillan was brought down. But, in the second half, the Scots were blown away. Cheered on by a raucous crowd of almost 80,000, Eintracht came flying out of the blocks, regaining the lead in the fifty-first minute. The goals kept coming, each one met by rockets and fireworks from the crowd, and each attack looking like it could result in a score. The final score was 6–1, leaving Rangers with no chance of making the final.

The torture continued in the second leg at Ibrox, where an astonishing 70,000 had turned out in hope of a miracle. It was not to be. Rangers managed to breach the German defence three times through McMillan (2) and Wilson, but Eintracht scored another six goals, giving them a 12–4 aggregate victory. The Rangers fans sportingly applauded the Germans at the end of the match and the players returned the compliment by standing in a line and raising their arms in acknowledgment, first to the supporters on the terracing then to those in the main stand.

The Eintracht performance was big news back home in West Germany, with the sportswear firm Adidas taking out adverts in the sports papers hailing the victorious team and showing them lined up before the match wearing the brand's distinctive three-stripe boots. It was a humbling experience for Rangers, but there may have been some sense of relief as they saw Real Madrid thrash Eintracht 7–3 in the famous Hampden cup final. Given their demolition of the team that had so easily dismantled the Scottish champions, what would the Spaniard maestros have done to Rangers? That question would be answered three years later.

Rangers winger Alex Scott later admitted the tactical shortcomings of the Scots were partly to blame for the Eintracht capitulation. He said:

> Ten minutes into the second half of the first leg it was one each. If we had a little bit of tactical know-how, like the Italians, and just held it, then it could have been different. But we only knew how to play one way and that was to go forward. The game finished 6–1 and they came over here and we did what we had to do which was all-out attack and it ended 6–3. So we scored four goals against them, but we lost twelve! The score flattered them a bit but they proved they were a good side when they gave Real Madrid a good game in the final. It was one of the best finals you were ever likely to see.

However, Rangers had finally made some significant progress in the European Cup, and while their first semi-final appearance had been something of a disaster, there did seem to be some signs, as the swinging sixties began, that the Ibrox club could make a serious and prolonged impact in Europe.

Football, like society, was changing too, particularly for the Rangers supporter. The fifties had often been trying for the club and there were dark moments, not least the humiliating defeats at the hands of Aberdeen (6–0 in the Scottish Cup semi-final in 1954) and Celtic (7–1 in the League Cup final of 1958). However, to paraphrase Harold Macmillan, the prime minister at the time, the winds of change were blowing at Ibrox and by the start of the 1960s there were signs that Scot Symon was creating a special team, befitting of the swinging new era.

This new Rangers squad dispelled many of the old stereotypes attached to Ibrox teams of the past; that they were dour, defensive and battered the opposition into submission. It was always a lazy description anyway, but the group assembled by Symon at the start of the sixties was one of the most talented ever seen in the south side of Glasgow. In fact, many fans consider it to be the best Rangers line-up of all time and the names still trip off the tongue today: Ritchie, Shearer, Caldow, Greig, McKinnon, Baxter, Henderson, McMillan, Millar, Brand and Wilson.

The success of the European Cup had led to UEFA introducing a second tournament for the 1960/61 season, contested by the winners of each country's national cup competition. The European Cup Winners Cup was less glamorous than its older brother, but it would prove to be a productive competition for Rangers.

With Scottish league winners Hearts competing in the European Cup,

Rangers qualified for the new tournament by defeating Kilmarnock in the 1960 Scottish Cup final. The opening match at Ibrox against Hungarian cup winners Ferencvaros was an uninspiring affair, with Rangers rarely reaching the heights they were capable of, and indeed the Hungarians were 1–0 ahead at half-time. The second-half performance saw some improvement and Rangers eventually ran out 4–2 winners.

For the second leg, Rangers paid £4,000 to charter a Douglas airliner to travel in style to Budapest. The plane remained at the airport throughout the team's stay, with the crew accompanying the official party everywhere they went, being wined and dined at the club's expense. It was typical of the style in which Rangers travelled in the pioneering days of European competition. The menu from a BEA flight chartered by Rangers for a journey between between Belgium and Glasgow a couple of years later reveals the luxury enjoyed by the travelling party. The five-course meal began with smoked Scottish salmon, followed by roast spring chicken, with chipolatas, bacon rolls, Parisian potatoes and minted garden peas. For dessert there was Bramley apple pie and dairy cream, followed by cheese and biscuits and sugared chestnuts, all washed down with coffee. It may not be haute cuisine by today's standards, but for the day it was the epitome of high-living. Quite what the sports dietitians who meticulously prepare balanced meals for today's footballers would make of such a spread is another matter.

In front of 25,000 at the Nep stadium, an injury-depleted Ferencvaros went into a two-goal lead and looked capable of pulling off an upset. However, as the game progressed the superior stamina of the Ibrox men began to tell and Rangers soon got a grip of the match. They got their just rewards in the seventieth minute, when Davie Wilson took advantage of defensive uncertainty to shoot Rangers through on aggregate by the odd goal in nine.

The next round saw Rangers drawn against West German opposition for the second successive season, in the form of Borussia Moenchengladbach. The team from Germany's Rhineland was an emerging force in a country that was slowly beginning to recover from the after-effects of war. The West German national team had shocked many by winning the 1954 World Cup in Switzerland against Hungary, and while professionalism was still (officially) outlawed, the humiliating defeat Rangers suffered at the hands of Eintracht the previous season meant no-one at the club expected anything other than a tough battle.

On a day when newspapers were reporting that Abbotsinch Royal Naval air station was to be taken over by the Ministry of Aviation and turned into the main civilian airport for the west of Scotland, Rangers were on foreign soil yet again. The decision to develop the navy airstrip into what would eventually become Glasgow airport was controversial at the time, but you can't help thinking that the minister, Peter Thorneycroft, had Rangers in mind when he made his decision. Having already racked up thousands of air miles on their sorties across Europe, the development of an international airport on their doorstep was a welcome gift from the authorities!

Such matters were far from the thoughts of the Rangers players as they prepared to tackle the Germans in the Rhinestadion. Having been so soundly beaten by Eintracht Frankfurt the previous season, the Rangers supporters had gone into the Borussia match with trepidation, but their concerns were allayed by a clinical away performance. The match was probably Alex Scott's finest hour. His name does not feature on the list of the players who make-up Scot Symon's best-ever team, but he was outstanding during his seven years at Ibrox. A fast and powerful right winger, he had the daunting task of replacing the legendary Willie Waddell when he signed from Camelon Juniors in 1955. He made things slightly easier for himself, by scoring a hat-trick on his debut against hometown team Falkirk, but it was on the European stage that he came to the fore.

Before the Borussia match, Scott had played in all eighteen of Rangers' games in Europe, scoring four goals in the process. He went on to make a total of twenty-eight European appearances, including twenty-seven in a row, and eventually took his goals tally up to eleven. Scott thrived on the unique atmosphere that the European ties created. As he recalled in an interview shortly before his death at the age of sixty-four in 2001: 'If you couldn't play football in that atmosphere, you couldn't play football at all.'

He considered the Moenchengladbach tie as one of his best performances, and the goal he scored in the first leg was his favourite. He took on the entire Borussia defence in an exhilarating run, which culminated in a clinical left-foot strike past goalkeeper Dresbech. Scott's goal was the second of three that Rangers scored without reply. After four good chances early on, Jimmy Millar opened the scoring from a pass by Ian McMillan, who had beaten four defenders during a mazy run. Scott doubled the lead before half-time and McMillan himself completed the scoring with a glorious shot in the fifty-sixth minute.

In typical European fashion, the game had been marred by rough play, particularly from the Germans. Bedfurtig found himself in hospital with a broken jaw and minus two teeth after one foul too many. Unlike the Anderlecht match a couple of years earlier, this time Harold Davis got his man, and landed a punch a heavyweight boxer would have been proud of.

The second leg at Ibrox was less towsy, and ranks as one of the club's most impressive results in Europe. Jim Baxter scored his first European goal in the second minute and set Rangers off on a goal spree that would remain a record victory for almost thirty years. Playing with skill and precision, Rangers toyed with the Germans, who had no response. By half-time, the Scots were five up, with Ralph Brand, McMillan and Millar adding to Baxter's strike and an own goal by Pfeiffer. The flood of goals was matched by a deluge from the skies, with torrential rain leaving huge puddles on the Ibrox turf, but the weather did little to dampen the Rangers performance. Brand and Millar scored again, with Brand completing his hat-trick in the sixty-fifth minute as Rangers ran out winners on the night by an astonishing eight goals to nil.

Scott recalled later, 'That must go down as one of the best performances ever by a Rangers team in Europe. To beat a German team by 11–0 [on aggregate] that's got to be one of the best performances. You don't beat German teams very easily as we've seen over the years. Everything just went really well for us.' Davis added, 'We were up to our knees in mud that night but we ploughed through and gave them a hell of a beating.'

The spectacular victory sent Rangers into the semi-final of the Cup Winners Cup, where they faced the much tougher proposition of English FA Cup winners Wolverhampton Wanderers. That tie, the first ever Anglo-Scottish clash in European competition, has gone down in Rangers folklore as one of the most famous encounters in the club's history.

3

'A sight I'd never seen when they sang God Save the Queen'

From all over Scotland they came with their Union flags and Scottish standards. Soaked to the bone from the torrential rain, ten thousand of them paraded through the streets of Wolverhampton. Despite the weather, many were without coats, but they didn't care. All they wanted was to enjoy the day away from home and see their team win. The red-white-and-blue flags that brightened the grey skies protected them from the elements anyway. The locals – bemused and amused in equal measure – may not have recognised the songs and chants, but they would surely have appreciated the passion with which they were delivered.

The battle cry of 'We Are the People' echoed off the red-brick buildings as the procession wound its way through the town centre. It had started early in the morning as the first trains rumbled into the station. By lunchtime, office workers were abandoning their desks and lining the streets to watch the show. In return, the Scots bellowed their anthems: 'There's Not a Team Like the Glasgow Rangers' and 'We Will Follow On'. Loyal to the Crown, and proud to be both Scottish and British, they broke into the national anthem, and were met with spontaneous applause from bystanders.

It may have resembled an army, but there was nothing hostile about this invading force. There was alcohol consumed, of course, and plenty were in high spirits, but no-one embarrassed themselves or their compatriots. It was simply a display of devotion to a football team that was then, and remains to this day, more than a just a club. On the streets of this industrial town in the Midlands, they were celebrating a way of life. 'The supporters were parading up the streets about ten abreast, waving flags and banners,' Rangers defender Harold Davis recalled. 'It was fantastic. They stopped the whole city; there were thousands of people there.'

19 April 1961. That was the day The Rangers came to Wolverhampton town.

Three weeks earlier, Wolves had visited Glasgow for the first leg of the battle for a place in the European Cup Winners Cup final. Interest in this cross-border clash of the giants was phenomenal. Rangers had sold 80,000 tickets and, such was the demand, could easily have sold at least half that number again. The Wolves fans weren't quite so keen to wander north, though, with less than a thousand making the trip. Casual callers to Ibrox on the morning of the game were surprised that they were able to buy terracing and enclosure tickets returned by the English club. Those without tickets had to put up with *Coronation Street* on the television instead, with only late-night highlights of the football being shown on both BBC and STV. Alternatively they could have visited one of Glasgow's many cinemas, where blockbusters *Ben Hur* and *Spartacus* were playing to packed houses.

That night's *Evening Citizen* devoted its entire broadsheet front page to the match. The headline 'Guardians of Ibrox' was emblazoned above a montage of pictures of the expected Rangers line-up, which had been superimposed over the stadium's famous iron gates. Injuries to key players like Jimmy Millar, Ian McMillan and Max Murray had hampered Scot Symon's team selection and he was forced into naming an experimental front line, featuring Doug Baillie at centre forward instead of his usual position of centre half. Bobby Hume, a 19-year-old outside left, was also drafted in for his first game of the season and Davie Wilson was switched to the right to accommodate him. Symon also gambled on the goalkeeping position, recalling Billy Ritchie at the expense of George Niven.

FA Cup holders Wolves were considered to be a strong, physical team more than capable of holding their own in a battle. These were their golden years: as well as lifting the FA Cup in 1960 the men from Molineux won the English title three times in the 1950s, including a very recent triumph in 1958/59. Wolves were packed with star names including defender Ron Flowers, who captained both his club and England, Bill Slater, also an England cap, and Peter Broadbent, another international star and considered by many fans to be the club's greatest-ever player. The manager was Stan Cullis, a Wolves legend as a player, and equally formidable as a coach. In many ways Wolves were similar in style to Rangers. But they were under-strength for the first leg, with Broadbent injured, and the Scottish press predicted a win for the Scots.

After just ten minutes of a tough-tackling encounter, Rangers suffered another injury blow, although it was entirely due to bad luck. Harold Davis overstretched and pulled a muscle in his leg. After lengthy treatment, he returned to the pitch with his right thigh heavily strapped but, in those days of no substitutes, Davis had to soldier on. He was moved to the right wing to keep him out of harm's way and the Rangers front line was reshuffled again. Davis performed out of his skin to help the cause. 'I got injured and finished the game on the wing,' he recalled. 'In those days you had no substitutes so you either finished with ten men or with eleven and the injured player remained on the park. Even if you had a twisted ankle or something, you were better out of the way than actually in the middle of the park.'

At this stage, even the most optimistic home supporter must have doubted whether a Rangers victory was likely. But thirty minutes into the first half, the Ibrox crowd erupted as Alex Scott scored a superb goal. He collected an overhead kick from Wilson and then beat two defenders before driving in an unstoppable shot from twenty yards. Wolves were stung by the goal and immediately set about trying to get an equalizer. Shortly before half-time Bobby Shearer had to make a goal-line clearance when Ritchie was beaten.

After the break, the game flowed back and forth as one team then the other gained the upper hand. Davis refused to remain a passenger on the wing and on more than one occasion tracked back to help out the defence as well as getting involved in attacking moves for Rangers. Wolves exerted more pressure on the Scottish defence as they sought the equalizer and Ritchie justified his selection by pulling off a string of saves. Then, with just six minutes to go, Ralph Brand pounced on a mistake by Wolves and smashed a low, hard shot past goalkeeper Finlayson to give Rangers a two-goal lead for the return.

The Rangers players and supporters were delighted at the win, especially as it had come in such difficult circumstances. Not everyone appreciated the efforts of injury victim Harold Davis, though. 'There was a comment made at the speeches after the game,' Davis remembered. 'The opposition manager Stan Cullis said something like, "If that guy who got injured and played on the wing was seriously hurt then I'm a bloody Dutchman." I ended up on the wing and I made a contribution and he didn't like it.'

Davis – a Korean War veteran who put his fledgling football career on hold as he spent two years recovering from gunshot wounds – now lives in Gairloch in the far north of Scotland. Coincidentally, the Scottish newspapers on the day of the game were running a story about an English laird who was embroiled in a dispute with local councillors over access to his 10,500-acre estate at Gairloch, part of which he wanted to turn into a holiday park. Oblivious to the sensitivities of the visitors from Wolverhampton, the *Daily Record* headlined their story 'Sassenach Laird Fights Land War'.

The second leg was to take place four days after the annual clash between

Scotland and England in the home-international championship. In 1961 the match was being played at Wembley and, as usual, thousands of Scots travelled to London. Many planned to return home via the Black Country and take in the Rangers game at Molineux.

Wembley was a disaster. With Celtic goalkeeper Frank Haffey between the sticks, Scotland suffered a humiliating 9–3 defeat. It was now down to Rangers to restore pride in the Scottish game, not that the travelling supporters in Wolverhampton had much sympathy for the unfortunate goalkeeper. According to journalist Hugh Taylor in his 1961 book *We Will Follow Rangers*: 'A derisive chorus filled the air: "Haffey, Haffey, Haffey." That was the Rangers supporters' way of poking fun at their great rivals, Celtic.'

Despite the huge prize at stake – the winners would make at least £20,000 from their appearance in the final – there were warm words from the English club towards Rangers before the match. The programme notes for the game showed the respect they had for their Scottish visitors:

> Since we qualified for one of the comparatively new international cup tournaments we have been privileged to receive on our ground some distinguished clubs from other countries. None of them however have been more welcome visitors to Molineux than the famous Rangers whom we see here tonight. Rangers are among the elite in Scottish football and all of us at Molineux are eagerly looking forward to seeing them.
>
> What we can promise is another ninety minutes of hard football in which this time the roars from the terraces will be urging the English side into action just as the tremendous crowd at Ibrox sought to inspire their favourites three weeks ago. Those who were privileged to be there on that occasion will not hurriedly forget either the scene, or the sound, as the crowd roared Rangers into action.

The bookmakers were offering generous odds of 5/2 for a Wolves win, but the English giants had a magnificent home record that season, losing just one of their seventeen matches at Molineux. The famous stadium had something in common with Ibrox, in that it was designed by Glasgow architect Archibald Leitch. The man who created the stunning main stand for Rangers began working on a new ground for Wolves in 1923 and, over the next sixteen years, developed the ground into one of the most distinctive in England. Unlike Ibrox the seats and terracing were covered on four sides, but with a capacity of only 55,000 it was dwarfed by the Glasgow ground. The vast south terracing was certainly something to be proud of, though. It was the second biggest in England – after Aston Villa's Holt End – and held almost 30,000 fans, many of them covered by a roof that was added in 1935. In the early 1950s, the stadium played host to a series of famous floodlit matches between Wolves and various exotic overseas opponents, which were a precursor to European competitions.

Molineux is barely a stone's throw from the town centre and, after congregating for a sing-song outside the hotel where Rangers had based themselves, the Scots fans marched to the ground to claim their spot on the terraces. From the start of the match to the end, the Rangers supporters roared on their team, to the amazement of the home fans. The local *Express and Star* newspaper said the thousands of visitors 'helped give the scene an atmosphere that has not been matched since the famous floodlit specials of '54'.

In their famous gold jerseys – and with star man Broadbent restored to the starting eleven – Wolves had the better of the opening exchanges, with Rangers limited to breakaways. But as the half progressed the Scots, in blue-and-white stripes, came more into it. Davie Wilson, one of three Rangers players who had appeared against England, was out to make amends for the Wembley fiasco and put in a man-of-the-match performance. Just before half-time Alex Scott and Ralph Brand combined to score and send the Rangers fans into delirium. Latching onto a long clearance from the Rangers penalty area, Brand evaded the challenge of defender Bill Slater and broke away, before laying it into the path of Scott, who carefully placed it beyond the keeper.

The cheers of the travelling fans were still reverberating around Molineux when Billy Ritchie was forced to pull off a magnificent diving save from a long-range shot. The save, which was greeted with almost as big a roar as the goal, broke English hearts. Wolves eventually found a way through and scored midway through the second half, but they would have needed another two to take the tie to extra time and, despite wave after wave of attack, that never looked likely.

Finally the final whistle blew, and Rangers were in the final, having won 3–1 over the two legs. Their supporters spilled onto the pitch to celebrate a famous victory over formidable opponents. The tolerant Wolverhampton constabulary stood back and let the Scots enjoy their fun as hundreds of fans hugged their heroes and carried them shoulder-high down the tunnel. Others danced with joy in front of the main stand before lining up in formation and starting a victory parade back to the town centre, where the late trains were waiting to carry them back north. 'We had a fantastic result,' said Harold Davis. 'Wolves were a great team in those days and that was one of our really good results. We were definitely helped by the fans. The backing of all those supporters was really super.'

Wolverhampton was an emotional occasion for many Rangers fans in exile down south, as they rarely got to see their heroes. The events were immortalised in song, and, even for those who weren't there, the words are stirring:

> I've been in exile for some years and my eyes filled up with tears when
> The Rangers came to Wolverhampton town
> So I took a trip along just to hear some famous songs
> When The Rangers came to Wolverhampton town.
>
> So I stood there all alone while the boys all down from home
> Sang of Rangers, that team of great renown
> And a sight I'd never seen when they sang 'God Save The Queen'
> When The Rangers came to Wolverhampton town.
>
> 'There's Not A Team Like The Glasgow Rangers'
> One of the famous songs they sung
> And a sight I'd never seen when they sang 'God Save The Queen'
> When The Rangers came to Wolverhampton town.
>
> Now on the field below, the boys put on a show
> The likes they'd never seen at Molineux
> And the football it was grand from McMillan, Scott and Brand
> When The Rangers came to Wolverhampton town.
>
> Now the league flag must come nearer with men like Bobby Shearer
> The way he played at Wolverhampton town
> And the world for ever after will sing of Jimmy Baxter
> For on his head they placed that noble Crown.
>
> Now I knew it had to happen I heard a mighty roar
> The famous Glasgow Rangers they had scored
> And the sky was white and blue, Wolverhampton shook right through
> The Loyal, Rampant Rangers had come through.

Fans launched a campaign for the song to be played over the speakers at Ibrox before matches and their wish was granted at the first home game of the 2006/07 season. At a time when so much attention was being focused on the chants inside the stadium, the club agreed that there was a place for a traditional song that celebrates one of Rangers' greatest triumphs.

The victory took Rangers into the final of the Cup Winners Cup, the first British club team to reach a major European final. Birmingham City had played in the previous year's Fairs Cup final, but technically they were a representative team appearing in a competition that was only open to cities that hosted trade fairs.

Having overcome teams from Hungary, Germany and England, Rangers now faced their biggest test against the Italians of Fiorentina.

4

May 1961: The First Final

After five years of trying, Rangers were only 180 minutes away from gaining the European crown to which their fans, players and officials believed they were entitled. In the two-legged final, Rangers, the newly crowned Scottish champions, faced Italians Fiorentina who had reached the European Cup final of 1957 and on their way to the final had knocked out Swiss and Yugoslavian opposition. They had only qualified for the Cup Winners Cup because Juventus – who had beaten them in the previous seasons *Coppa Italia* final – were playing in the European Cup. Nevertheless their performances in the earlier rounds, including a 9–2 aggregate victory over Lucerne, showed they would be a tough proposition, as did the fact that they had made it to the *Coppa* final again, where this time they would beat Lazio by two goals to nil.

Rangers went into the final having stuttered their way to the championship. In the title run-in a 2–0 defeat against Kilmarnock, followed by a 6–1 thrashing at Aberdeen, ensured a nervous finish to the season. However, a 7–3 victory over Ayr United on the final day meant that the Light Blues won the league by a single point from Kilmarnock.

The contrast in styles between the two finalists could not have been greater. Rangers – strong, direct and honest but somewhat limited in technical ability – were the epitome of the northern-European style of football that had dominated the first half of the century, but by now was considered to be old-fashioned. Fiorentina – coached by the former Hungary international Nandor Hidegkuti – played intelligent, skilful football that allowed them to counter-attack at pace. It was coupled with a cynical determination to use any means necessary to gain the upper hand, and they used both these tactics to good effect in the first leg of the final at Ibrox on 17 May 1961.

Rangers – wearing blue-and-white stripes instead of their normal light-blue jerseys – enjoyed the bulk of possession but their approach was one-dimensional and relied on long balls being thrown into the Fiorentina penalty area. Invariably, though, it was the tall defenders who came out on top in the aerial battles, marshalled superbly by their captain Alberto Orzan, a veteran of the 1957 European Cup final.

Sweden international winger Kurt Hamrin and inside left Luigi Milan were Fiorentina's biggest attacking threats, the latter in particular causing problems for the Rangers defence. It was a defensive blunder by Davis that led to the opening goal, his short pass back being pounced on by Gianfranco Petris. He squared to Milan who stroked the ball into the empty net.

Rangers had the chance to get back on level terms just six minutes later when the Austrian referee Erich Steiner adjudged that Ian McMillan had been fouled inside the penalty box. His decision sparked anarchic scenes; Fiorentina furiously protested that it had been a fair tackle and the official was surrounded by wildly gesticulating Italian players. Moments later incensed assistant coach Beppe Chiapella raced onto the pitch to join the protests, and had to be restrained by Hamrin.

It took several minutes to restore order, before the Rangers captain Eric Caldow was finally allowed to take the penalty. As he began his run-up, goalkeeper Albertosi bounced up and down and, by the time the ball was struck, he was more than six yards off his line. The antics obviously distracted Caldow and he pushed the penalty past the post. Calls for a retake were waved away.

From that point on the game turned ugly, with the Italians resorting to the sort of ruthless tactics that *Serie A* has become infamous for. As Rangers toiled to overcome the Fiorentina defence, the Ibrox crowd's mood grew darker. Every trip was met with a shout of protest, every body check with a howl of derision, every kick with a catcall. Most notably, a scything foul by Rimbaldo on Bobby Shearer sparked outrage and led to a torrent of bottles and cans being thrown onto the field.

Milan scored a second goal a minute before the end, leaving the Rangers support even angrier, so much so that on the final whistle the Italian flag, which had been flying above the covered enclosure, was ripped down. It was an act of frustration, brought about by the behaviour of the Fiorentina players, but most Rangers fans felt it was disrespectful. As the Italian players stood in the middle of the pitch, saluting the baying crowd, police stormed into the mob and rescued the flag from whatever fate it was about to befall.

The return leg, ten days later, seemed a forlorn hope for the Scots. However, there was a sense of optimism, perhaps borne more out of hope than expectation, that they could somehow reverse the score in Florence. The city has roots dating back as far back as 200 BC and is rich in culture and history, renowned for the development of art, music and poetry. Its art and architecture were a Mecca for tourists, even in the 1950s, and for the six hundred Rangers supporters who travelled to the game it was an unforgettable experience.

Given the events of the first leg, the chief of police in Florence was perturbed at what the Sunday night match might bring in its wake. Fearing repercussions for the insult to the Italian *tricolore* at the first leg, he cancelled police leave and ordered two hundred officers to report for duty, three times the normal complement.

Temperatures were in the eighties in the run-up to the match and the kick-off was delayed until 9.30 p.m. to allow the weather to cool down. On the night of the match, the streets of Florence were packed with cars heading for the Stadio Comunale and in stereotypical Italian style the drivers were sounding their horns wildly and flashing their headlights.

Inside the ground, there were almost 30,000 fanatical Fiorentina fans, but observers with a finely tuned ear would just have been able to pick out the familiar refrain of 'Follow, Follow' amid the tumult. 'Everywhere, anywhere, we will follow on' is how it goes, and the players were grateful that so many had done just that, in an era when air travel was still the reserve of the privileged few. Businessmen Ross Bowie and Joe Welsh were two regular travellers with Rangers in the early days and they had even spent a week in Italy before the match, compiling a dossier on Fiorentina.

Any hope Rangers had of turning the tie around quickly evaporated when Milan notched his third goal of the final. Just like in the first leg, he scored in the twelfth minute, chesting home a cross from Hamrin. The skilful Swede had already had a goal disallowed for offside and there were some who feared Rangers could be on the end of a heavy defeat.

However, to their credit the Scots fought back and produced a performance full of skill and effort that earned applause from the Italian crowd. In the second half, Alex Scott became the first British player to score in a European final, when he drove home a shot from fifteen yards. Scott was later denied what seemed, to many observers, a stonewall penalty. Had it been given and converted, Rangers might well have gone on to take something from the match.

Jimmy Millar, who was returning for his first game in the front line after a lengthy period of injury, had an excellent game, as did Baxter, Caldow and Scott, but it was Fiorentina's Hamrin who stole the show with the decisive goal late in the game. He weaved his way past a handful of Rangers defenders before blasting an unstoppable shot into the net from what seemed an impossible angle. That was the end of the scoring and the end of Rangers hopes of winning a European trophy for another year. But the rancour of the first leg was forgotten as the Scots applauded the Fiorentina players, who paraded the new trophy in front of their delirious fans.

Ralph Brand, who was a regular scorer in Europe and played in both legs of the final, struggled against the well-organised Italian defence. It was a situation Brand – and the other Rangers forwards – repeatedly encountered in Europe. Back in the early sixties, he advanced an argument for the annual struggle Rangers faced in the European arena; one that would be trotted out regularly for the next forty years. 'The ordinary league games we play now are definitely getting easier to win,' he declared in the book, *Playing For Rangers*. 'Things do not seem so difficult for the Rangers now as they did in the days when I broke through to the first team. And I feel that is one of the reasons we have not done so well in the Continental tournaments.'

On the surface, the argument that the Scottish league is too easy for clubs successfully to compete in Europe is compelling, but it bears little serious analysis. Did the league suddenly become more competitive in 1967 when both Rangers and Celtic reached European finals? Or what about 1972, when Rangers finished third, level on points with fourth-placed Hibs, yet won the Cup Winners Cup? Did the much-maligned SPL enjoy a sudden surge in quality the season Celtic reached the UEFA Cup final or in 2006, when Rangers reached the last sixteen of the Champions League and finished third in the league? The reality is that it is neither the standard of the league nor the quality of the opposition that is to blame, but rather the approach that Scottish teams have taken and the lack of thought given to the opposition.

Brand touched on this in his sixties interview:

> I feel that we must play more games against Continental opposition before we can really find out how to tackle them, how to break down their blanket defences. It is one of the most difficult situations in football to find yourself suddenly faced with a wall of defenders who simply will not venture up-field and leave you the tiniest chink to get through. It has been our inability to beat this kind of defence which has led to our failure in the European Cup. Only experience of playing against these tight defences can eventually help us win.

Rangers had gone far in 1961, but they did not yet have the tactical nous of the Italians. Nor did they have a world-class player like Hamrin or Milan, both of whom could turn a game with a single pass, although in Jim Baxter they had someone who would soon scale those heights, albeit for a frustratingly short period of time.

Baxter was at the heart of the new team Scot Symon was gradually creating. Signed from Raith Rovers for £17,500 in 1960, he possessed a combination of skill and arrogance that marked him apart from every other Scottish player of his generation. His talents were more akin to those of the Continental and seemed ideally suited to the European stage. Baxter's first match in Europe was against Ferencvaros in the European Cup Winners Cup of 1960/61, and while he performed well during the run to the final, it was not until the following season that he would show his true ability on the European stage.

Appropriately enough for Britain's first pop-star footballer, the playboy's paradise of Monte Carlo was the scene of Baxter's first great European performance. For the third time, Rangers had been drawn to face the French champions in the European Cup. This time their opponents in the preliminary round of 1961/62 were AS Monaco, whose home in the tiny principality on the Mediterranean coast meant they actually played outside of France.

A crowd of six thousand crammed into Monaco's stadium – carved into the rocks below Prince Rainier's palace – keen to see the high rollers of Scotland, who had come so close to winning a European trophy the season before. Rangers, and Baxter in particular, did not disappoint. At times their play was more Vegas cabaret than football, and the home fans enjoyed every minute of the entertainment, even though their own team was the butt of the joke.

The Scots were 2-0 up at half-time with Baxter scoring the first from a twenty-yard drive after just ten minutes. Thirteen minutes later, Rangers went two-up and Baxter was involved again; this time his lob was half cleared and fell to Alex Scott who finished clinically. As a left half, Baxter was ostensibly a defensive player but he was acting as a sixth forward, bringing the ball from defence and starting virtually every Rangers attack.

Rangers swept the ball about the pitch with pinpoint accuracy and baffled their opponents with dazzling footwork, Ian McMillan the main challenger to Baxter for the title of entertainer-in-chief. The crowd cheered every move by the Scots and jeered the Monaco team for its inadequacies. It was a fantastic performance and challenged the assumptions that Scottish football was all about running and brute strength. It was also a remarkable transformation from the stale and static performance Rangers had put in just four months earlier against Fiorentina, especially in the first leg.

However, this exhibition of skill had just one flaw; Rangers had failed to add to their goals tally. So when Monaco finally rallied in the second half, Rangers suddenly had cause to worry, especially when the French champions scored twice to level the game. Rangers were forced to abandon their show-boating in a bid to score a winning goal and they did just that, through yet another strike from European-specialist Scott; this time it was a header with eight minutes left on the clock.

In the second leg at Ibrox, Rangers and Baxter didn't scale the heights of the first game and were forced to scrap for a 3–2 victory in front of a 65,000 crowd. Alex Scott once again scored the winning goal, using his pace and skill to capitalise on a defensive blunder and give Rangers a 6–4 aggregate victory.

The first match was considered Baxter's finest to date for Rangers and commentators were quick to highlight the contrast between the opulence of Monte Carlo and the Fife mining village of Hill O' Beath, where Baxter was raised. Similar contrasts could be drawn between the casinos and fast cars of Monaco and the austere surroundings of communist East Berlin, where Rangers found themselves taking on ASK Vorwaerts in the first-round proper.

A brief look at the complicated history of this club shows how much European football has changed over the last fifty years, especially in the former Eastern Bloc. The club has had a confusing time of it, to say the least, since being formed in 1951 shortly after the creation of East Germany. Founded as the army club KVP Vorwaerts Leipzig, the authorities took the view that the lack of immediate success meant a change was required, so two years later they moved the club one hundred miles to Berlin and renamed it ZSK Vorwaerts Berlin.

The next season it underwent another subtle transformation, being renamed ASK Vorwaerts Berlin, a decision that clearly had the desired effect, setting the club off on a period of success that saw four Oberliga championship wins between 1958 and 1965. A further name change to FC Vorwaerts in the mid-sixties preceded another couple of league wins, before the club moved again, this time to the city of Frankfurt an der Oder, to replace the local secret-police-sponsored side. After reunification in 1990, the club dropped its affiliation with the army and became FC Victoria Frankfurt/Oder before changing again to Frankfurt/Oder FC Viktoria 91. These days the club plays in the depths of German non-league football, a far cry from their Oberliga-winning peak in the 1950s and 1960s and their regular forays into the European Cup.

It was during one of those European jaunts that the players of Vorwaerts and Rangers found themselves at the centre of a political storm. The first leg in East Germany took place on 15 November 1961 only months after work had begun on the Berlin Wall, which would physically divide the two halves of the city. The decision by East German leader Walter Ulbricht – and approved by Soviet leader Nikita Khrushchev – to create the partition was made in a bid to stem the flow of economic migrants from east to west and secure the future of the East German economy. With defectors facing being shot if they tried to cross the wall, tensions were high on both sides of the Berlin divide.

Rangers won 2–1 in Germany through a penalty by Eric Caldow and a header by Ralph Brand. Although he had not been prominent in what was a scrappy match, Jim Baxter had thrilled the twenty thousand East German fans with his skill in setting up the second goal.

Under normal circumstances, Rangers of course would have defended their lead at Ibrox. However, with the Cold War at its most intense, these were far from normal circumstances. The East Germans were denied visas to travel to Glasgow for the second leg, so the game was moved to the Swedish city of Malmo.

Despite fears about the thick fog which had hung over Malmo for much of the day, the match got under way in front of around four thousand spectators at seven. A mere forty-five minutes later the game was over, having been abandoned due to the reappearance of the heavy, grey fog that was rolling in from the sea. Rangers apprentice Willie Henderson – making his European debut at the age of seventeen in place of the injured Alex Scott – had been the only scorer in the first half, and in fact, was the only player to provide any sort of entertainment for the miserable crowd.

In a somewhat unusual move, the match was rescheduled for ten o'clock the following morning, meaning an early rise for the players and a surreal atmosphere. Just 1,800 spectators attended the game, which Rangers eventually won 4–1. Henderson, making his second 'debut', scored again and put in a man-of-the-match performance. Back home in Caldercruix, Henderson's dad John was waiting for a full account of the game. It was the first match he had missed since his son had started playing – and he only missed it because he couldn't get a passport in time.

European football then, as now, was a money-spinner for Rangers. A home tie with a capacity 80,000 crowd could have pulled in £20,000 for the Ibrox coffers. In the case of Vorwaerts, two overseas trips meant Rangers actually lost £6,000 from the tie, a fair amount in those days.

The match was also notable for the appearance in the stands of the legendary Danish forward Carl Hansen, who, in the 1920s, became the first foreigner to play for Rangers. Hansen – known in his homeland as Carl Skomager (Shoemaker) – was a superb player who specialised in scoring against Celtic, but his Rangers career was blighted by two leg-breaks that eventually forced him to return to Denmark. During the war he was part of the Danish resistance and was arrested by the Gestapo and sent to a concentration camp, for shouting 'Quisling' at a local who was too friendly with the occupying Germans. After the war, Hansen divided his time between coaching and journalism, and he was working at the Danish paper *Politiken* when Rangers were playing across the sea in Sweden. He joined up with the Rangers party and, when he couldn't get a room in the team hotel, bunked up on a chair in the room of a Scottish reporter.

The night before the replayed game there was more controversy, as two of the Vorwaerts party, including interpreter Karl Ernst Zrem, defected to the West. They vanished from the hotel where both teams were staying. Earlier, at a party organised by Rangers, Zrem had approached Ibrox secretary James Simpson and some of the players, pleading for help in his bid to be reunited with his fiancée in West Germany. Suspecting they were being set up by the East German government the Scots declined to help, but the officials still managed to make good their escape and turned themselves in to the Swedish police.

After the difficulties of the previous round, Rangers would have been expecting an easier time of things in their next tie with Belgian champions Standard Liege. Certainly there were none of the off-field difficulties encountered against the East Germans but, on the pitch, the Scots were found wanting yet again.

The first leg in the historic 'Glowing City' was played out in front of a passionate crowd of 37,000, many of whom had broken through the barricades and lined the pitch to get a better view of proceedings. The half-time break lasted for a full twenty-five minutes, and, to add to the surreal atmosphere, the players were introduced to Prince Albert of Liege on the pitch before the restart.

The game itself was a disaster for Rangers. They went down 4–1, with Davie Wilson's goal one of the few bright spots on a grim night. Back home in Scotland, the press described the result as a 'humiliation' pointing out, quite rightly, that Standard was nothing more than an average team of plodders. The biggest positive Rangers could take from the night was the performance of the two eighteen-year-olds who had been drafted into the side because of injuries. Willie Henderson had already made his mark in the competition, but the match in Liege was the European debut of a certain John Greig. He gave an assured performance on the right, and along with Henderson was the biggest threat to the Standard defence during the short period when Rangers were in the ascendancy.

Edinburgh-born Greig had been a Hearts supporter as a boy but, as is often the case, the local club was too slow to sign him and he was snatched away by Rangers. He made his debut in September 1961 against Airdrie and his goal was the first of eight he would score in just thirteen domestic appearances that season. He would go on to play almost nine hundred times for Rangers, winning five championship medals along the way, and in 1999 was voted by fans as the greatest-ever Ranger. For many supporters, his never-say-die attitude sums up the Rangers ethos, although his image was tarnished somewhat by his unsuccessful period as manager.

Ironically, for a player who never possessed the technical skills that are considered a prerequisite for European success, Greig played in two European finals, captaining Rangers to their only trophy win on that stage in 1972. He also enjoyed some success as a manager in Europe, showing unexpected tactical ability to record impressive wins against Juventus and PSV Eindhoven. In his recent autobiography, Greig wrote that Standard Liege were one of Europe's leading sides at the time; however, one wonders if his view was clouded by their only notable victory on the European stage, a 6–3 aggregate victory against his boyhood heroes Hearts in 1958.

Certainly, there were few signs that Liege belonged in Europe's elite in either match against Rangers. The second leg, in front of an impressive crowd of 75,000, was won 2–0 by the Scots but there was precious little quality on view. Greig was out of the team again and the Rangers attack was hindered by the absence of fellow teenager Willie Henderson. The youngster had been due to play but got caught in traffic on his way to Ibrox, and turned up late. With fifteen minutes to go before kick-off – and Rangers reserve players scouring the streets for Henderson – his place went to Alex Scott, who had one of his less impressive European performances. He was outplayed by the strong tackling left-back, Thellin, and the match was his last in Europe for the club before his move to Everton the following season. The two-goal victory, gained through a goal from Brand and a last-minute Caldow penalty, was not enough to put Rangers through; after reaching the previous season's Cup Winners Cup final, and the impressive first-round performance against Monaco, it was another disappointment.

The following season's campaign – in the Cup Winners Cup of 1962/63 – was also depressing. Once again it started brightly, with a Jimmy Millar hat-trick helping the Glasgow side to a 4–0 victory against Spanish Cup winners Sevilla at Ibrox. The second-leg was a typically fiery affair, which exploded in the closing minutes when a twenty-two-man brawl erupted. From the start of the match, the Spaniards made their intentions clear, charging into wild tackles, throwing fists and elbows and even spitting at their opponents. Rangers were goaded into retaliation, with the smallest man on the park, Willie Henderson, lashing out after yet another vicious foul. Luckily, Bobby

Shearer, himself the victim of an earlier punch, was on hand to rescue the little winger from a beating at the hands of his towering opponent.

Then with a few minutes to go, and with Rangers safely through, despite being two goals down, the Scots decided to get their revenge for the foul play they had endured. The Portuguese referee, sensing that trouble was brewing, wisely brought the game to a halt two minutes early and fled the pitch. He left behind all twenty-two players to slug it out, as some fans started to invade the field and others hurled hundreds of cushions from the terraces.

Defender Harold Davis later confessed that he was one of the prime instigators of what became known as the Battle of Seville. He recalled:

> We had the match sewn up; we had been sitting back and we were home-and-dry. I personally asked for 'the shout' when there was two minutes to go and when I got the signal I said, 'right lads, let's give them a taste of their own medicine!' By that time it was all boiling up, people were kicking each other left, right and centre. That was when the referee blew the whistle, ran off the park and left twenty-two guys battling it out. I don't think there's ever been anything like the Battle of Seville in the history of football. But because there wasn't so much telly in those days, it wasn't recorded. It really must have been the worst case of two football teams battling it out on the park that ever happened. But we got through that match; it was a great European result for us.

Still nursing their wounds, the Rangers players attended the post-match banquet laid on by the Seville club with some trepidation. Although it turned out to be a friendly affair, Henderson sensibly made sure he steered clear of his earlier adversary. 'I didn't want to take any more chances', he said afterwards.

The next round saw Rangers drawn against English opposition again; this time they were to face Tottenham Hotspur, considered by many to be the greatest team in English football. Spurs had international stars galore – including Danny Blanchflower, Dave MacKay and Jimmy Greaves – and had won the double of league and FA Cup as recently as 1960/61. It was therefore hardly surprising that they proved much too strong for the Scots.

The hype that surrounded the game was enormous, with even legendary Tottenham manager Bill Nicholson joining in the hyperbole by declaring it the 'greatest game on earth'. Thousands of fans queued up to get tickets for the match when they went on sale at White Hart Lane, including many thousands of Scots who had travelled south just to ensure they got a brief. All 60,000 tickets were sold out within two hours, many going to Rangers fans, meaning that the Scottish contingent would be much larger than the official party of 3,000.

On the morning of the match, London was flooded with Rangers supporters, who descended on the capital by plane, train and automobile. Euston station was the unofficial gathering point and estimates of the number of Scots present ranged from 10,000 to 30,000. Inside White Hart Lane, the Rangers supporters sang themselves hoarse, but, on the pitch, the players failed to match their performance, losing 5–2.

The three-goal deficit proved too much to overcome in the second leg, despite the best efforts of a partisan Ibrox crowd of almost 80,000 and the promise of a £200 bonus. In his autobiography, *From Me to You*, England forward Jimmy Greaves recalled the electric atmosphere inside Ibrox. 'When the teams took to the pitch the noise was deafening, the atmosphere intimidating in the extreme,' he wrote. But just nine minutes into the match, Greaves silenced the home supporters and effectively ended the tie, as he strode through the Rangers defence and drilled a powerful shot past Billy Ritchie. As the ball hit the net it was as if a switch had been flicked immediately to mute the crowd. 'It was eerie,' said Greaves.

Rangers battled hard for an equaliser and in the second half finally broke through, Brand heading home Henderson's looping cross. But the fans' joy was short lived; a few minutes later, Spurs regained the lead through Smith. Further goals from Davie Wilson for Rangers and another from Smith, meant the game ended 3–2 to Tottenham, giving the Londoners a comprehensive 8–4 aggregate victory. As some consolation for Rangers, Spurs went on to win the competition, beating Atletico Madrid in the final.

With Rangers competing in Europe almost every season, it was almost inevitable that they would eventually come up against Real Madrid. Since the inauguration of the European Cup in 1955, no other club had enjoyed as much success as the Spanish giants. Inspired by superstars like Puskas, di Stefano, Kopa and Gento, Real won the first five European Cups. The run included the greatest final of them all: the 7–3 victory at Hampden in 1960 over Eintracht Frankfurt (who, of course, had thrashed Rangers in the semi-final) was an astonishing display of attacking football, which has probably never been equalled.

Three years later, even though many of their biggest stars were nearing the end of their careers, Madrid's return to Glasgow for a European Cup tie was eagerly anticipated by the locals. As usual, a capacity crowd packed out Ibrox to see Rangers take on the Spaniards and they were rewarded with a fantastic performance from the depleted home team.

The fearless young Rangers team attacked the Real defence, and were unlucky not to take the lead. Henderson in particular was a thorn in the side of the Spaniards, his close control and speedy runs causing mayhem and providing several openings for the Rangers strike force, none of which was taken. Strangely, Baxter was the one Rangers player who did not play to his full potential, although it may have been that he was planning the post-match entertainment. In defence Rangers comfortably contained the threat of di Stefano, Puskas and Gento; Ronnie McKinnon, David Provan and Bobby Shearer in particular were pillars of strength. Then, inevitably, came the killer blow. With just three minutes to go, Puskas fired past Billy Ritchie after receiving a pass from Gento. In typical Scottish fashion, Rangers had contrived to lose a match they could easily have won.

Puskas may have scored the winning goal that night but his visit to Glasgow was far more memorable for what went on after the final whistle, although just how much the Hungarian legend would have remembered is debatable. Puskas had met Jim Baxter at a world-select match a few months earlier, and the party-loving Scot felt it was only good manners to invite his old pal out on the town. Surprisingly, the Real star accepted the invitation, and so it was that two of the world's greatest players found themselves boozing the night away at a flat . . . in Drumchapel.

In an interview in 2001, days after Baxter's death from cancer, former teammate Alex Willoughby recalled how he watched incredulously as the pair drank themselves into a stupor in the most unlikely of surroundings. 'Jim asked him if he'd like to go to a party. "Of course," said Puskas. The next thing you know the two of them are lying steaming at a party in Drumchapel.' Willoughby, who himself died prematurely in 2004, bumped into Puskas again many years later, and the first thing he asked him in pidgin English was 'How's Jimmy? How's Jimmy?' As Willoughby pointed out, 'Anyone who can take Puskas to a knees-up in Drumchapel deserves not only some credit, but a bloody medal as well.'

There is no record of how Puskas felt the next morning, but the experience did not have any long-term effect, as the 'Galloping Major' inspired his teammates to a crushing 6–0 victory over Rangers in the second leg at the Santiago Bernabeu stadium. Puskas scored the opening goal in three minutes before setting up the second for Evaristo. The Hungarian and his fellow superstars destroyed Rangers in the first half, scoring four without reply. Another two goals after the break completed the rout.

After the game Puskas went into the Rangers dressing room and gave Alex Willoughby his famous white shirt. In a 1964 interview, George McLean recalled the lessons that were learned by the young Rangers team. 'It was a humiliating experience being beaten so soundly in Madrid,' he said. 'But as

I watched the great Puskas that night I realised just how much more I had to learn about the game. Puskas was the complete player that night. He seemed to be able to hit the ball with such wonderful accuracy from almost any position.'

Fellow forward Jim Forrest said Rangers had been 'whipped mercilessly' and chastised those who believed pace was all that was required for success in modern football. 'Real Madrid hammered home that lesson to me in the Bernabeu stadium,' he recalled. 'The sheer poetry of Puskas and Di Stefano overwhelmed me that night.'

Madrid's 7–0 aggregate victory propelled the veterans on the way to their seventh European Cup final, but it was to prove a bridge too far for Puskas and co. Real lost 3–1 to Inter Milan, signalling the end of an era. To reinforce the point, European Cup top scorer Alfredo di Stefano left the club for Espanyol in the summer. A much younger Real team won the European Cup again in 1966, but it was a false dawn: the famous all-white strip would not be seen in a final again until 1981, and Madrid would not lift the trophy until 1998.

For Rangers, the defeat had little impact on their season. Scot Symon's team had youth and experience in perfect harmony, and in 1963/64 finally fulfilled its potential. Rangers won the domestic treble for the second time. Greig, Henderson and McKinnon provided the youthful exuberance, while stalwarts like 'Captain Cutlass' Bobby Shearer, Eric Caldow, Jimmy Millar and Ralph Brand supplied the maturity required to carry the youngsters. Jim Baxter was the creative genius who brought the two elements together and provided Rangers with the 'X factor' that every great team requires.

That season would be the last of any significance for many of the older players, and in many respects it was the end of a great era. However, the following season would, in the eyes of many supporters, be seen as a missed opportunity to land the much-sought-after first European trophy.

5

What If?

Football is full of what-ifs and could-have-beens. *What if* that penalty had been given? *What if* the linesman hadn't flagged for offside? We *could have been* champions if we were given that corner in the twenty-first minute of the first game of the season. Supporters of certain clubs expend huge amounts of energy gnashing their teeth over such imponderables, wallowing in misery about something they have absolutely no control over. It's not a trait exhibited by Rangers fans, who tend to take a more relaxed view of such matters, presumably because history has taught them that for every disappointment, there will be another success around the corner.

But even the most philosophical of bluenoses have wondered whether things would have turned out differently if an Austrian by the name of Walter Skocik had not lost his head with twenty seconds left of a match in which he had been tormented by one of the greatest talents Scotland had ever seen: Jim Baxter. Rapid Vienna right half Skocik was in direct opposition to Baxter on the night that the Fifer had what many consider his best game. In a moment of madness, the Austrian may have changed the course of football history in Scotland, and denied Rangers the chance to win the greatest prize in European football.

His rash tackle in the final minute of the European Cup tie on 8 December 1964, with the Scots cruising into the next round, broke Baxter's leg two inches above the ankle. Skocik, who was full of remorse the next day, could not have known at the time, but the foul would have a profound impact on the fortunes of Rangers Football Club. With Baxter missing, the Light Blues failed to win the European Cup and slumped to a catastrophic fifth-place finish in the league.

Baxter returned to the team before the end of the season, but in the summer of 1965 he was sold to Sunderland for £72,000, following a dispute with Rangers over money. Whether his broken leg was a factor in the decision not to give him a pay rise, or whether Rangers were of the view that the honour of playing for the club transcended financial reward, is not clear. Whatever the motive, his departure had a major impact. Celtic won the league in 1965/66, but Baxter was a talisman in Old Firm games, losing only twice in eighteen appearances, and a strong case can be made that, with him in the team, Rangers would have regained the title. Of course, if Rangers had won the league, they would have qualified for the European Cup the following season and not Celtic; this would have denied Jock Stein's team the historic triumph in Lisbon, which has stuck in the craw of the Rangers support ever since.

But enough of what-ifs. The 1964/65 European Cup campaign kicked off with a difficult draw against Yugoslavian champions Red Star Belgrade. The team was packed with internationals, with several of the side that faced Rangers in the first leg at Ibrox having been members of the Yugoslavia team that won the gold medal at the 1960 Olympics in Rome. Two years later, Yugoslavia reached the semi-final of the 1962 World Cup in Chile, with playmaker Dragoslav 'Sekki' Sekulara the inspiration. Considered the best inside-forward in Europe he was the subject of a big-money bid from Juventus, although he had a suspect temperament that led to his suspension from football for a total of three years. Luckily for Rangers, he missed the tie with the Scottish champions because of a knee injury.

Professional sport was banned by Yugoslavia's communist rulers, so theoretically Red Star's players were amateurs. Most were students at Belgrade University – Sekki was studying meteorology – and as a result received government grants. Clubs were also allowed to pay up to £40 a month for expenses, however an investigation was launched by the authorities after it emerged that some clubs were making illegal payments of up to £120. When you consider that Jim Baxter was being paid just £35 a week by Rangers, it's easy to see why he felt aggrieved – he would have been better rewarded if he played as an amateur in a communist state!

Rangers won the first leg 3–1, with Ralph Brand's late goal giving them a great chance of progressing to the next round. However, the second leg in front of a 70,000 crowd at Red Star's spectacular new stadium was a different proposition, with the Yugoslavs racing to a 4–1 lead after half-time. It was left to defender Ronnie McKinnon to rescue Rangers when he headed a goal in injury time to level the aggregate score. With the away-goals rule, extra time and penalties still some way off, the tie went to a play-off at Arsenal's Highbury stadium.

Like the play-off against Sparta Rotterdam at the same ground four years earlier, there was huge interest in the match and it attracted an impressive crowd of 34,000, most of them Scots. Despite their poor league form, Rangers went into the game on a high, having recently beaten Celtic in the League Cup final and hammered St Mirren 7–0 at Love Street. Willie Henderson missed the match as he was shortly to undergo an operation to remove a bunion, which was to keep him out the team for several months. He was able to watch the last twenty minutes of the game live on the BBC on a television set installed in his hospital room.

Inspired by Baxter, Rangers were impressive. While Red Star knocked the ball around with ease, they lacked penetration and the direct approach of the Scots was far more effective. Baxter's sudden changes of direction and incisive passes confused the Yugoslavians and the wing play of promising youngster Willie Johnston was just as productive.

Jim Forrest, who was proving to be a prolific striker, opened the scoring in the twelfth minute and sparked wild celebrations among the thousands of Scots on the Highbury terraces. He added a second after a left-foot shot from Brand, set up by an excellent Baxter pass, was parried into his path by the goalkeeper. In the seventy-third minute, Johnston sealed the tie with the third goal, again after build-up play from Baxter. Red Star scored a late consolation through Cop, but Rangers were safely through to the next round to meet Austrian champions Rapid Vienna.

In front of 60,000 fans at Ibrox, Rangers found it difficult to break down the well-disciplined Rapid defence in the first leg and gained only the narrowest of advantages, Davie Wilson converting a perfect pass from Baxter. The Rangers front line of Forrest, Wilson and Johnston were regularly caught in the Austrians' offside trap and there were concerns that the Scots would struggle in the return. Jim Baxter did not share those concerns. He was convinced that Rangers had the ability to beat the Austrians on their own ground and went about proving it in the best way possible – by turning in a virtuoso performance.

When Rangers arrived in the Austrian capital, the pitch at the Prater stadium was covered in a blanket of snow, and although a shower of rain cleared the field in time for kick-off, the playing surface was heavy and there were piles of snow on the running track. Just as in the first leg, Rapid utilised the offside trap, and again the Rangers attackers initially found it difficult to break down. However, the tactic backfired spectacularly as Baxter carefully hung onto the ball until he was certain that his forwards were onside, before sliding a perfect pass through to Jim Forrest. The Rangers number nine raced past the static defenders and, from just inside the penalty box, flicked the ball first time over the body of the advancing goalkeeper, Veres. It was a simple goal, but also a quality goal; and it was poetic justice that the offside tactics of the Austrians had proved to be their downfall.

The goal allowed Rangers to relax, and Baxter in particular was able to express himself on the slushy pitch. Time and again he turned defenders inside out, before chipping perfectly weighted passes to his forwards. He later recalled nutmegging the unfortunate Skocik 'dozens' of times during the match. It wasn't only Baxter who was on top form; the entire Rangers team was playing to the best of its ability and it was no surprise when the Scots scored again in the fifty-first minute. With Eric Caldow off receiving treatment for an injury Willie Johnston suddenly burst through the Rapid defence and cut back an inch-perfect cross for Davie Wilson, who coolly side-footed home under pressure from a defender.

With the aggregate score now 3–0 and the tie won, Rangers enjoyed themselves as they played out the remainder of the half to the cheers of the 70,000-strong crowd. Then with seconds to go, the tormented Skocik lunged in with his leg-breaking tackle. As Baxter put it many years later, 'If it had been him against me, I would have kicked me much sooner. I can assure you of that.'

After having his leg encased in plaster at a local hospital, the story goes that Baxter spent the night guzzling champagne and brandy with a newly-acquired lady friend in his room at the team hotel. It is almost certainly apocryphal, but no-one who knows anything of his off-field antics would be surprised if it were true. The following morning Skocik and his wife visited Baxter's room and presented him with a huge bunch of flowers and a box of chocolates by way of an apology for the injury. One can only hope that Baxter's supposed overnight visitor had left and that he had gathered up the empty bottles before they arrived!

Back home in Scotland, the injured hero was met at the airport by his parents and his fiancée, Jean Ferguson, twenty-one, who breathlessly told reporters, 'As Jim hugged me it was the most wonderful moment of my life.'

But it was for the events on the field that Baxter will be remembered most. Even Rapid coach Bimbo Binder was full of praise for 'Slim' and his team-mates, saying, 'They played it with all the flair of a top Continental team, dictating the play, slowing it whenever they felt like it.' Many Rangers supporters believe it was the high point of Baxter's career, and the player himself agreed in a 1996 interview. 'Looking back on it, I think it was the best game I ever played for Rangers and I'm not saying that because I played well – which I did – or because I broke my leg, but because it was the best team performance Rangers managed during the time I was at Ibrox.'

So with their most influential player recovering from injury, Rangers now had the daunting task of taking on Milanese giants Internazionale, the holders of both the European Cup and the World Club Championship. Owned by millionaire businessman Angelo Moratti, and coached by Helenio Herrera, Inter were the polar opposite of the Real Madrid dream team. The Italians had built their success on impenetrable defence, as opposed to Madrid's reliance on attacking flair.

Under former Barcelona coach Herrera, Inter used a system known as *catenaccio*. It was frustrating to play against and ugly to watch, but at the same time proved to be a highly effective, if extremely unpopular, tactic. Herrera deployed a sweeper (*libero*) behind a bank of four defenders; the sweeper's job was to block any forwards who managed to break through the first line of defence. The midfield would also be packed, leaving just one player up front; his job was to score on the break.

During the previous season, 1963/64, Inter had beaten Real Madrid 3–1 in the European Cup final (at the Prater stadium of all places), with striker Sandro Mazzola scoring twice. Luis Suarez – European player of the year in 1960 – controlled the midfield displaying all the creative talents that had persuaded Inter to pay Barcelona a world record £200,000 for his services. For all that their defence captured the headlines the *nerazzuri* (black and blues) had plenty of attacking flair in their team, particularly Suarez, Mazzola, Angelo Domenghini and Mario Costa.

Rangers ran out for the first leg at the San Siro on 17 February 1965 hoping to capitalise on their good form in the tournament and to pull off what would have been a major shock. For the first forty-five minutes the Scots more than held their own and for once it was the Inter attackers who were left frustrated. In fact the Italian goalkeeper, Sarti, had to make two good saves early in the game, including a twelfth-minute stop from a Ralph Brand header.

But, in a devastating spell shortly after half-time, Rangers conceded three goals, through Suarez and two from Peiro. The Scots were shell-shocked but somehow found the character to fight back and gave themselves a glimmer of hope for the second leg when Jim Forrest scored with a powerful shot. It was only the second goal Inter had ever conceded at home in the European Cup.

Snow was piled up around the Ibrox pitch as a crowd of more than 77,000 braved a bitterly cold February night; they saw Rangers literally come within inches of a historic result against the European champions. Kitted out in an all-white change strip, the Scots had a stunning start to the second leg when Inter goalkeeper Giuliano Sarti fumbled a fierce thirty-yard shot from Roger Hynd and Forrest pounced to open the scoring. Another goal would have taken the tie to a play-off in Stuttgart but, following the shock of the goal, the Italians closed ranks in typical fashion. Inter captain Picchi was outstanding in the *libero* role, sweeping-up anything that got past the man-markers in front of him. He only blotted his copy book once with a heavy tackle on Willie Henderson, which resulted in a booking.

As the game progressed, Inter grew stronger; Rangers found it increasingly difficult to string passes together and appeared to run out of ideas. Henderson failed to make any progress against the superb Inter left back, Giacinto Faccheti, while on the opposite wing Willie Johnston was starved of service. Just as they had done in previous European ties Rangers too often resorted to the old Scottish tactic of the big punt up the park.

Then, with just nine minutes to go, Rangers came agonisingly close to levelling the tie. George McLean hit a tremendous shot from twenty yards that flew past the helpless Sarti, but it smashed off the crossbar and rebounded to safety. It was a typical hard luck story for Rangers in Europe but, in fairness, they had done little during the game to merit a draw. As an attacking force, Inter were almost non-existent. Raymond Jacobs in the *Glasgow Herald* noted, 'They played their retreating game as expected, and could not, in their position, I suppose, be blamed for that, however unappealing the game was made as an alternative to a warm fireside.'

The one unanswered question from the game is whether a fully fit Jim Baxter would have had the craft to break down Inter's *catenaccio* defence. No doubt the ever-confident Baxter would have answered in the affirmative; but, of course, it is impossible to say. Even if he had inspired Rangers to victory over the Italians, we cannot be sure that Rangers would have gone on to win the competition, as others have hypothesised. In the semi-final, Inter went on to defeat English champions Liverpool – certainly no pushovers – and they had to overcome Benfica in the final, albeit on their own San Siro pitch, to win the cup again.

Rangers left back Eric Caldow was one member of that Rangers team who did not subscribe to the theory that it was Baxter's absence that cost Rangers against Milan. 'I don't think Baxter being injured made any difference,' he argued. 'It was always a team effort.' Nor was Caldow of the view that Baxter's talents merited the praise bestowed on him. 'How could Baxter be one of the best players in the world?' he asked, 'He was slow, couldn't tackle, couldn't head the ball and he had only one foot! How could he be the greatest?' Caldow's views may well have been clouded by the fact that he was the one who had to pick up the slack caused by Baxter's less than impressive work ethic. 'He played in front of me and used to say: "This inside right's fast Eric, will you take him?" Give him the ball yes, he was a great attacking wing half but to me he was not the greatest player I've seen at Ibrox.'

Baxter never played in the European Cup again for Rangers, although after his disappointing spells at Sunderland and Nottingham Forest, he returned briefly to Ibrox in 1969 and played in the Cup Winners Cup. The end of the 1964/65 campaign was also the beginning of the end for Scot Symon's great team of the early sixties. With no European football the following season, the likes of Bobby Shearer, Eric Caldow and Ralph Brand never played again in any of the Continental tournaments. Billy Ritchie, Jimmy Millar and Davie Wilson had a handful of appearances between them in 1966/67 but by the end of that season only Ronnie McKinnon, John Greig and Willie Henderson remained.

It was a new-look Rangers team that began the 1966/67 campaign with their first tie against Irish opposition, in the shape of Glentoran. The first leg in Belfast was a less than dazzling performance against a team that was packed with Rangers supporters. George McLean opened the scoring in the fifteenth minute after running onto an Alex Smith flick and finishing clinically from just inside the penalty area. It was expected that the floodgates would open and Rangers would run up a cricket score befitting the name of the Oval ground, where the game was being played. Instead, the Glens put up a spirited resistance and carved out as many chances as their illustrious visitors. Then in the final minute, Rangers conceded a free kick twenty-five yards out. Player-coach, and Celtic supporter, John Colrain touched it to Sinclair, who drove a low shot in off the post for a late equalizer. In the second leg at Ibrox, Rangers had a comfortable 4–0 victory without ever scaling the heights.

Rangers were drawn against Cup Winners Cup holders Borussia Dortmund in the first-round proper. The West Germans had won the trophy at Hampden the previous May against Liverpool in a dour final played out in dreadful weather. Liverpool manager Bill Shankly had declared that his team would win easily and then go on to lift the European Cup the following season. Having just won the English title comfortably, most pundits agreed with Shankly that the Anfield team were the overwhelming favourites but, as so often, the Germans defied the odds and won in extra time.

It was the first European trophy won by a West German club and signalled the arrival of the country as a force to be reckoned with in club football. The creation in 1963 of a national league, the *Bundesliga*, and the belated introduction of professionalism were the catalysts for an upturn in its fortunes. In the summer of 1966, West Germany reached the final of the World Cup, losing a classic match to England. The team, which arrived home to a rapturous reception, included three Dortmund players: goalkeeper Hans Tilkowski and forwards Siegfried Held and Lothar Emmerich. All three were in the Dortmund squad that faced Rangers in the first leg.

In a hard-fought match at Ibrox, Rangers won 2–1. Danish right-back Kai Johansen opened the scoring before Dortmund equalized with a controversial goal. A deflected shot appeared to be going harmlessly wide, until Held, who had left the pitch after an earlier attack, re-entered the field and diverted it back towards goal, where Threshold collected the ball and scored. A late goal from Alex Smith gave Rangers a slim lead for the second leg. A magnificent defensive performance in Dortmund, where Rangers played with ten men for most of the game after an injury to Watson, secured a goalless draw and a passage into the next round.

For first-leg goal scorer Kai Johansen, the tie was memorable, particularly for his own performance. 'One of my finest hours was in that match against Borussia Dortmund,' he recalled. 'A lot of people said the game was like a final.' Johansen had not had the best of starts to his Ibrox career after signing from Morton the previous season. But his stock among the Rangers support rose enormously when he scored a spectacular winning goal against Celtic in the Scottish Cup final. It was a goal that instantly elevated him to hero status and secured Rangers' place in the Cup Winners Cup.

'I didn't really know until then what it meant to be a Ranger – but I soon found out,' he said. 'We went to the hotel in St Enoch's Square after the game and I came out like a king to see the crowds. It was embarrassing but never before in the history of Rangers was something like that needed. It was in the middle of Celtic's period of dominance. We needed this and it took us into Europe.' Johansen would be a key player in Rangers' run to the Cup Winners Cup final, but what the fans did not know was that every trip overseas filled him with dread. A fear of flying meant he had to down a couple of whiskies before he could face getting on a plane.

His phobia came from a tragic incident in 1960, when eight Danish footballers lost their lives in a plane crash on their way to a training camp. But for a twist of fate, Johansen would have been on the flight. He was called up to play for the Danish under-23 team in an exhibition match against the full national side in Jutland as a warm-up for the Olympics in Rome. Instead of travelling with his teammates, Johansen, who was doing his military service at the time, got permission to leave a day early so he could travel under his own steam and claim the expenses.

The grieving Danish squad, who assumed Johansen was on the doomed flight from Copenhagen as planned, got a shock when he arrived for duty.

'When I got to the training camp all the flags were at half-mast, he said. 'When they saw me walk in they did not understand how I survived.' The incident affected Johansen badly. 'I am not a religious person – but I could not understand why I had survived,' he said. 'I got doctor's treatment and the army put me off for about a week. But I could not get over it and the result was I became scared of flying. I did not want to fly at all, but if I wanted to have a career in football I had to do it. When they came back from the Olympics I got promoted to the national team. I had to have a couple of whiskies to fly every time.'

In an attempt to cure their player's phobia, Rangers took unorthodox action, although it didn't quite have the desired effect. 'The club paid for lessons so I could get a pilot's licence,' recalled Johansen. 'On one occasion, I was flying over Loch Lomond at 1,500 feet when they suddenly cut-off the engine and put the plane into a spin. I got so sick when we landed. I only had four or five flying hours left to get my licence but I never did it again.'

Always popular with the Rangers support, Johansen – who opened a pub on Govan Road, not far from Ibrox, as well as a bar and restaurant in Glasgow city centre – left Ibrox in 1970 and moved to South Africa, where he forged a successful coaching career. In the eighties he lived a nomadic lifestyle, before moving into the sunbed business in Denmark. He later returned to Scotland and opened a successful chain of tanning salons, before moving into property development. In April 2006, at the age of sixty-one, he was diagnosed with terminal cancer.

A month after the Dortmund tie was won Johansen was in the Rangers eleven that took part in the club's most humiliating defeat of all time. Rangers were beaten 1–0 by lowly Berwick Rangers in the opening round of the Scottish Cup. The result shocked Scottish football and reverberated around Europe. Even today, it is cited whenever there is a major cup shock; a recognition of the standing of Rangers as Scotland's most eminent football club. While others quite regularly find themselves on the end of defeats by lower-league opposition, it simply does not happen to Rangers. Well, on 28 January 1967 it did, and the repercussions were enormous.

In an era when tracksuit managers were becoming the norm, Scot Symon's outdated approach to management came under fire following the Berwick defeat, but publicly at least, he was backed by the board. Instead, chairman John Lawrence turned his ire on the players, and two in particular were made to pay for the humiliation. The scapegoats were forwards George McLean and Jim Forrest, neither of whom played a competitive match for Rangers again. The treatment of the young strike pair was harsh. They had racked up twenty-eight goals between them that season, and Forrest in particular, with an astonishing 145 goals in 164 games, was a player who could have been a Rangers scoring legend. As it was both he and McLean were shipped out, and it could be argued that their departure cost Rangers the chance to win their first European trophy.

In March, having recovered somewhat from the trauma of Berwick, Rangers found themselves facing tournament favourites Real Zaragoza in the quarter-final of the Cup Winners Cup. After ten years of competing in Europe, the clash with the Spaniards was seen as make-or-break, and would prove once and for all whether the Scottish giants had what it took finally to win the much sought-after European trophy.

It was exactly the sort of game in which Rangers had come up short in the past, but on a night of heavy rain, driving sleet and high winds in Glasgow, they put in a superb performance. The stormy weather only added to the electric atmosphere created by the 65,000 crowd; the sort of ambience that only Ibrox can generate on special European nights under floodlights. In fact, the crowd was swollen by representatives from several European countries, who were at the match primarily to see the stadium's new lights in action. Ironically, given the Spanish opposition, it was the same system used to illuminate the Rock of Gibraltar.

The performances of inside left Dave Smith, a £45,000 close-season signing from Aberdeen, and 18-year-old Sandy Jardine caught the eye as Rangers mastered the weather conditions and dominated the Spaniards. Smith scored the first goal in ten minutes, had another disallowed ten minutes later and set up the second goal midway through the first half. Jardine, on his European debut, was a revelation, setting up countless Rangers attacks with his accurate passing, and almost scored in the first five minutes with a twenty-yard drive that produced a spectacular save from goalkeeper Yarza. Jim Forrest's cousin Alex Willoughby who, ironically, had become a regular in the team in the aftermath of Berwick, scored the second goal, which gave Rangers a great chance to progress.

Jardine could have been forgiven for being overawed at the experience of his European debut, but he took it in his stride as only an 18-year old could:

> To be honest I was just happy to be playing. It was a brand-new experience for me but I didn't feel any pressure, probably because I didn't understand or appreciate the level I was playing at. You don't know what you've got to lose and you just think these things will come around all the time. We got a really good result at Ibrox though. The one thing I remember about that game was that it was absolutely lashing with rain and the pitch was really muddy. The conditions were the complete opposite over there, which was something I had never experienced before.

The second leg at *La Romerada* was one of the most dramatic nights ever experienced by Rangers in Europe, and in the end was decided by a silver two-franc coin. Rangers were without defensive stalwart Ronnie McKinnon – who had suffered a broken nose in a match against Ayr United – and pitched young centre half Colin Jackson into the cauldron. Aided by Greig, Johansen and Provan, he had a good game under enormous pressure from the Spanish attack, known as *Los Cinco Fabulosos* (The Magnificent Five). Rangers did concede a goal in the twenty-fifth minute when a speculative free-kick deceived goalkeeper Norrie Martin but, with just four minutes to go, the Zaragoza players, seemed to accept that they would fail to break down the Scottish defence. Then they were awarded the softest of penalties. A cross from the left struck Greig on the shoulder, but the French referee Michel Kitbadjian pointed to the spot and Santos levelled the tie on aggregate.

The match moved into extra time and, with just three minutes on the clock, Rangers were handed a golden chance to seal the tie. Davie Wilson was fouled as he worked his way in from the left and a penalty was given, the referee perhaps attempting to 'even-up' his earlier dubious award. Unfortunately for Rangers, Dave Smith couldn't take advantage and Yarza saved his shot. Despite numerous chances in an exciting last twenty-seven minutes, neither team could score again. The play-off system had by now been scrapped by UEFA and with penalty shoot-outs still in the future the rules dictated that the toss of a coin would determine the tie.

Rangers captain John Greig and his Spanish opposite number Reija were brought together, face-to-face on the halfway line, by Monsieur Kitbadjian. Greig had already correctly called two tosses of the coin, one before the match kicked off and one before extra time, so he decided to share the burden of making the decision with Scot Symon. In front of a disbelieving crowd, he ran to the sideline for a short consultation before returning to the centre circle to announce his choice.

With the 35,000 Spanish supporters now waiting in silence, and many of the Rangers team in the dressing room unable to watch, Greig called 'tails'. The coin sparkled under the floodlights as it was tossed, before landing on the turf. It was indeed tails and the Rangers players who were still on the pitch went crazy with delight. The spin of the coin had guaranteed Rangers at least £35,000 and put them into a semi-final with Slavia Sofia. Forty years later, Greig still has the silver coin as a souvenir of one of the most surreal European matches in Rangers' history.

The first leg of the semi-final in the Bulgarian capital – Rangers' fiftieth match in European football – proved to be the most straightforward tie of the competition. But when the Rangers players arrived at the National

Levski stadium they feared that the state of the pitch would cause problems. It was small, bumpy and almost entirely devoid of grass. After a training session on Slavia's ash-covered training pitch, Scot Symon declared Rangers would not be taking a negative approach to the game. He told reporters, 'We came here to win. That is still our main aim.'

On an uninspiring afternoon of football, a goal from Davie Wilson in the thirty-first minute gave Rangers the win that Symon craved. The victory should have been more comprehensive, when Dave Smith scored what appeared to be a second goal after taking a pass from Willoughby. However, after a moment's hesitation, the referee disallowed the goal, much to the annoyance of the Rangers party; not least chairman John Lawrence, who was heavily critical of the official.

It wasn't the first controversy the Soviet referee, Tofik Bakhramov, had been involved in with a British team. A few months earlier he had officiated in the World Cup final between England and West Germany, and it was on his say-so that Geoff Hurst's infamous shot was ruled to have crossed the line. As a result, he has gone down in English football folklore as the 'Russian linesman' who helped England win the Jules Rimet trophy – although he was actually from Azerbaijan, where he became a national hero.

Rangers went onto the second leg of the semi-final, knowing that their rivals from across the city had already claimed a place in the final of the European Cup. Failure to emulate that achievement was simply unaccept-able for the Rangers support. Given the importance of the match, there was some surprise at Scot Symon's team selection, particularly in attack. Roger Hynd – a hitherto unheralded defender who had not played a first-team game for more than three months, and had been on the transfer list at the beginning of the season – was called up as a centre forward at the expense of Alex Willoughby. Solid and powerful, Hynd played himself into con-tention for a place against Slavia by scoring four goals in a reserve match the weekend before.

Willoughby, who had only just agreed terms for another season at Ibrox, was stunned by the decision and immediately handed in a transfer request. The 22-year-old had scored fifteen goals in seventeen matches since he broke into the team and was skilful, if slightly built. Symon felt he needed a more powerful presence in the number-nine shirt and gambled on Hynd. Ably supported by wingers Willie Johnston and Willie Henderson, Hynd put in an impressive performance; he constantly harried the Slavia defenders and gave a new drive to the attack. All three were involved in the winning goal, Hynd heading on a Johnston corner towards Henderson, who sent a twenty-yard drive high into the net past goalkeeper Simeonov. It was the only goal of the game, but Rangers were comfortable winners, and only a series of saves by Simeonov kept the score down.

Sandy Jardine recalled, 'They were a very physical team. They didn't have a lot of flair but were very well organised. It wasn't quite a kicking match but it was very tough and we did well to get a win over there and there was more of the same at Ibrox.'

For the second time, Rangers were in the final of the European Cup Winners Cup and this time failure was not an option.

6

Nuremberg, May 1967: Victory Was a Must

They arrived in Nuremberg by plane, train and automobile. Some even made the journey on foot. It started with a trickle on the Monday and by Tuesday it had become a flood. Many had taken a week off work, while others simply headed off to Bavaria without telling their boss, and without knowing if they would have a job to return to. In an era when package holidays were still in their infancy and foreign travel was something of a luxury, for some it was the first time they had ever been abroad.

Rangers were in the final of the European Cup Winners Cup, with Bayern Munich the opposition, and thousands of dedicated fans were determined to be there. With Celtic having just won the European Cup a week earlier, victory was a must. Getting to the south of Germany was not easy. The straightforward option, for those who could afford it, was to fly. Glasgow travel firms had laid on charter flights and, as late as the Monday before the match, one company was offering fans a last chance to make the trip. The advertisement for Holiday Enterprises of Partick Cross even said that planes could be laid on at an hour's notice if there was enough demand. A fleet of coaches also left Scotland for the trip to Bavaria. Nuremberg is a thousand miles from Glasgow, which would be bad enough in the luxury coaches that are available today; in the late sixties a bus journey of that magnitude was a test of endurance.

Then there were those who hitchhiked their way across Europe, spending money only on a cross-channel ferry at Dover. They arrived looking bedraggled, with barely a pfennig to their name, but clutching their flags and flutes and proudly wearing their red-white-and-blue scarves. Bobby Sorbie was a 17-year-old apprentice commercial artist from East Kilbride, who followed

Rangers home and away in Scotland. Going to Germany for the most important match in their history seemed logical. So he got his first passport and set off with his pal, Malky, on an epic journey; they had just a few pounds in their pocket and no real plan. They were dropped off in Hamilton by the side of the main road to England and started looking for a lift. Bobby, now a Lanarkshire businessman, said:

> We got to Beattock where we went into the transport caff. A lorry driver saw us walking in with our Union Jacks and scarves and asked us where we were going. We replied Nuremberg! Luckily he was able to give us a lift right down to London and my pal had worked for British Rail so we got cheap tickets to Dover and then a ferry to Ostend.

On the boat they befriended a Belgian student who, it turned out, was also going to Germany and he gave the pair a lift all the way through Belgium and as far as Munich, less than one hundred miles from their destination. 'What an experience that was,' remembered Bobby. 'He was a nutcase! He was driving through the night, steering with his knees and playing the mouth organ. We were teaching him all the songs and he was playing along.'

After being deposited in Munich, Bobby and Malky fell foul of the police, who issued them with an on-the-spot fine of five marks for hitchhiking. The police apparently didn't appreciate the fact that they were standing at the side of the *autobahn* with their Union flag on prominent display as cars raced past at 100 miles per hour. Having escaped the attentions of the authorities, the duo then managed to get lost in a wood, which they later found out was the Black Forest.

'Next we jumped on a log train, even though we had no idea where it was going!' said Bobby. 'We ended up coming across a shop somewhere that had a statue of a British policeman inside so we assumed they could speak English. It turned out to be a tourist agency and amazingly they all had a whip-round when they heard about our plight. They pointed us in the right direction and told us where to stand so we wouldn't get done by the police again.'

The final leg was completed with the help of a German Scoutmaster ('We told him we were Scouts, which was why we had a big Union Jack') and they arrived in Nuremberg thirty hours after setting off from Scotland. In the city they bumped into a journalist from the *Evening Times*, Gair Henderson. 'We gave him our story and they gave us money so we could spend a night in a hotel,' said Bobby. 'The night before we had slept in a ploughed field with the flag to keep us warm.' When the article appeared, the lads became minor celebrities with Scottish and German papers desperate to tell their story. They happily agreed – for a small fee of course.

They used Nuremberg's grand railway station as a base during the day, passing the time in the bars where they drank beer from giant steins. Dozens of other Rangers fans in the same position also descended on the station and turned it into an unofficial headquarters. The people of Nuremberg took the young supporters to their hearts and delivered them food and beer. Some were even invited back to family homes and presented with traditional Bavarian tankards as mementoes.

With its chocolate-box houses, beautiful churches, cobbled squares and medieval city walls, Nuremberg looks like a picture-postcard Bavarian town. But its very name is enough to conjure up images of the darkest period in Europe's history. The city was the site of the notorious Nazi rallies of the 1930s and the municipal stadium where the final was to be played was part of the rally grounds. It was also used as a parade ground for the Hitler Youth.

During the war, Nuremberg was a centre for the production of aircraft and tank engines and as a result large parts of the old centre were destroyed in Allied air raids, only to be rebuilt in almost identical form in the post-war years. Between 1945 and 1949, Nazi officials who took part in the Holocaust were tried in what became known as the Nuremberg trials. In the late sixties, these events would still have been painfully fresh in the minds of those who travelled from Scotland, yet there were no reports, either in the media or from the local police, that it was an issue.

Bobby, Malky and a few other early arrivals went to the airport on the Monday morning to meet the team as they arrived. After chatting at length to players like Willie Johnston and Kai Johansen they managed to get precious tickets for the game from John Lawrence and Scot Symon, a wonderful gesture. That night, they were among a group of around thirty fans who ended up in bunks at a local Catholic mission, of all places.

'The people there were really nice,' remembers Bobby. 'All the people in Nuremberg were fantastic in fact. They fed us and gave us gifts. One young family took about eight of us back to their home and fed us. It was amazing and I don't think it would happen here.'

There was not a hint of trouble from the Rangers fans, although the local chief of police did find it necessary to issue a warning following the invasion by Celtic fans at the National stadium in Lisbon the previous week. He said sternly, 'There will be no repeat here.'

While the Rangers players were staying at their hideaway far out of town, the club officials were based in the heart of Nuremberg. Chairman John Lawrence held court at the luxurious Grand Hotel; it was a minute's walk

from the main railway station, where most of the Rangers suppo.
spending their time. Coincidentally, England's World Cup squad s.
the same hotel before their match with Trinidad and Tobago in su.
2006. Like the Rangers party, Beckham, Rooney, Owen and co had to .
up with the racket created by noisy fans until the early hours.

As Wednesday, the day of the match, arrived, the scramble for tickets
began in earnest. The Nuremberg stadium could hold a crowd of 70,000
but with Munich less than one hundred miles away, the vast majority of the
fans would be backing the Germans. For the five thousand or so Rangers
fans in town it was going to be difficult to get in. Touts were selling briefs
for four times their face value on the main thoroughfare, *Konigstrasse*.

One supporter who was determined to get his hands on a precious ticket
was the Govan-born songwriter Bill Martin. His song 'Puppet on a String' had
just won the Eurovision Song Contest for Sandie Shaw and was actually at
number one in the West German charts at the time of the final. He was desperate to be in Nuremberg for the match and set about pulling every string
he could for a ticket. He cabled one journalist at his hotel in Nuremberg,
'If you have tickets I will travel. If you haven't I will still travel.' Martin –
who later co-wrote the England World Cup song 'Back Home' and claims to
have written more number ones than any other Scot – flew in to Germany
on the day of the match and used his family connections to see his heroes,
as he explained to the author:

> The BBC's football commentator Kenneth Wolstenholme was the godfather of
> the girl I married and he managed to get me into the ground to see the match.
> My heart was always with the Rangers and still to this day, if I'm asked
> who I support, it's the Rangers. I was desperate to see them win the cup. I
> was a promising footballer myself, and I ended up in South Africa playing
> for a team called Johannesburg Rangers. My father used to tell everyone I
> played for the Rangers, and no-one ever checked.

In May 2004 current Rangers chairman David Murray declared: 'They
always say that football chairmen are sensible but they leave their brains
outside when they go into the stadium.' He was referring to the baffling
habit of prudent businessmen abandoning their usual financial acumen as
soon as they take the reins at a football club. It may even have been an
admission that he had made some mistakes during his own tenure. But the
comment could also apply to the inexplicable outbursts that so many chairmen have been guilty of over the years; not least the one that preceded what
was the most important game in Rangers' history at the time.

g, construction-company boss John Lawrence
from all over Europe and launched a scathing
the Rangers team. That he was club chairman
nouncements came on the eve of the team's
up Winners Cup final made it unforgivable.
won the European Cup against Inter Milan in
____rg, Rangers had the chance to achieve an unprece-
____ double for Glasgow. No city had won both of UEFA's major club
tournaments in the same season. But, more importantly for Rangers fans,
victory was essential to offset the agony of watching their rivals celebrate
lifting the Champions Cup.

As the players trained at their hideaway in the village of Neundettelsau,
twenty miles from the city, Lawrence announced that chief scout Jimmy
Smith was being pensioned off, with the implication that he had failed to
identify a sufficient number of good players. The chairman then went on to say
he felt the team wasn't good enough and that the board would break the
bank to bring in two new forwards. His argument was that Rangers could
not compete with Celtic, or Europe's other top clubs, as long as they were
playing with three halfbacks in the forward line.

The fact that many Rangers supporters actually agreed with his assessment
was irrelevant. The decision to go public in the middle of preparations for
such an enormous game beggared belief and it was difficult to comprehend
the motivation for such an outburst. Surely it was Lawrence and the rest of
the board who were responsible for the state of the club? And given that the
chairman was widely thought to be responsible for the hounding out of
Ibrox of Jim Forrest and George McLean, the comments about the forward
line were bizarre. But it was the timing that brought the most criticism for
Lawrence.

Sandy Jardine remembers there was a sense of disbelief that Lawrence
had spoken out in such a fashion:

> We didn't know that on the morning of the game, because we were in
> Germany and didn't see the papers. But after the game, everyone was a bit
> depressed and we were relaxing in a café at our training camp when we
> were told about the chairman's comments. All the players were very, very
> angry and disappointed that he could come out with a comment like that
> prior to one of the biggest games the club had.

Having knocked out the holders Borussia Dortmund earlier in the competition, there was a genuine belief that Rangers had the ability to defeat Munich.

Although they are now the undisputed kings of German football, in the 1960s Bayern were still establishing themselves as a force. Indeed the club had been overlooked when the *Bundesliga* was set up in 1963, with rivals 1860 Munich getting the city's place instead. However, Yugoslavian coach Zlatko Cajkovski formed a talented team based around the axis of three of Europe's best young players: goalkeeper Sepp Maier, midfield general Franz Beckenbauer and prolific striker Gerd Muller.

The team's undoubted star was 21-year-old Beckenbauer. His style and supreme confidence, bordering on arrogance, earned him the nickname of *Der Kaiser* and he was vital to everything Bayern achieved. In his first season, the club gained promotion to the *Bundesliga* and in its debut campaign finished third. During that season he made his first international appearance, and played for West Germany in the World Cup final against England in 1966. Bayern also won the German Cup in 1965/66, to take them into the European Cup Winners Cup for the first time.

Bayern had reached the final by defeating Tatran Presov from Czechoslovakia, Shamrock Rovers, Rapid Vienna and Standard Liege. Only in the semi-final against the Belgians did Bayern show anything like convincing form, winning 5–1 on aggregate; it was the only tie in which they managed a winning margin of more than one goal.

In the build-up to the final the talk centred on whether Muller would be allowed to play. He had broken his arm playing for West Germany against Yugoslavia three weeks earlier and his arm was strapped up with a heavy leather bandage. Rangers were unhappy at the prospect of him playing with the bandage and demanded that the Italian referee, Concetto Lo Bello, carry out stringent safety tests. On the day of the game the official compromised: he ordered Muller to modify the strapping and allowed him to play with a much smaller bandage than the striker wanted.

Rangers named the team that had overcome Slavia Prague in the semi-final and drawn with Celtic in the closing stages of the league campaign. That meant physical-education teacher Roger Hynd continuing in his unfamiliar role at centre forward. The full Rangers team was Martin; Johansen, Provan; Jardine, McKinnon, Greig; Alex Smith, Dave Smith; Henderson, Hynd and Johnston. Much would depend on Henderson and Johnston on the wings. Henderson had suffered a loss of form earlier in the season but was still seen as a danger man by Cajkovski, who described him before the match as the finest winger in Europe. The coach shuffled his team to combat the threat posed by the little Scot, putting Kupferschmidt to left back in the belief that he was the only man capable of thwarting Henderson's jinking runs forward.

As expected the stadium was a sell-out and it was a magnificent scene. The terraces were almost full an hour before kick-off and they were covered with the red-and-white flags of the Bayern fans, who took up most of the stadium. Exploding fireworks lit up the overcast sky, and the small band of Rangers fans among 65,000 Germans did their best to make themselves heard. But the cacophony of noise coming from the German supporters was deafening. Shortly before the game started there was the bizarre sight of a Rangers fan being carried round the track on a stretcher, but doing his best to get away from the ambulance men. Then, a German band in full traditional dress took to the field to provide a fanfare for the trophy, and the stadium erupted again as the teams appeared; Bayern in their change strip of white tops and red shorts, Rangers in light blue and white.

Sheer weight of numbers meant the Scots were outperformed on the terraces but on the pitch it was Rangers who were on top throughout the first half. Chance after chance went unclaimed as the Scots took the game to Bayern. The best chance fell to Roger Hynd after half an hour. Dave Smith evaded Beckenbauer and cut the ball back from the goal line into the path of the temporary centre forward, who stabbed it left-footed towards goal. Maier managed to get a hand to the shot and as the ball rolled agonisingly towards the net he dived on top of it for a second time. The Rangers pressure continued but they couldn't put the ball in the net.

The pattern continued in the second half, and although Beckenbauer made occasional forays forward, he was largely limited to defensive duties. However, even in his own penalty area *Der Kaiser* was a joy to watch. At one point he intercepted a through ball that was meant for John Greig. Running back towards his goal, and with Greig in hot pursuit, he suddenly turned and moved off to his left, in the same movement hurdling a lunging challenge from the Rangers man with balletic grace. Most defenders in the same position would have taken the easy option and hoofed it out for a corner, but Beckenbauer's willingness to take a chance allowed him to turn defence into attack.

While Beckenbauer was demonstrating his class and Maier was making a string of saves, Gerd Muller, the other member of the famous Bayern trio, had less impact. He was well marshalled by Ronnie McKinnon, and on the rare occasions when he did get a chance he was off the boil. Still Rangers pressed forward, to no avail. Sandy Jardine – known by his real name, Willie, at that time – was involved in many of Rangers' attacks and thoroughly enjoyed the experience:

> I had just turned eighteen and at the time I was the youngest person to play in a European final. I was just so happy to be playing. My first final wasn't a

domestic game, but a European final, and that was a very unusual set of circumstances. I watched a video of that game recently and we played really well. We were by far the better team and controlled the game but we just couldn't score any goals.

After a gruelling ninety minutes the match remained goalless and moved into extra time. Two minutes into the first period, Roger Hynd had a back-post header tipped over the bar by Maier. Four minutes later, the Rangers players and fans thought they had finally got the breakthrough. Hynd rose in the penalty area with Maier and the ball broke loose; the Rangers man was first to react and rolled it into the net. Before the celebrations could begin, the Italian referee had blown for a foul on the goalkeeper. There was contact between the two, and in the current era it would have been a foul, but in those days it was a highly contentious decision.

The incident almost killed the game stone dead. The exhausted players slowed to walking speed and seemed content to hold out for a replay. Then, in the second period of extra time, disaster struck for Rangers. A long ball into the penalty area looked harmless enough, but, as it dropped, Franz Roth, 'The Bull', managed to twist his body and stuck out a leg to hook it past Martin into the net.

Rangers desperately tried to get an equalizer but it was too late. After a brave battle they had lost; what made it more difficult to take was that they had been the better team. At the final whistle, thousands of Germans invaded the pitch to celebrate, and many of them even joined the players on their lap of honour. There was no disgrace in losing to Bayern but the sense of disappointment was amplified by the thought of what might have been and tears flowed as the players left the pitch. Roger Hynd, unfairly branded the scapegoat, hurled his runners-up medal into the crowd such was his despair.

Sandy Jardine is in no doubt where the fault lay for the lack of a goalscorer:

> I wouldn't blame Roger. The blame lies with the directors at the time, who took umbrage at the result at Berwick and made sure that Jim Forrest and George McLean were pushed out of the club. They forced the hand of Scot Symon but never gave him the money to re-invest in another centre forward. As a result we went to the final with no recognised player for that position. Roger himself will admit he was a stopgap. He would always give 100 per cent but he wasn't really a centre forward. But having said that we were still the better team and we should have won but we just didn't have that wee bit of luck on the night.

Jardine was desperate to win, but the naivety of youth softened the blow of defeat. He recalled:

> A lot of the other players were hugely disappointed, and with Celtic win-
> ning the European Cup, losing the final put pressure on the club. It would
> have been fantastic for us to achieve that but I was just in the team and I
> was just happy to play. I was eighteen and I assumed I would get another
> chance, and I was lucky enough that I did get another chance, but you kind
> of take it for granted at that age. Rangers at that time had a fantastic time
> in European competitions, as did all the Scottish teams in fact.

Contrary to most observers, Danish full back Kai Johansen felt that Bayern were worthy of their win. 'This was Bayern Munich's first year in Europe with players like Beckenbauer and Maier. That was the first major final they had been in and look what happened to them since. The result was a fair reflection of what had happened but it was an unbelievable disappointment not to win that game.'

For the fans, the result was a huge disappointment after a wonderful trip, as Bobby Sorbie recalls:

> The whole game went by in a flash but we should have won. There were
> about six thousand of us in there but the majority were Bayern Munich fans.
> Afterwards the German fans were brilliant too; they had never seen any-
> thing like us and wanted to swap scarves as souvenirs. The whole trip was
> a great experience although getting home was a nightmare and even worse
> than coming over, because there were so many of us looking for a lift.

Bill Martin shared the disappointment of the supporters:

> It wasn't the greatest of games if I remember, but there was so much pres-
> sure on Rangers to win because Celtic had done it the week before. It came
> too soon after their game. But it was a thrill to get there nonetheless. Scot
> Symon was a very nice man but he was never my favourite manager. He
> was almost too nice, and didn't have the personality of someone like Jock
> Stein. To be honest I don't think we had the tactics correct that night. Scot
> Symon was maybe from a different era and things had passed him by.

It was a sombre Rangers party that arrived home at Glasgow airport on the following afternoon. The city's Lord Provost John Johnston and Celtic chairman Bob Kelly were on hand to dispense commiserations. John Lawrence was first off the plane and immediately issued a denial that he was quitting as chairman.

At Ibrox, a small band of supporters were present to welcome the team home. It was a sad end to what could have been a glorious trip.

7

The Battle of Newcastle

After the crushing disappointment of the 1966/67 campaign, which Rangers ended without silverware, the following season saw the Ibrox club compete for the first time in UEFA's third tournament, the Inter Cities Fairs Cup. The competition was inaugurated in 1955, and it took three years to complete the first tournament. For reasons best known to the organisers, it was only open to cities that hosted annual trade fairs and, in the first contest, London entered a representative team. The London XI actually reached the final, where they were thrashed 8–2 over two legs by Barcelona. As time went on, the rules were amended to ensure that only clubs could enter, rather than representative selects, and eventually the baffling link with trade exhibitions was dropped. In 1971 the competition was renamed the UEFA Cup.

In the first round, Rangers were again paired with German opposition, this time from the eastern side of the divide. Dynamo Dresden had been formed in the early 1950s but had grown in stature within the East German game. The tie with Rangers was their first in European competition, however, and there was huge interest in the city, which was still struggling to recover from the devastating Allied bombing raids during the war.

The Heinz Steyer stadium was packed with more than 40,000 fans, and they applauded both teams off the pitch at the end of what was an entertaining match. Dynamo had much the better of the game, winning eight corners to Rangers' none, and the Ibrox club's new Danish goalkeeper, Erik Sorensen, had to perform well to keep the Germans at bay. Rangers actually took the lead through a certain Alex Ferguson, who had recently been signed from Dunfermline. Ferguson, of course, went on to achieve European success as a manager, first with Aberdeen, then Manchester United. Dieter Riedel finally managed to breach the Rangers defence in the second half, but Rangers were happy with the 1–1 scoreline.

In the run-up to the second leg, Rangers chairman John Lawrence paid tribute to the East German club in typically verbose style. He wrote, 'The road was arduous, but none shirked the task, and by dint of shrewd planning and overwhelming enthusiasm, brushed aside the problems as they arose.' Undeterred by the heroics of their opponents, Rangers took the lead in the first half through Andy Penman, and seemed to be cruising comfortably into the next round when, with seconds to go, Hans Kreische equalised. Extra time looked inevitable but, with ninety-one minutes on the clock, and the Portuguese referee poised to blow for full time, John Greig stepped up to score an unlikely winner.

By coincidence it was German opposition again in the next round, this time from the west. However, it was a Rangers team in a state of flux that hosted Cologne on 8 November 1967. With the team at the top of the first division, having already beaten European champions Celtic, and having successfully negotiated a tricky European tie, the directors had decided that Scot Symon's time as manager was up. Whether or not it was the correct decision is debatable – and certainly the timing was open to question – but the way the sacking of a loyal club servant was handled was disgraceful.

Symon – the manager for thirteen years – was summoned to the home of chartered accountant Alex McBain, told he was no longer wanted and urged to tender his resignation. Understandably, Symon took the view that if the directors had agreed that they no longer wanted him then that was tantamount to dismissal, and he wanted nothing more to do with the club. To the shock of players and supporters alike, a devastated Symon issued a statement that he had been sacked.

It seems astonishing that John Lawrence delegated such a task to some-one with no connection to the club. Common courtesy, not to mention Symon's years of loyal service, demanded that he be told the news in person by those who made the decision. In a typically high-handed statement to the Press Association, the club arrogantly announced that Symon was no longer wanted, 'for reasons which appeared to the board to be adequate'. It went on to claim that Mr McBain had been sent because he was best placed to advise Symon on the financial implications of his departure and suggested that they had done everything possible to make the move as smooth as possible. Nevertheless, it is impossible to escape the conclusion that Lawrence and his colleagues had taken the cowardly option. It was not the first time in the history of Rangers that the directors had treated employees with a lack of respect, and by no means was it the last.

Assistant manager Davie White was the man chosen to succeed Symon. He was a modern, 'tracksuit' manager; he had never played at the highest level, but thought deeply about the game. He had joined Rangers from Clyde, after travelling to Germany to watch the 1967 Cup Winners Cup final to enhance his football education. His appointment was seen as a positive one by the players, although many supporters were more dubious, concerned about his lack of top-level experience.

White's first match in charge was a 3–2 away victory at St Johnstone, but his first real test came three days later in the Fairs Cup. The new manager took the team to Largs to prepare for the visit of Cologne and the team-bonding session certainly worked. Rangers secured a superb 3–0 win, including a tremendous headed goal from Alex Ferguson, one of two he scored.

The return match at the Mungersdorfer stadium in Cologne seemed a formality, but, in predictable fashion, Rangers made heavy weather of getting through to the next round. In his pre-match team talk, White stressed the importance of not losing an early goal, but before he had taken his place on the bench the Germans were a goal to the good. It was scored in twenty-five seconds by World Cup star Wolfgang Overath, one of the world's leading players at the time; he went on to inspire Cologne to a 3–0 lead, taking the game into extra time. Then, with just three minutes left, and the dreaded toss of a coin looming, Rangers won a corner. Danish winger Orjan Persson swung in a cross, which goalkeeper Milutin Soskic could only palm out to Willie Henderson, who struck a sweet shot into the net.

The goal put Rangers through on a 4–3 aggregate to the quarter-final and another Battle of Britain, this time against Leeds United. Renowned for its hard-tackling, no-nonsense style, Don Revie's team was packed with quality players. It included Gary Sprake, Billy Bremner, Jack Charlton, Norman Hunter, Jimmy Greenhoff, Peter Lorimer and Johnny Giles. If Rangers were to overcome this emerging power of the English game they would have to perform at the top of their game – and take any chances that came their way.

A crowd of 80,000 packed into Ibrox for the first leg, with around 20,000 watching on big screens at Elland Road. Most commentators believed a two-goal lead was essential to give the men from Govan any chance of progressing, and had they taken even a small percentage of their chances, they would have done so. Alex Ferguson was the worst offender as Rangers repeatedly penetrated United's much-lauded defensive shield but failed to take advantage by putting the ball in the net. For all their chances, Rangers allowed Leeds back into the game and Bremner was soon able to dictate the pace and direction of the game. The Yorkshiremen came close themselves on a number of occasions, with Lorimer having two good chances late in the game and Giles forcing Rangers goalkeeper Erik Sorensen into a good save.

Ten thousand Rangers fans were expected to descend on Leeds for the return match, sparking a massive police operation. Two hundred police were on duty along with a team of ten dogs, as the local assistant chief constable Brian Molloy warned the Scots, 'Behave or else.' Police urged fans without tickets not to travel, insisting that the match was a sell-out. However, the Scottish supporters knew differently, with the Rangers Supporters Association revealing that one tout alone had 1,500 tickets. In the end the night was trouble free, leaving police delighted and full of praise for the travelling Scots. There were just sixteen arrests at the ground; unsurprisingly thirteen were for drunk and disorderly behaviour.

Back in Glasgow, a huge crowd of 43,177 turned up at Ibrox to watch the beam-back. Giant screens were put up on the goal line on either side of the goals at the Copland Road end and the terracing was packed. Unfortunately for the massive Gers support in Govan and Yorkshire, Rangers were out-played at Elland Road. Giles scored a penalty and Lorimer added a second goal before half-time and, although Leeds did not add to their tally, Rangers never looked like getting back into the game and were knocked out.

As the sixties drew to a close it seemed that Rangers were slowly but surely falling down the pecking order of European football. While Real Madrid were no longer the power they had been, a new order was emerging. English teams were now coming to the fore, illustrated by Manchester United's European Cup triumph of 1968 and the victory by Leeds United in the Fairs Cup the same year. West Germany had also arrived as a major power on the European stage, not least due to the efforts of Bayern Munich and Borussia Dortmund. The countries of Eastern Europe were also producing better teams than before: Hungary's Ferencvaros lost to Leeds in the Fairs Cup final and Partizan Belgrade from Yugoslavia had reached the European Cup final two years earlier.

Trips behind the Iron Curtain were still fraught with difficulty for Western clubs, and matters worsened in August 1968 when Russian tanks led an invasion of Czechoslovakia, overthrowing the regime of Alexander Dubcek. The Soviets were supported in their action by the rest of the Warsaw Pact countries, namely Hungary, Bulgaria, Poland and East Germany, but the rest of Europe was alarmed at this turn of events. Western clubs, including Celtic and AC Milan, who were drawn against teams from these countries threatened to pull out of the tournament rather than complete their fixtures, and as a result UEFA decided to redraw the first round. Unfortunately, their suggestion that Eastern and Western teams should be kept apart in the first round was seen as discriminatory by the communist bloc, which promptly withdrew en masse. Yugoslavia was one of the few Eastern European nations to compete that season, and it was there that Rangers found themselves in the first round of the 1968/69 Fairs Cup.

Opponents Vojvodina – narrowly beaten by Celtic in the 1966/67 European Cup – came from the historic city of Novi Sad, which sits on the banks of the Danube in the area now known as Serbia. Although Yugoslavia was a relatively liberal state by communist standards, and not under Soviet control, a visit was still uncomfortable, and with a 2–0 lead from the first leg, Rangers were relieved to escape with a 1–0 defeat in Novi Sad; the black spot being the sending-off of John Greig for retaliation.

After their trip across the Iron Curtain, the second round saw Rangers crossing another divide, this time far closer to home. The match against Dundalk would be the first time Rangers had played a competitive tie in the Republic of Ireland and the fact that the opponents were from a staunchly Republican town on the front line of the IRA's terrorist campaign made it all the more fraught. As it turned out, both matches passed largely without incident.

However, there was off-field controversy and perhaps predictably it concerned the flying of flags. It was the custom in European football for the home club to fly the national flag of their opponents. Rangers, unsurprisingly, did not have an Irish tricolour to hand and were forced to borrow one from a club that did: Celtic. It was actually the flag displayed at Celtic Park on match days. But the tricolour was never run up the Ibrox flagpole because, according to the Rangers public relations officer, Willie Allison, Dundalk did not ask for it to be flown. The Irish club was surprised by Allison's statement and after the game manager Tommy Rowe rather pointedly remarked: 'Oh, you have to ask do you?'

The diplomatic controversy had no impact on the Rangers players as they recorded a comprehensive 6–1 victory. Alex Ferguson and Willie Henderson both scored twice, but the match was most notable for the return to right back of Kai Johansen. He had been dropped by Davie White and spent several months in the reserves, much to his annoyance. He said:

> I had never before been so long out of first-team football. I was not sure how long it would take me to settle, nor to what extent my bosses and the fans would make allowances for me. Well I was soon to know. The reception I got that evening was the most moving thing that has ever happened to me. I felt ten-feet tall.

For the second leg, Rangers travelled across the Irish Sea to Northern Ireland before driving south to their base on the outskirts of Dundalk. Extra police were drafted in to protect the three hundred or so Rangers supporters who were expected to make the same trip from Ulster. Thankfully, the match passed without incident and the travelling fans made it home safely, delighted at a 3–0 victory.

Dutch team DWS Amsterdam were disposed of 4–1 on aggregate in the third round and this was followed by an impressive 4–3 aggregate victory over Basque side Athletic Bilbao. Temperamental winger Willie Johnston was sent off late in the away leg for fighting, but Rangers made it through, and for the second season in a row came up against English opposition, this time in the shape of Newcastle United.

Despite constant pressure from Rangers, the first leg at Ibrox ended goalless in front of a 70,000 crowd. Northern Ireland international goalkeeper Willie McFaul, who had been in top form throughout the competition, pulled off a stunning penalty save from Andy Penman. In a 1997 interview, the goalie admitted, 'It was pure guess work. Nothing else. Mind you, I had to save it as I had conceded the penalty by whacking one of their players. To come away from Glasgow without conceding a goal was a hell of a result.'

A huge travelling support made the short trip across the border for the second leg, sparking the usual warnings of crowd trouble. Unlike previous visits to England, this time an element of the Rangers support decided to live up to the negative expectations and embarrassed the club.

Thousands of Rangers fans were in the north-east of England from early on match day and many bottles of the famous local brew, Newcastle Brown Ale, were consumed. By the time kick-off came around, the boisterousness that had marked most of the day had started to turn slightly ugly. Minor scuffles and unrest broke out in the crowd early in the match as tempers flared on the field. This only worsened when exiled Scotsman Jim Scott (brother of former Rangers star Alex) scored early in the second half. Then, with ten minutes to go, Jackie Sinclair scored the second and decisive goal. Moments later, hundreds of Rangers fans burst onto the pitch. It has been claimed by some that this was an attempt to have the game abandoned, but those who were there believe the invasion was more to do with the crushing on the terraces.

John McMahon, who was seventeen at the time, had hitched down from Glasgow for the game after finishing his school exams. 'Mine had finished but my mate had Higher Art that day', he recalled. 'We slagged him for not making the game and left early doors that day to hitch down the road. We got there about dinner time and wandered about the town centre in the afternoon with a bunch of similar degenerates.' A couple of hours before kick-off, John and his pals congregated at the ground. That's when he saw his friend Alex, who he thought was up the road sitting his Higher Art.

'He'd got to the lunch break at twelve o'clock and thought "fuck this afternoon's paper". He'd got his arse to the Hamilton bypass, stuck out his thumb, and here he was!'

The fans without tickets came up with an ingenious way of getting in to the match, as McMahon recounted:

> The front of St. James's was nothing like Ibrox. It was about twelve-feet high at the turnstiles. A relay had been set up where one guy would stand back to the wall, hands joined in front providing a foothold, the next would do a runny towards the wall, put his foot in the hands, and would get launched high enough to grab the top and get over. It would then be the launcher's turn. I launched one supporter and got launched by another. I remember balancing on the wall top as the police grabbed for my legs. Thankfully I tipped over into the terracing.

From his vantage point he could see hundreds of Rangers fans without tickets. Near the turnstiles there were large wooden gates and, with the police too slow to react, the crowd charged towards the gates and burst them open. Supporters surged onto the already-packed terracing, as McMahon described:

> You could hardly move. As the game progressed and we got beat, the pressure from the terracing became so great that fans had to escape on to the pitch. This was later interpreted as a pitch invasion because we were getting beat. That's shite! The crush was such that we couldn't stand it. Thankfully we weren't penned in like other English grounds were then. Yes we were on the pitch, but thank God we weren't behind cages where we'd have been crushed to death. There were thousands more in the ground than tickets sold.

As the police tried to clear the invasion, fighting broke out between fans and officers. Bottles and cans were thrown and Newcastle coach Dave Smith got involved in a confrontation with some of the invaders. It was only a matter of time before Newcastle fans retaliated and, sure enough, a full-scale battle soon broke out. Despite bringing dogs onto the pitch, the police were hopelessly under-resourced to cope with the trouble.

Welsh referee Jim Gow held the match up for seventeen minutes as the police attempted to restore order. After the invasion was finally cleared, there were piles of bottles and cans behind the goals at the Rangers end. An estimated twenty-seven fans were arrested, according to police reports, and thirty people were injured in the fighting. Newcastle's chief constable Clarence Cooksley said at the time, 'It was an explosive situation brought about by Glasgow supporters. It was not all of them, just a section of drunken hooligans.'

The Rangers players were also disappointed in the behaviour of the fans. 'It was very unsavoury,' said Sandy Jardine. 'That sort of trouble going on disrupts your game and your concentration. And it is an embarrassment for the players because people who behave like that embarrass the club.'

Having met up with his brother after the game, John McMahon tried to get a lift home on supporters buses with empty seats, but none would take them. A kind-hearted shift manager at an all-night café gave them free tea and coffee and let them stay until dawn. They headed for the road north, breakfasting on milk from the doorsteps of suburban Newcastle and the fresh bread that came with it. 'A Geordie lorry driver picked us up and told us we were bastards for our performance the night before and should be ashamed,' said John. 'He dropped us at Carlisle but nobbled one of his mates going up the A74 to give us a lift.'

Meanwhile there was a major fall-out following the trouble. FIFA vice-president Harry Cavan, from the Irish FA, was the UEFA observer at the match and didn't hold back when asked by newspapers for his take on events. Cavan, who died in 2000, said: 'The attitude of the Rangers fans was disgraceful; there is no doubt they were to blame. If this is the attitude of Rangers and Scottish football supporters then there is a danger that Rangers and other Scottish clubs will be prevented from playing in Europe.'

It did not come to that, but the reputation of the Rangers support was severely damaged as a result of the actions of a loutish element. Although, as unacceptable as they were, it has to be said that such events were hardly out of the ordinary at the time. Just a week before, there had been trouble at Old Trafford during a match between Manchester United and AC Milan. For all the damage they did to the club's reputation, as the police pointed out, it was a minority of the Rangers supporters who were involved in the trouble. Most had enjoyed a great day out in the city.

Quite apart from the trouble off the park, Rangers had failed once again in Europe. Although it could be argued they had underachieved in most of their European campaigns in the fifties and sixties, almost all the teams they had lost to were from the European superpowers. Over the years Rangers had been defeated by opponents from France, Italy, West Germany, England and Spain. Granted, some of those defeats had been humiliating, but there was some comfort in knowing that top-class teams, like Real Madrid and AC Milan, had inflicted them. Despite the claims of John Greig, Standard Liege were hardly from the top bracket when they beat Rangers in 1962, but at least they were from a recognised football nation. However, 1969 brought a new and unwelcome development – defeat to a team of unknowns from an Eastern European country considered by most Scots to be a backwater.

It wasn't just the fact that Rangers were knocked out of the European Cup Winners Cup of 1969/70 by Polish minnows Gornik Zabrze; it was the manner of the defeat. A 3–1 loss in Poland on 12 November 1969 may have been considered retrievable, but to crash to the same score at Ibrox was simply inexcusable. The defeat led to the sacking of Davie White and heralded a new era at Ibrox, which ironically resulted in the much longed-for capture of a European trophy.

Davie White's final European campaign with Rangers had started with a satisfactory defeat of Steaua Bucharest of Romania. By now, Jim Baxter was back in the Rangers team after his spell in England. His signing from Nottingham Forest, shortly after the Newcastle debacle of the previous season, was seen by many as White's last throw of the dice.

Although his time away had done him few favours, and he was a shadow of the player he had been before going south, Baxter still performed fairly well against Steuau. In the first leg at Ibrox, Rangers secured a 2–0 victory through a double from Willie Johnston. A crowd of 90,000 packed into the national stadium in Bucharest for the second leg, but were left disappointed by a grim 0–0 draw, which was enough to see Rangers through to the next round to face Gornik.

Gornik, from the industrial Silesia region of Poland, had won the national league eight times since 1957 and had given Manchester United a tough game in the previous season's European Cup. They also possessed a genuine world-class player in the shape of Wlodek Lubanski, who had a seventeen-year international career that began in 1963 when he made his debut at the age of sixteen. However, Gornik were not a big-name team and most Scottish observers expected Rangers comfortably to progress. Even White declared before the game that he planned to go for all-out attack.

His brave words backfired, though, as Gornik raced to a two-goal lead early in the match, sending the 60,000 crowd at the Slaski stadium in the Silesian city of Chortzow wild with delight. Lubanski scored the first in four minutes, taking advantage of an error by Baxter. He allowed the ball to run out of play and, following a quick throw-in, Polish football's golden boy burst free of Baxter, played a quick wall-pass with a teammate and fired home a low drive past Gerry Neef in the Rangers goal.

The goal sparked a riot of colour and noise on the terraces and the atmosphere helped drive the home team forward. After a string of chances, a second goal seemed inevitable and it came in twelve minutes, albeit in controversial circumstances. Szoltysik hit a long-range shot, which beat Neef, but crashed off the crossbar and bounced down onto the turf. Neef grabbed the ball, and was preparing to kick it out, when the Belgian referee awarded a goal. Neef was incensed and after the game he insisted, 'It was not a goal. I could not believe it when the referee walked to the centre circle.' Davie White was also furious that the goal was given, and even now the decision rankles with Harold Davis, who had been drafted in as a coach. He told me, 'The ball hit the crossbar, full on, and bounced out to the eighteen-yard line. But it was raining that night and when it hit the bar, the net jumped and all the water sprayed up off the net. The referee gave it, which was unbelievable.'

Despite the early blow, Rangers fought their way back into the match and had a number of opportunities that went begging, with goalkeeper Kotsca pulling off two great saves. But, in the fifty-seventh minute, Rangers got their breakthrough. Henderson, who had switched to the left side, picked the ball up on the edge of the penalty area, weaved past the lunges of two defenders and cut back for Orjan Persson to score.

As the game entered its closing stages, Rangers looked like holding onto the 2–1 scoreline, which would have given them an excellent foundation for the return leg. Then, with just ninety seconds to go, the Poles won a free kick on the edge of the penalty area. With Rangers still preparing their wall, the Poles took the kick quickly and Lubanski shot home before the defence had the chance to react. Despite Scottish protests the goal stood, and Rangers were 3–1 down.

There was tragedy on the return journey from Poland, when one of the party on the official Rangers charter flight died. *Evening Times* sports writer Peter Hendry collapsed as the plane flew into Amsterdam to pick up a replacement crew. Despite attempts by Rangers coaches Davie Kinnear, Harold Davis and Lawrie Smith to revive him he died before the medical team waiting on the ground could help. Rangers chairman John Lawrence, who had sat with Hendry during the flight, was deeply upset by the death. When Rangers eventually returned to Glasgow, the chaotic journey from Poland had taken more than fifteen hours and involved two, 200-mile coach trips.

Rangers had performed well in the first leg and the two-goal deficit was not considered insurmountable. But on the day before the vital return match, the Ibrox preparations were thrown into turmoil. White had taken the squad to Largs to prepare, but as the players gathered for their morning training session the day before the game, two significant names were missing. Star players – and hotel roommates – Jim Baxter and Willie Henderson had slept in. Rather than holding everyone up and dragging the wayward duo from their beds, the furious White decided the session should go ahead without them. Baxter and Henderson were instead ordered out in the afternoon for a tough workout after the rest of the team had finished.

Both players were told they were to be disciplined; but both were also told they would play against Gornik. Critics saw this as a mistake by White, believing he should have shown that he would not tolerate lack of discipline and dropped both men. One of the main criticisms levelled at the manager was that he was too easy on the players and that, as a result, the renowned Ibrox discipline instilled by William Struth was a thing of the past.

In the end both players did turn out against Gornik, and didn't play too badly. In fact Baxter opened the scoring in eighteen minutes with a powerful finish from a Persson cutback. It seemed that it was only a matter of time before Rangers got the second goal that would take them through on away goals as they went on to dominate the match for almost an hour.

Then, in the fifty-fourth minute, the Rangers collapse began. Olek broke away on the right, evading feeble challenges from Brian Heron and Baxter. His shot somehow squeezed past Gerry Neef into the net. The goal was a killer blow. Rangers now needed three to go through, and the task seemed beyond them. As Rangers pushed forward, Gornik, and Lubanski in particular, took advantage. With less than fifteen minutes to go, he broke clear of the last defender, Ronnie McKinnon, and rounded Gerry Neef, dragging the ball in from the touchline before lashing an angled shot into the roof of the net.

That was the cue for many of the 70,000 Rangers fans to leave Ibrox and five minutes later the Poles piled on even more agony for those who remained, when Neef failed to cope with a long-range shot. The third goal sparked chants of 'Gornik, Gornik' from the remaining fans, designed as much to insult the Rangers players as it was to honour the Poles. At the end, those fans who were still inside the stadium gave Gornik a huge ovation, but it was the jeers aimed at the home players that were ringing in the ears of the Rangers board. Chants of 'White must go' rang round Ibrox and it seemed that finally the manager's time was up.

Sandy Jardine admits the players were stunned at the defeat but insists there was a massive overreaction to the result:

> It was a shock to the system to get knocked out by an unfashionable Polish team but to be honest Gornik had a fantastic team, probably one of the best their country has produced, and Lubanski was a world-class player. He caused all sorts of problems and we actually got knocked out by a top-quality team, although no-one really knew about them.

The next morning, White arrived at Ibrox as normal, only to be summoned by the board. Seventy seconds after stepping into the boardroom, he was sacked from his £4,000-per-annum post. Shell-shocked White left the boardroom, said his farewells to the coaching staff and within five minutes was driving his bronze Ford Capri to his home in the Mount Vernon area of the city.

It was the second managerial sacking in two years and threw the club into turmoil again. Sandy Jardine said:

> Scot Symon had been treated very shabbily by the club and because of Gornik there was another massive upheaval when Davie White was dismissed. Davie was popular with the players and we weren't doing badly in the league but it was that result in Europe that did for him. Celtic were also doing so well and that put added pressure on the club.

Newspapers criticised the Rangers board for their treatment of White, describing him as a 'scapegoat', just like Scot Symon two years before. But as embarrassing as the Gornik defeat was the sacking was in no small part down to a vitriolic column by Willie Waddell in the *Daily Express*, in which he fiercely attacked White's abilities as a manager. Harold Davis believes it was the words of the legendary winger that did for White. Davis recalled: 'Your man Waddell wrote some bloody stinking reports on him. It was terrible, so Davie got the heave.'

The Davis view of Waddell was not shared by the Rangers support, and it was to almost universal acclaim that he was appointed as White's successor. This was a man who had played at the highest level for the club under its greatest-ever manager. He had already proved a successful manager, leading Kilmarnock to an unlikely league championship in 1965 before moving into journalism. Waddell remained as manager for a relatively short period, but he laid the groundwork for the club's revival and steered the team to its greatest-ever European achievement.

With Waddell at the helm, Rangers entered the new decade with an optimism that had been lacking for five years. Waddell was determined to restore the club to the glory days of the Struth era and he immediately set about clearing out players he felt were not up to the task, the most notable casualty being Jim Baxter. The backroom staff was also given a major overhaul, as Waddell tried to bring the squad up to the fitness levels he required. Key to this was the appointment of Hearts assistant manager Jock Wallace as trainer. Wallace – who was player-manager of Berwick when they defeated the big Rangers in 1967 – was a fitness fanatic who oversaw gruelling training regimes for the players, including the notorious sprints up the sand dunes at Gullane beach.

Waddell's first full season in charge was a tumultuous one. October saw a famous victory over Celtic in the League Cup final, with 16-year-old Derek Johnstone scoring the goal that brought silverware back to Ibrox for the first time since 1966. The league campaign was a disappointment though, with Rangers finishing a lowly fourth, and the season ended with a Scottish Cup final defeat to Celtic. However, the football was overshadowed by the tragic events of 2 January 1971, when sixty-six Rangers fans lost their lives in a stairway crush as they left Ibrox after the New Year Old Firm match.

In the Fairs Cup of 1970/71, Rangers were drawn against old foes Bayern Munich in the first round. Bayern had gone from strength to strength since their Cup Winners Cup defeat of Rangers in 1967 and were fast becoming part of Europe's elite. In 1969 they won their first Bundesliga title, as well as the national cup, and their three star players formed the backbone of the West German team that had done well at the World Cup in Mexico a few months earlier. Sepp Maier, Franz Beckenbauer and Gerd Muller had of course also faced Rangers in Nuremberg. Of the 1970 team, Franz Roth and Dieter Brenniger also remained from the 1967 final; while Jardine, McKinnon and Greig were the only survivors in the Rangers team, largely thanks to Waddell's clear out.

The imperious figure of Beckenbauer was the driving force behind the German team's success and he was the difference between the two teams in the first leg at the Grunwalder Stadion in Munich. Rangers had played well, with Maier being called on to produce a series of saves. When the Light Blues eventually beat the goalkeeper, the woodwork saved the Germans, John Greig's close-range header rebounding off the bar. Then Beckenbauer decided it was time for an intervention; stepping out of midfield, he played a one-two with Paul Breitner before firing a shot beyond the outstretched arms of Rangers goalkeeper Peter McCloy.

Beckenbauer's strike was the only goal of the game, and Rangers went into the second leg at Ibrox with high hopes of overturning the Germans' narrow lead. A massive crowd of 83,000 packed into the stadium and watched Rangers dominate the match, but fail to turn their superiority into goals. During a rare attack in the eightieth minute, the Germans were awarded a free kick on the edge of the penalty area by Swiss referee Pius Camber. As Gerd Muller prepared to take the kick, the official stood over the ball with his arm raised, clearly indicating an indirect free kick. But to the surprise of just about everyone in the ground, not least Peter McCloy, instead of aiming a cross at a teammate, Muller thrashed a powerful shot into the net.

Initially, McCloy assumed the goal would be disallowed and made to place the ball for a free kick but, as the Germans celebrated, it quickly became apparent that the referee had changed his mind. Despite the protests of the Rangers players, the goal stood. From being on the verge of equalizing, Rangers were suddenly two goals behind, and because of the away goal, needed to score three times to go through. Within seconds Colin

Stein pulled one back, but the task was too great and Rangers went out, with an understandable sense of injustice.

It was the thirteenth season Rangers had competed in Europe and after seventy-three matches they seemed no closer to winning a trophy. But the following season, to the surprise of many, Willie Waddell's team achieved what no other Rangers squad had managed before or since – a European title.

8

April 1972: Beating the Kaiser

In the eighteenth century, it was part of the education process for young British aristocrats to take part in the Grand Tour. Travel was arduous and expensive, but the idea of the trips was to expose these young men to the finest art and culture Europe had to offer and introduce them to the fashionable society of the Continent. The itinerary would invariably include France, Italy, Germany and Spain, and even Portugal on occasion. The Grand Tourists would return home with souvenirs of their journeys as well as a new understanding of the culture of Europe.

In 1971, Rangers embarked on their own Grand Tour. Just like the noblemen of the past, they visited France, Portugal, Italy, Germany and Spain, finishing up in Catalonia's magnificent capital, Barcelona. It's doubtful if the aristocrats of Scottish football were exposed to much in the way of high culture on their travels, but it was certainly an education and they brought home a wonderful souvenir in the shape of the European Cup Winners Cup.

The road to Barcelona began in the picturesque French city of Rennes, the capital of Brittany. Local club Stade Rennais – always known as Rennes in Britain – were flying high in the French league. Rangers manager Willie Waddell would have preferred an easier opponent in the first round, particularly given the nightmare start his team had endured in the league. Defeats to Celtic and Partick Thistle had left Rangers languishing near the bottom of the first division. In a bid to nullify the threat from France midfielder Raymond Keruzore, Waddell adopted a 4–4–2 formation in the first leg, relying on the front pair of Colin Stein and Willie Johnston to try to get an away goal. The tactic worked perfectly, with Johnston scoring the opening goal in the sixty-ninth minute. Rennes equalized but they were left frustrated and Rangers were favourites to go through.

French coach Jean Prouff attacked the Scots' tactics, claiming his team would go to Ibrox and win the tie because Rangers would have to attack in front of their own supporters. It didn't quite work out that way. Rangers continued to adopt a cautious approach and it paid off when Alex MacDonald scored just before half-time. The red-shirted Frenchmen had no answer and Rangers moved into the next round 2–1 on aggregate. MacDonald remembers the difference in approach between league games and European matches:

> At home you would know everybody you played against. You wouldn't have to study them; you would know what they would do and how they acted. The thing that sticks in my mind about Europe is that there was a lot more interest in tactics. We would be given photographs of the guy we were up against and told exactly how they would play. It made it far more interesting and I loved it.

The second round paired Rangers with Portuguese opposition for the first time in the shape of Sporting Lisbon. If Barcelona was to prove the greatest occasion in Rangers' fifty years in Europe, then the second leg in Lisbon was surely the most dramatic. The drama began when Rangers arrived at Glasgow airport on the morning of 1 November 1971 and ended late on the Wednesday night, deep in the bowels of the Jose Alvalade stadium.

The first leg at Ibrox was exciting enough. In front of a 50,000 crowd, Rangers raced into a three-goal lead in the first half through a Colin Stein double and a fine strike from Willie Henderson. However, the Portuguese, in their green-and-white hooped jerseys, fought back after half-time and pulled back two goals to give them a great chance of progression.

Rangers were due to leave Glasgow early on the Monday morning for the return match and should have touched down in the Portuguese capital in early afternoon, giving plenty of time for acclimatisation and training. However, industrial action at Heathrow airport meant the party missed its connecting flight and faced another lengthy delay as attempts were made to find an alternative. A decision was made to head for Stansted airport in Essex and it eventually took until Tuesday afternoon to get a flight and the weary travellers didn't touch down in Portugal until the evening. It was now more than thirty-six hours since they had first gathered at Glasgow airport.

It was not the ideal preparation for such a big game, but Rangers were determined to make the best of it. A light training session was hurriedly arranged at the Jose Alvalade on the Wednesday morning and only a few hours later they walked out at the same stadium for the second leg. The ground was now a cauldron of noise, the chanting of a 60,000 crowd being orchestrated by a cheerleader over the stadium's loudspeaker. A drum provided a constant, if slightly irritating, backbeat to the action on the pitch. 'The two things I remember most about the game were the drums and the green-and-white hoops on the Sporting Libson strips,' said Alex MacDonald. 'I've got to be honest; I think their colours helped me!'

Despite all the problems that had gone before, it was a fantastic match, the action raging from end to end until the last minute. Sporting went a goal up in twenty-four minutes but just sixty seconds later Colin Stein got an equalizer. Just before half-time, the Portuguese went 2–1 ahead, but moments after the break Stein again brought Rangers level on the night. Rangers were now 5–4 ahead on aggregate but they suffered a major blow when defensive stalwart Ronnie McKinnon suffered a sickening broken leg in a clash with a Sporting attacker. Alex MacDonald said, 'When somebody breaks their leg you imagine they would be rolling about all over the place, but Ronnie was just lying there with his hand in the air. We were all shouting at him to get up. But he just said, "I think I've broke my leg" just as simple as that.' Minutes from the end, there came another blow, as Sporting levelled the tie and took it into extra time.

Against all the odds, Rangers steeled themselves for one last push. Henderson managed to put them into a 6–5 aggregate lead meaning the Portuguese now needed to score twice to go through because of the Ibrox club's greater number of away goals. In the closing minutes, Peres scored a penalty to make it six each but it wasn't enough and Rangers were through. Except, no-one told the Dutch referee Laurens Van Ravens. In a remarkable display of incompetence, the official decided that the away-goal rule did not apply in extra time, that the tie had actually finished level and that a penalty shoot-out was required.

As the Sporting fans scaled the barriers and crowded round the touchline, the pressure finally got to Rangers and they blew the shoot-out, missing all four of their kicks. As the Portuguese fans carried their goalkeeper above their heads in triumph, the disconsolate Rangers players trooped back to the dressing room believing they had suffered a cruel defeat. The Rangers supporters who had followed the team to Lisbon left the stadium and flew home in the belief they were out of Europe.

'The penalty shoot-out was absolutely unbelievable, we just missed everything,' recalled Alex MacDonald. 'We were sitting in the dressing room absolutely gutted.' But moves were afoot behind the scenes. With the help of journalist John Fairgrieve, Willie Waddell was now in possession of the rulebook that showed Rangers should have gone through. The official UEFA delegate, Andres Ramirez of Spain, was already aware of the blunder and had pointed out the mistake to the referee. After a summit between the clubs and the officials, UEFA's general secretary Hans Bangerter was contacted at home in Switzerland to make a ruling and he declared Rangers the winners. 'It's hard to explain the feelings in the dressing room when we found out,' said Alex MacDonald. 'We went from being six-feet under to flying with the angels. It was amazing.' Sporting were furious at the ruling and lodged an appeal but they were unsuccessful and Rangers were into the next round.

Although they had gone through, the return journey to Scotland was a sombre affair because of Ronnie McKinnon's injury. An X-ray revealed he had suffered a double-break and he flew home with his leg encased in plaster in the almost certain knowledge that his season was already over in November.

Europe was put on the back burner for four months as Rangers attempted to get themselves back into contention in the league. A defeat against Celtic on 3 January 1972 was a serious blow to their hopes and their domestic form continued to fluctuate. By the time the next round of the Cup Winners Cup came around in March, Rangers league challenge was over. Italian Cup holders Torino were Rangers' opponents in the quarter-final. It was another tough task, as *i Granata* (the Maroons) were doing well in *Serie A*. They had finished eighth the season before but started the new season well and would eventually finish in third place. Torino had once been the leading team in Italy until tragedy struck in 1949. After winning five league titles in a row, the team was returning from an exhibition match against Benfica in Lisbon when their plane crashed into the Superga hills near Turin. Eighteen members of the squad known as the *Grande Torino* were killed in the disaster. Torino would not win *Serie A* again until 1976.

History was not on Rangers' side ahead of the first leg at the Stadio Comunale. In three previous ties with Italian opposition, Rangers had been beaten over two legs on each occasion. The second round of the 1957 European Cup saw a 6–1 aggregate defeat to AC Milan, and in 1961 they were beaten 4–1 in the two legs of the Cup Winners Cup final by Fiorentina. Three years later, Rangers managed a 1–0 victory over Internazionale at Ibrox, but they had already been beaten 3–1 in the San Siro.

But, in 1972, Rangers won a victory before a ball had been kicked. Torino wanted the venues switched so they would be at home in the second match. But Rangers insisted that the original dates should apply and were backed by UEFA. As a result, Rangers and Celtic would both be playing

European quarter-finals in Glasgow on the same night, a scenario that would not be countenanced today.

Rangers set up base in a hotel in the wine-producing town of Asti, home of the famous Asti Spumante sparkling wine. Having assured the Italian media that he would be adopting an attacking style, Willie Waddell was in fact drawing up plans for a defensive approach that the local team would have been proud of. With Ronnie McKinnon out injured, Colin Jackson was partnered in the heart of defence by young centre forward Derek Johnstone. Dave Smith was played as a sweeper behind the two centre backs, who were given the task of marking the Torino forwards Paolino Pulici and Gianni Bui. In midfield John Greig was tasked with sticking as close to Italy international Claudio Sala as possible, a job he fulfilled to the letter. A crunching tackle by the Rangers captain in the opening minute set the tone for the battle to come.

The night before their match, the Rangers squad made the hour-long journey into Turin to watch their opponents' city rivals Juventus draw 1–1 with Wolves in the UEFA Cup. The trip let them sample the atmosphere in the municipal stadium and broke the routine of the training camp. The tactics of the English team impressed Rangers but their own approach the next night was equally praiseworthy.

A crowd of 35,000, including 500 Rangers supporters, turned out for the first leg in Turin paying gate receipts of more than sixty-six million lira. Despite their defensive set-up, Rangers took the lead in just twelve minutes, Willie Johnston forcing home after the goalkeeper failed to hold a cross from Willie Mathieson. Torino showed little sign in the rest of the first half that they would be a threat but, after the interval, they launched wave after wave of attack, most foundering on the twin rocks of Jackson and Johnstone. If they managed to get past that pair, the cool presence of Dave Smith eased the pressure. Torino eventually got a goal through Pulici but Rangers held out and returned with a valuable 1–1 draw. Willie Waddell singled out Johnstone for praise. 'The Italian fans must have been amazed at him; a player who can be the new John Charles,' he said, in a reference to the Wales international legend who had starred in both defence and attack for Juventus in the fifties.

Smith also came in for praise for his performance at sweeper, a role that would see him win the Scottish player-of-the-year award at the end of the season. No-one was more impressed by Smith than Alex MacDonald:

> Dave Smith was absolutely brilliant. I remember years later I was player-manager for Hearts and he was player-manager for Berwick, and we played each other in the cup. He absolutely ran the show and that was about ten years later. I played a sweeper system when I was in charge at Hearts because it worked so well back then.

As was common for big games right up until the 1990s, Rangers headed for the Ayrshire coast to prepare. A couple of miles along the coast, at Seamill, Celtic were also getting ready for their European Cup quarter-final against Ujpest Dozsa. A total of more than 140,000 fans would watch the two matches at Ibrox and Parkhead and the Rangers fans expected victory. But Waddell cautioned, 'Torino can play a bit. They wouldn't be so high up in the Italian league if they couldn't. They will be very, very hard to beat.' Rangers' eightieth match in Europe proved to be a closely fought affair but the home team got the vital breakthrough shortly after half-time. Tommy McLean took off down the left and sent a dangerous cross into the box. Willie Johnston leapt with the Torino keeper Luciano Castellini and just beat him to it, flicking the ball on to Alex MacDonald, who bundled it over the line. Reports at the time suggested the midfielder put it in with his knee or his chest, but he is adamant that it was a header. Whatever the case, it may not have been the goal of the season, but it was enough to put Rangers through to the semi-final and a chance to gain revenge on old rivals Bayern Munich.

Rangers could be forgiven if they were apprehensive about facing the West Germans. The memory of the 1967 Cup Winners Cup final was particularly painful for players like John Greig, Sandy Jardine and Willie Johnston who had endured the agony of extra-time defeat. And the previous season's loss in the Fairs Cities was also a tough one to take. Furthermore, Bayern had developed into a formidable unit over the past five years. The youngsters of '67, like Beckenbauer and Muller, were now superstars who made up the backbone of the West Germany international team. Just ten days after the second leg of their tie with Rangers, no fewer than six Bayern players featured in the national team's humiliating defeat of England at Wembley in a qualifying match for the European Championship. The 3–1 win was the springboard to glory for West Germany: it began when they became European champions with a 3–0 defeat of the USSR in June 1972 and culminated in a victory over Holland in the World Cup final two years later. In 1974, Bayern won the first of three consecutive European Cup titles and were without question the best team on the Continent.

Any trepidation Rangers had going into the first leg at the Grunwalder stadium in Munich on 5 April 1972 seemed fully justified as Bayern pummelled them from the start. Gerd Muller hit the crossbar with a header in eight minutes to set the tone for the first half. Despite a battling performance, it was little surprise when left back Paul Breitner shot home from six yards in the twenty-first minute after a one-two with Muller. But Rangers had gone into the match with the same starting eleven that had performed so well against Torino and defensively they were strong, Dave Smith again performing admirably as sweeper. 'To be honest they were giving us an absolute doing over there,' recalled Sandy Jardine. 'You hear of teams that can't get out of their own half, well we couldn't get out our own eighteen-yard box for periods of that game.' Bayern were unable to add to their lead and, as the half progressed, Rangers came more into the game. The frustration of the Bayern players was clearly demonstrated when Muller punched substitute Alfie Conn on the way to the dressing rooms at half-time.

Shortly after the break, Rangers got the goal they had been desperate for. Colin Stein and Willie Johnston broke from the halfway line and Stein drove a hard cross into the middle that Rainer Zobel headed into his own net. The goal inspired Rangers into attack, Mathieson twice forcing Maier into saves. Beckenbauer, who had spent the first hour of the game in midfield, retreated back into defence. Muller looked increasingly isolated up front as Rangers took control of the game, and might even have gone on to win. 'We had superb fitness and were able to last the game far better than them,' said Jardine. 'In the last ten or fifteen minutes we were running a lot stronger than them.' For the third match on their run, Rangers secured a 1–1 draw away from home. It had been a tremendous performance. Willie Waddell was delighted by the draw in Munich. 'This was definitely one of our best performances in Europe,' he said. The Bayern coach Udo Lattek was less happy though, accusing Rangers of roughhouse tactics.

John Greig had played through the pain barrier in the first game, having suffered serious bruising to his legs after falling victim to a two-footed challenge in a league match against Motherwell. Four days before the second leg, the Rangers captain was injured again, this time in the Scottish Cup semi-final against Hibernian. He suffered severe bruising to his ankle although X-rays showed there was no break. He underwent intensive treatment and was included in the nineteen-man pool that travelled to Largs. Right up until the day of the match it was hoped that he could play, but in the end it was a bridge too far.

On another remarkable night for Glasgow football, an all-ticket crowd of 80,000 packed into Ibrox on 19 April 1972 while on the other side of the city there were 75,000 at Parkhead for Celtic's European Cup semi-final against Inter Milan. It was an odd coincidence that the two teams the Old Firm faced that night had also been their final opponents from five years earlier. There was a huge sense of anticipation before the matches and the Scottish newspapers were full of souvenir pull-outs and page after page of build-up.

The papers speculated that Alfie Conn or Jim Denny would replace Greig, but instead Waddell opted for 18-year-old Derek Parlane. The youngster had only played four first-team games and it was a major gamble. He was asked to mark Bayern's midfield star Franz Roth, who had scored the extra-time winner in 1967, and had he failed to perform there could have been dire consequences. Happily that was not to be the case.

The Germans did not have a huge travelling support, but those who did make the trip from Bavaria were colourful and noisy. Some were dressed in traditional German attire (lederhosen and leather hats) while others bizarrely adopted full Highland regalia. The atmosphere inside Ibrox was electric as Rangers, all in blue, lined up to salute the fans. Forty-five seconds after the start there was bedlam, as Rangers took a stunning lead. The goal came from right back Sandy Jardine, who had been quietly efficient throughout the European run. Derek Johnstone started the move after intercepting a Beckenbauer pass. He knocked it through to Jardine and the defender hit a left-foot shot past Maier, who stood stock-still as the ball sailed into the net.

The goal stunned Bayern and they were very nearly two behind after five minutes when Colin Stein hit the bar with a header. But the delirious Rangers fans didn't have too long to wait for the second goal. In twenty-three minutes, Stein outjumped Maier and flicked on a Willie Johnston corner. The ball fell to Parlane and the teenager lashed it home off the underside of the bar to make it 2–0 on the night. It was a stunning moment for the youngster and for the Rangers fans, who knew there was no way back for the Germans.

Beckenbauer, the epitome of Teutonic calm, suddenly lost his cool. He seemed to lose interest as the match progressed, only coming to life when he was falling out with teammates, as Alex MacDonald explains:

> I don't think the stars like Beckenbauer and the lads up front liked the Ibrox park. I think at that time we just left the pitch to be in its natural state of mud and I don't think they were too happy about that. Beckenbauer was hitting it with the outside of his boot and it was going straight into the enclosure. It was brilliant. They were world-class individuals but you could sense on the pitch that there was something not right with them. But Sandy and Derek Parlane scored brilliant goals.

The final whistle brought a tremendous outpouring of emotion. The injured John Greig had watched the game from the dugout alongside the Rangers backroom team and to a man they raced onto the pitch to celebrate. Rangers coach Jock Wallace described the performance against Bayern as the best he'd seen since joining the club. 'When you saw the way the Bayern men played against England you realised just how great our victory had been.'

Bayern captain Beckenbauer was gracious in defeat and he acknowledged: 'Rangers were magnificent; they will go on to win the cup. I have no doubts about that.'

Sandy Jardine is clear about the magnitude of the victory over Bayern:

> That team went on to win the European Cup three times and if you talk to people from Munich they will tell you that it was the best team in their history. It was such a fantastic achievement to beat them but the way it transpired it was actually one of the easiest games of the tournament. They just folded and Beckenbauer was arguing with Maier.

The celebrations among the Rangers fans were made all the sweeter when they learned that the other semi-final had gone to a penalty shoot-out and that Celtic had been eliminated. Rangers were through to the final and would be able to enjoy their moment in the sun knowing that, unlike 1967, Celtic would not be able to steal the limelight. The songs rang out into the night and the tune on everyone's lips was 'Barcelona Here We Come'.

9

One Night in Barcelona

The build-up to Scotland's biggest away day began in December 1971 – a full five months before tens of thousands of Rangers fans would eventually descend on Barcelona. At that stage Rangers hadn't even reached the semi-final, but at least one 17-year-old was optimistic. Gordon McGilvray phoned Rangers to find out the date and venue of the final. It was Barcelona, 24 May 1972. He got straight onto his boss at Bearsden post office and booked time off. If Rangers were going to be there he was determined to be with them.

From the moment the referee brought the semi-final to a close a few months later, the plans could begin in earnest. Even as the fans celebrated their victory over Bayern, they were already working out how they were going make it to Barcelona. The final was more than five weeks away and no-one even knew who the opponents would be yet, but it didn't matter. McGilvray was one of many who rushed to travel agents to get booked up. 'I booked my trip to Barcelona through Holiday Enterprises, who operated from a shop near Partick Cross,' he said. 'The flight, one night's hotel accommodation in Lloret de Mar, coach transfers to and from Barcelona, plus of course the match ticket, cost around £35. It seems like such a bargain now.' The lure of the match was so great that Glasgow car dealership Croft was giving away flight, hotel and match-ticket packages with every new or used Ford Capri. Or perhaps it was a free Capri with every trip to Barcelona.

Communication from behind the Iron Curtain was slow in those days so it was a day before word came through that Dynamo Moscow had defeated Dynamo Berlin on penalties in the other semi-final. Rangers and Dynamo had history. They first met in a famous clash at Ibrox in November 1945 when the Dynamos toured Britain. The visit to Scotland sparked a frenzy of interest. Fans queued for hours for tickets when they went on sale in Glasgow and when they quickly sold out, some offered up to £30 for a seat. The match itself lived up to expectations. Dynamo, demonstrating skills and technique never seen before in Scotland, raced into a two-goal lead, but a brave fight-back from Rangers followed and goals from Jimmy Smith and George Young earned the Scots a battling 2–2 draw.

More significantly in terms of the Cup Winners Cup final, Rangers and Dynamo had met again at Ibrox in November 1970. The friendly had ended in a 1–0 victory for the Scots and eight of the Russian team that played that day were still in their squad. But although Dynamo were far from an unknown quantity, Willie Waddell was keen to continue his routine of watching each of his European opponents in the flesh.

After weeks of diplomatic wrangling he finally obtained a visa to travel to the Soviet Union for a spy mission, although his difficulties didn't end with his arrival in Moscow. Officials went out of their way to be as unhelpful as possible, without actually being hostile. Waddell had problems even finding out who Dynamo were playing against and when. At his hotel in the shadow of the Kremlin, the Rangers boss was told he would have to buy a ticket for the match – although the Russians generously offered him a pass that would allow him to jump to the head of the queue at the stadium! Eventually, he managed to get himself a seat for the league match against Kairat and was impressed by what he saw. The manager had already identified wingers Estrekov (supposedly the Russian Garrincha) and Evriuzhikin as threats, but it was the performance of international midfielder Josef Sabo that caught the eye.

Legendary goalkeeper Lev Yashin, a coach with Dynamo, predicted that Sabo would be a key player. 'His deep knowledge of the game and the many years he has played in European and international football have helped us reach this final,' he told the *Daily Record*. 'Sabo has the great thing about his play that means you never have to worry about him losing form.' Head coach Konstantin Beskov – who played against Rangers in 1945 – played down his team's chances, pointing out that his team was mostly made up of young players. He refused to be drawn on Rangers' abilities, but did offer up a classic manager's cliché: 'There are no easy matches in Europe at this stage.'

Dynamo had enjoyed by far the easier run to the final, beating Olympiakos of Greece, Eskisehirspor of Turkey, Yugoslavia's Red Star Belgrade and Dynamo Berlin. Yashin said, 'Instead of teams with worldwide reputations we have played only one club who can compare with these clubs who have lost to Glasgow Rangers. We defeated the Yugoslavian team – that was our proudest moment in the tournament so far. We know that we will have to equal that form if we are to beat Glasgow Rangers in Barcelona.'

Waddell's painstaking preparatory work ensured Rangers had the edge in terms of facilities. He made an advance trip to Spain to find a suitable headquarters for the team and booked the squad into the luxurious and secluded Hotel Rey Don Jaime in the coastal resort of Castelldefels, around fifteen miles from Barcelona. The hotel was a fortress on a secluded hilltop overlooking the Mediterranean. Waddell specified all their requirements well in advance, including transport and menus, and booked Espanyol's Sarria stadium for training sessions. The wives of the Rangers players were booked into another hotel in nearby Sitges.

The Russians, on the other hand, had very little advance contact with the Spanish authorities, who were organising the final on behalf of UEFA. The party of twenty-four from Moscow, including a television commentator, arrived an hour after Rangers on the Sunday before the game and checked into a beachfront hotel in Castelldefels. It was right in the centre of the town, and they had to endure the sound of music blaring from bars all day and all night. It was made worse by the fact that the resort was filled with holiday-makers from Barcelona enjoying a public holiday. On their arrival the Russian players went out training on the beach, jogging among the sun-worshippers stretched out on the sands. From their rooms, the Dynamo stars could see their rivals' peaceful base in the distance and must have cast an envious glance in that direction as the car horns sounded in the street outside.

At the Rey Don Jaime, the Rangers players relaxed in the sunshine by the pool, playing dominoes to while away the time between training sessions. The squad was well away from the hustle and bustle of the resort and there was no chance of any outside disturbances. As the match approached the players gathered for a team meeting, during which they vowed to leave the stadium as winners. John Greig, Sandy Jardine, Dave Smith and Willie Johnston had suffered the heartache of the 1967 final and they had no intention of repeating the experience. 'We all got together in the hotel before the game and, having come home a loser in 1967, I wasn't going through that again,' Johnston said later.

It wasn't all going smoothly for Waddell. John Greig was still recovering from the injury that had ruled him out of the semi-final and was by no means certain to play. Colin Jackson was even more of a doubt, having damaged an ankle in the run-up to the final. Sadly, his injury flared up again during a training session at the Camp Nou, twenty-four hours before the big game. It was a devastating blow for the centre half and he found himself on the sidelines along with Ronnie McKinnon, who was still recovering from his broken leg.

Meanwhile, the Rangers fans were arriving in Barcelona in their droves;

it was the biggest travelling support Europe had ever seen. Spanish customs officials said they had processed 110 charter flights filled with fans from Scotland as well as 203 buses. With many more travelling independently by car, train or by hitching a lift, the total number who descended on the Catalonian capital exceeded twenty thousand. The atmosphere in Barcelona before the match was good humoured. The Rangers fans took over the city centre and a lot of alcohol was consumed, but there was no trouble as the Scots mixed happily with locals. Union flags and lions rampant were draped everywhere that there were Rangers fans; hanging from the windows of hotels, bars and taxis. Unfortunately, in the searing heat, the travellers were dressed for a Scottish spring in long trousers, sweaters and jackets.

Gordon McGilvray recalled:

> My flight left Glasgow airport around nine on the morning of the match and arrived at Barcelona airport around lunchtime. A coach took us the fifty miles or so to our hotel in Lloret de Mar, where we just had time to check-in, and have dinner – then it was onto the coach again for the journey back to Barcelona. As the coach approached, and travelled through Barcelona, the city appeared to be a sea of red, white and blue, with buses, taxis and private cars having flags and scarves waving from the windows. What a fantastic feeling it was when I entered the stadium that evening. I just knew that we would win that cup.

Some fans visited the team hotel on the afternoon of the game in the hope of catching a glimpse of their heroes. Unfortunately for them, the players were ensconced in their shuttered rooms, enjoying a siesta before gathering for a light meal. Sprint coach Tom Paterson sat at the end of the corridor to keep out any curious passers-by as Willie Waddell made his final preparations.

The team set off for the Camp Nou in confident mood and their spirits were raised even further as they approached the stadium and were faced with that sea of red, white and blue. Thousands of Rangers fans were thronging the street leading to the ground and they surrounded the team bus as it inched forward. 'As we approached the stadium the scenes were absolutely incredible,' remembers Alex MacDonald. 'Next thing, my brother-in-law was up shouting for his tickets at the back window of the bus! I had to hand them out the window to him in the middle of all that.'

For those who hadn't been able to travel to Spain, the ever-helpful Scottish Football Association wrecked their hopes of watching the action live. The match was being shown in virtually every country in Europe, except Scotland, where it was banned because there was a match against Wales at

Hampden the same night. SFA bosses feared live coverage would affect the attendance. In the event, a meagre 21,000 bothered to turn up anyway, the majority of football fans obviously preferring either the delights of Western star Glenn Ford in the long-forgotten series *Cade's County* or spy-thriller *Callan* to the thrills of the home internationals. Both BBC and STV showed the complete match later that night, resulting in countless Rangers fans re-enacting the famous episode from the *Likely Lads* by trying to avoid finding out the score.

Back in Barcelona, there was the bizarre sight of hundreds of sombrero-wearing Rangers supporters, draped in red-white-and-blue flags and scarves, wandering all over the Camp Nou pitch before the match. Far from being alarmed, Franco's police positively encouraged them, happily posing for pictures and taking snaps for fans. 'I even spotted an old school-friend of mine kicking the ball around with a couple of the Russian players before the match,' noted Gordon McGilvray. 'The fans on the park were obviously in high spirits, but there was no malice. However, at the time, I remember being surprised that the police who were positioned around the pitch hadn't ushered the fans away.'

As kick-off approached, it became clear that Rangers were going to have a massive support inside the cavernous stadium. The scenes inspired the players. Having already given them their instructions, Willie Waddell felt there was no need for a team talk. Instead, he simply told the players in the dressing room, 'You can see what it means to these people; don't let them down.'

At last the waiting was over. The teams emerged from the tunnel to a cacophony of noise from the Rangers fans. There were some neutral Spaniards, and even a handful of Russians, in the crowd but you would have struggled to find them. The Camp Nou may only have been a third full, but Rangers flags and banners hung from every balcony and stairway, and the noise generated rivalled an Old Firm game.

The contrasting images of the players as they emerged highlighted yet another difference between East and West. Dynamo's players – in crisp, white V-neck shirts – sported clean-cut, military-style hairdos redolent of the 1950s. With long hair and mutton-chop sideburns that Mungo Jerry would have been proud of, many of the Rangers players looked more like roadies for Slade than finely honed athletes. Alfie Conn, drafted in as a replacement for Colin Jackson, sported the finest pair of sideboards ever seen in Scottish football, although Alex MacDonald ran him close.

But, if their appearance left something to be desired, there was no doubt about how well prepared Rangers were. After a slow start, in which Dynamo created several chances, the Scots took control. Dave Smith was outstanding as a sweeper and was involved in most of Rangers' creative play. And in the twenty-fourth minute he provided a superb fifty-yard pass that set up the first goal. Colin Stein got away from his marker and, as the ball dropped, he fired it first time on the half-volley past Dynamo goalkeeper Pilguy and into the net. It was the cue for bedlam. As the Rangers players celebrated, they were joined on the pitch by dozens of fans. The Russians were visibly rattled as the Camp Nou terraces shook to the sound of Rangers songs.

The noise inspired the Ibrox men to greater heights. Smith continued to dominate at the back while Greig and MacDonald harried and hustled in midfield. Stein and Willie Johnston were immense up front, battling for everything and holding the ball up well. A second goal seemed inevitable and it came five minutes before half-time. Again Smith was the architect, picking the ball up just inside the Moscow half and carrying it forward. It looked as if he might have knocked it too far in front but he managed to reach it, checked onto his left foot and chipped a wonderful cross into the penalty area. Willie Johnston rose above the defence and headed past the goalkeeper from six yards. Two goals up at the interval and Rangers were halfway there. But there was plenty of drama to come.

During the break the Rangers players swapped their jerseys so they could keep their special shirts with the words 'European Cup Winners Cup Final 1972' stitched around the crest. Unfortunately, the replacements weren't exactly ideal for the Spanish heat. Alex MacDonald recalled, 'The strips we wore in the second half were like polo necks!' It didn't seem to have any immediate effect because Rangers extended their lead just four minutes into the second half. It was a goal of incredible simplicity. Peter McCloy launched an enormous kick from the edge of his penalty area into the Dynamo box. Willie Johnston brought it down and quickly shot low past Pilguy. The Russians claimed it was offside but Johnston remains adamant that he timed his run to perfection and there was no doubt about the quality of his finish.

The scoreboard now read, 'R.F.C. Glasgow 3 Dinamo Moscu 0'. It seemed that Rangers were out of sight. John Greig was convinced that Rangers had the cup won and told Johnston as much as they celebrated. His words almost came back to haunt him. Dynamo pulled a goal back in the fifty-ninth minute when Evriuzhikin took advantage of uncertainty between Mathieson and Jardine and squared it for substitute Estrekov to put the ball into the empty net. Rangers were forced onto the defensive as Dynamo pressed hard. It seemed that the Scots had weathered the storm when, with three minutes to go, the Soviets scored a second. Makovikov cut through the Rangers defence with ease and played a one-two with Gerschkovitch before firing the ball high into the net as he was falling over.

The second goal meant a nerve-shredding few minutes. Sandy Jardine must have been alone in the stadium in being entirely confident of a Rangers win. 'I didn't feel nervy even though they scored a second goal late on' he said. 'I didn't ever think we were going to lose it.' The fans in the stadium were desperate for the final whistle to blow. Gordon McGilvray relates how they were put through an emotional wringer:

> By the time wee Bud had scored our third goal that was it – we had definitely won the cup. It was a fantastic atmosphere, although Dynamo did give us a huge fright towards the end of the game. After each goal that we scored, some fans ran onto the park. Again, there was no malice, just joyful celebrations. They shouldn't have been there, but there was no stewarding in those days, like we have now, and the police just sat in their positions, and watched.

When the match finished, the invasion started in earnest. Just like Lisbon in 1967 (and in Nuremberg the same year, for that matter) hundreds of ecstatic fans poured onto the pitch to celebrate. As the fans raced onto the field the disappointed Dynamo players trooped past them, unhindered, to the tunnel. The Rangers players, on the other hand, were in serious danger of being crushed as they were mobbed by crowds of supporters, and needed to break free from the mêlée as quickly as possible. Some fled to the tunnel but others were overwhelmed by the crowds.

'When the supporters came on to the pitch at the end I was too knackered to do anything,' recalled Alex MacDonald. 'I felt like I was having a heart attack with the heat and everything else. A big friend of mine called Stewart Daniels came on to the pitch and got me out. He lifted me up and carried me to the tunnel; and thank Christ for that.'

Eventually, all the players extricated themselves and reached the dressing room, where they patiently awaited the call to return to the pitch and receive their medals and the trophy. As time wore on it became clear that things were not going to plan. Up on the pitch there was mayhem. Having previously tolerated the exuberance of the Scots, the police suddenly had a change of heart. Rather than allowing the fans to calm down, and then making public-address announcements asking them to clear the pitch, the police attempted to restore order by attacking anyone who came near them with batons. Such brutality inevitably provoked a response from the fans, who retaliated by launching a charge towards the police.

'Franco's fascist thugs didn't discriminate between man or woman or child,' said Gordon McGilvray, 'but I don't think the local Catalans, most of whom hated the Franco regime, had seen anyone stand up to the police before.'

Sandy Jardine recalled:

> We didn't know anything about it because we were taken off the park. We
> had to get off because so many fans were on the park, but there was no
> badness involved, it was only exuberance because we had won a European
> cup. It was very similar to what happened with Celtic in Lisbon. The dif-
> ference was the Spanish police were extremely heavy-handed. Everybody
> understood they had to clear the park, but they did it in a manner that was
> totally unacceptable. They were hitting the Rangers supporters with batons
> and some of them took exception, and that was when the trouble started.

As the battles raged on, John Greig and Willie Waddell were presented with the
trophy in a small anteroom deep in the heart of the stadium. Having worked so
hard, it was a major disappointment not to be allowed to lift the trophy
with his teammates in front of the Rangers support. Celtic had suffered a
similar anti-climax in 1967 when the behaviour of their fans prevented the
players from receiving their medals in public. Celtic captain Billy McNeill
described it as being one of the biggest regrets of his career.

However, the players refused to let the trouble spoil their night, and the
party began as soon as Greig returned to the dressing room with the trophy.
Back at the Rey Don Jaime the champagne flowed as the wives joined in.
The celebrations went on until five and they resumed again later that morning
as the players gathered round the pool for a 'hair of the dog'. Willie
Waddell described his team as 'Ibrox immortals'. He said, 'They have done
something that no other Rangers team has ever done. I could not be happier.'
The medals were duly dished out and, to this day, Alex MacDonald wears his
on a chain around his neck. 'We weren't that bothered about the trophy,'
he recalled. 'We knew we'd won it and we'd get it some time along with the
medals. I'm wearing mine right now, in fact.'

Back home, the newspapers focused on the post-match trouble rather than
the result. The coverage predictably condemned the Rangers fans. Rather than
examining the role of the fascist police in the events, newspapers blamed the
Scots. It was a self-fulfilling prophecy, as many columnists had been predict-
ing trouble long before the final. Under a headline 'The Shame in Spain'
Alex Cameron in the *Daily Record* described the game as 'the most unruly
major European soccer match ever'.

Having escaped from the mayhem that was the Camp Nou, Gordon
McGilvray and his fellow travellers returned to Lloret to celebrate, and met
some very interesting barmaids:

We had a great time, both Bears and local Catalans, even though the police ordered bars and clubs to close early. Sitting poolside on the Thursday enjoying our beers in the sun was another great experience worth waiting for. I say worth waiting for, as there were only two girls 'working' behind the hotel bar. They were both prostitutes – which meant that there was only ever one of them serving behind the bar, while the other served in a bedroom. It wasn't until naive young me went to the bar and complained about the slow service, that an older and wiser Bear put me right. Anyway, I stuck to the beer.

The Rangers team flew back to Glasgow on the Thursday morning and headed straight for Ibrox, where they were welcomed by a piper playing 'Amazing Grace'. More than twenty thousand fans turned out in torrential rain to welcome the victors home. Some were still wearing the sombreros they had acquired in Spain, although most of the travelling supporters were still making their way back from the final and missed the victory parade. The Rangers players toured the stadium on the back of a coal lorry draped with a Union flag and red-white-and-blue bunting. Among those paying tribute in the rain was the legendary 'Captain Cutlass', Bobby Shearer.

For a suffering Alex MacDonald, the glimpse of Shearer helped make the lap of honour that bit more bearable:

> The problem was that being redheaded I got sunstroke from getting burned by the pool up in the hills. I was feeling ill on the plane and everyone was laughing at me saying I'd had too much to drink. Then we got back to Ibrox and the doc came up to me and told me I had sunstroke. Half of me was bright red! So we went out on that lorry and went round Ibrox in the pouring rain so I get even more ill. Then we saw Bobby Shearer in the crowd standing in the rain and clapping us and that was fantastic.

Rangers were back in Glasgow with the trophy but the drama wasn't over yet. Dynamo lodged a protest claiming they had been intimidated by the Rangers support and demanded a replay. Despite the mini-invasions, the Spanish referee Jose Ortes de Mendibil had at no point felt a need to stop the game. He said later, 'I did not think they were going to be violent. They were excited. They were exuberant. Probably too exuberant, but I was never concerned.' Waddell was furious at the lack of crowd control and condemned UEFA for their organisational failures. He also pointed out, 'There were fans on the field at Wembley last year when Ajax won the European Cup. There were fans on the field at Nuremberg in 1967. There were Celtic fans on the field at Lisbon when they won the European Cup. I don't see how Rangers FC can be discriminated against when this has happened before.'

After an investigation, UEFA threw out the Moscow protest and the result stood, but Rangers were horrified to be told they had been kicked out of Europe for two years. Waddell cut short a Spanish holiday and rushed to Switzerland to lodge the appeal. He managed to get the ban halved but it might not have happened without the help of one Barcelona veteran. Gordon McGilvray explains:

> I was a friend of John Lawrence's secretary, and because I worked in the Post Office, she came to see me with an A4-sized envelope containing the appeal documents and said, 'Gordon, this has to be in Switzerland for the day after tomorrow at the latest, or it will miss the appeal deadline.' She left the envelope – and the problem – with me. What a responsibility to have! I can't remember the exact service that I used for the appeal envelope but I ensured that it would have been traceable all the way through its journey, and I made sure it left Glasgow safely. Anyway, it got there. Willie Waddell also got there, and the ban was reduced to one year.

It was still a serious blow to the club. Waddell later hit out at the 'certain few' whose misbehaviour tarnished the club's reputation. 'The actions of those irresponsible fans that night could have cost the vast, well-behaved majority of Rangers fans the opportunity of seeing the club in action against the best European teams until 1975.' But any doubts about how the people of Barcelona viewed Rangers were put to rest two years after the final, when the Catalans invited Rangers back to the city to compete in their prestigious Joan Gamper tournament along with Ajax and Athletic Bilbao. A capacity crowd turned out at the Camp Nou to see the Ibrox side.

With all that followed, the achievement of that team in winning the European trophy is often overlooked. Unlike Celtic's run to the European Cup final in 1967, the teams Rangers had knocked out were all from major football powers: France, Portugal, Italy, West Germany and the Soviet Union. The defeat of Bayern Munich must rank as one of the greatest-ever victories achieved by a Scottish team. Sandy Jardine argues, 'The team probably didn't get the credit it was due. That season Davie Smith was absolutely fantastic at sweeper. We had a lot of ability in the team and all the way through we had to beat teams from major nations. There was no easy draw.' The 1972 team has never inspired the sort of dewy-eyed adulation accorded to the Lisbon Lions or even to Aberdeen's 1983 Cup Winners Cup-winning squad. It is probably because, unlike Celtic and Aberdeen, few Rangers fans consider the team that won a European trophy as their best. In fact, for most supporters it probably wouldn't even be in the top five of all time.

Nevertheless, Jardine believes Waddell's legacy was to create a team that would go on to end Celtic's domination of Scottish football and bring honours back to Ibrox:

> When he came in, Waddell set about restoring a lot of the traditions of the club. A lot of personnel left and others came in. We had a much younger team and initially we started off terribly in the league. But we were fantastic in Europe and the Cup Winners Cup win laid the foundations for the team that won the trebles later in the decade. It set Rangers up to be the dominant team in Scotland of the seventies.

At long last Rangers had landed that elusive European trophy. Shortly after the victory over Dynamo, Waddell stepped down as manager and took on an administrative role as general manager. Coach Jock Wallace was the obvious successor. His first task would be to regain some domestic credibility and hopefully go on and build on the Barcelona success with more triumphs in Europe. The triumphs at home under Wallace came soon enough, but unfortunately European success wasn't quite so forthcoming.

10

January 1973: The First European Super Cup

Cast into the European wilderness by UEFA for a year, Rangers were left for the most part to concentrate on domestic matters in 1972/73 and as a result enjoyed their best season on that front for seven years. The championship went to Celtic for the eighth season in a row, but Rangers finished just one point behind in second place. And then Jock Wallace picked up his first piece of silverware as manager in the final game of the season when Tom Forsyth's 'sclaff' from a couple of inches won the Scottish Cup against Celtic.

Rangers did play one European tie that season, albeit an unofficial one. Not content at seeing Dutch clubs dominate the European Cup, journalist Anton Witkamp wanted a way of definitively deciding the top club in Europe. He also wanted to celebrate the masters of total football, Ajax, and arguably the world's best player at the time, Johann Cruyff. Witkamp's dream was for a European Super Cup, played over two legs between the winners of the Champions Cup and the Cup Winners Cup.

Witkamp's thinking, as recorded on UEFA's website, was more profound than most football writers:

> More than money and glory, they were pursuing the right to be called the best. But which was the strongest team in Europe, or which team ought to have been the strongest? The team that won the European Cup? In principle, yes, this team ought to have been the strongest. Football is often a hymn to relativity and, for this reason, can be an imprecise art. So why not pit the holders of the European Champion Clubs Cup against the winners of the Cup Winners Cup? Why not throw down a challenge to Ajax?

He took his proposal of a match between Ajax and Rangers to the Dutch team's president Jaap Van Praag, who loved the idea. Witkamp and Van Praag travelled to Zurich to seek official approval for their new competition.

Unfortunately, UEFA's suspension of Rangers meant the governing body was unable to endorse the match, but with the backing of Witkamp's newspaper, *De Telegraaf*, it went ahead.

Rangers grasped the opportunity to take part, and linked the games in with their centenary celebrations, even though some believed the club should have marked the landmark anniversary a year earlier. The reason for the dispute is the confusion over the year Rangers were formed. The official version is that the club was started in 1873, possibly because this was the year of the inaugural general meeting, when office bearers were first elected. But the history books tell us that the group of young men who founded the club played their first game a year earlier at Flesher's Haugh on Glasgow Green.

Either way, 1973 was declared centenary year and it is difficult to imagine a better way of marking the occasion than with a glamour match against Europe's best team. A week after Rangers had defeated Dynamo Moscow, Ajax destroyed Internazionale in the final of the European Cup. The 2–0 victory was a triumph for football purists. The flowing football of Cruyff, Johann Neeskens, Gerrie Muhren, Ruud Krol and Arie Haan was the polar opposite of Inter's dreary and cynical approach to the game, and only the *nerazzuri*'s own fans would have been disappointed with the result. It was the second season in a row that Ajax had won Europe's top trophy, having beaten Panathinaikos in 1971. The year before, their biggest rivals Feyenoord, of Rotterdam, had beaten Celtic to win the trophy. For a country that had been considered one of European football's minnows until very recently, Holland's pre-eminence was remarkable.

When they faced Rangers in the Super Cup in January 1973, Ajax were in the middle of a third consecutive European Cup-winning run. On the way to their victory over Juventus in the final, the Amsterdam team disposed of CSKA Sofia, Bayern Munich and Real Madrid, scoring fourteen goals in the process. So it was no embarrassment for Rangers to lose 3–1 in the first leg at Ibrox. In front of a 60,000 crowd, the teams put on a fine exhibition of attacking football that included a tremendous volleyed goal from Cruyff. In the return leg at the Olympic stadium in Amsterdam, Rangers opened the scoring through Alex MacDonald in the third minute and, by half-time, it was two apiece with Quinton 'Cutty' Young also getting on the score sheet. Inevitably, Cruyff scored the winner in the second half, but Rangers were by no means out of their depth against the best team in the world.

Although the 6–3 aggregate defeat was comprehensive, the young Rangers team had given a good account of themselves and gained valuable experience. The success of the matches was also noted by UEFA, who decided to make the competition an official annual event, one that continues to this day.

Back in official European competition the following year, 1973/74, Rangers were drawn in the Cup Winners Cup against a Turkish team for the first time, in the form of Ankaragucu. Based in the Turkish capital, Ankara, they had made their European debut in the previous season's Cup Winners Cup, losing narrowly to Leeds United. Rangers made easy work of progressing past the Turks, winning 2–0 away and 4–0 at Ibrox. Two Ankaragucu players were sent off in the second leg as they inexplicably lost control, even though the game was well beyond them.

The next round brought a tougher test, although they were on more familiar ground. For the ninth time, Rangers faced German opposition, this time old foes Borussia Moenchengladbach. The World Cup in West Germany was a matter of months away and the country's football was on a high at the time. Bayern Munich were on their way to winning the European Cup for the first time, while the national team were the reigning European champions and would soon add the world crown.

The last time Rangers and Monchengladbach had met, the Scots had recorded one of their best European victories, winning 11–0 on aggregate. The Borussia team of the early seventies were a far tougher proposition. Along with Bayern, the club had risen to the top of West German football with the advent of the professional era and the creation of the *Bundesliga*. The teams were deadly rivals, dominating the league in the late sixties and the start of the new decade.

Bayern were usually dismissed as the epitome of Germanic efficiency, lacking in flair and more interested in winning than the beautiful game. Gladbach, on the other hand, were seen as the radical football team, whose cavalier approach was as entertaining as it was effective. Similar comparisons have been made over the years about Scotland's two biggest rivals, with Rangers taking Bayern's 'bad guy' role and Celtic being lauded as the 'good guys'. In Germany, as in Scotland, such stereotypes were never supported by the facts. Inspired by Beckenbauer, Bayern often played scintillating football that rivalled Ajax at their peak, while Gladbach founded their success on a strong defence, epitomised by *Der Terrier* Berti Vogts, who was limited as a footballer but effective as a stopper.

Gladbach won their first Bundesliga title in 1970, and followed it up with another league win the following season. They lost their talisman Gunter Netzer to Real Madrid in 1973, but came back strongly to win three titles in a row between 1975 and 1977.

The Borussia team that faced Rangers was packed with stars, including Vogts (who went on to become a figure of fun in Scotland after his shambolic time in charge of the national team) cultured midfielder Rainer Bonhof (later to become the Scotland Under-21 coach), Josef Heynckes and Bernd Rupp. Nevertheless, Rangers settled comfortably into the match and restricted the Germans to a handful of attacks in the opening twenty minutes.

Then came one of the most farcical goals Rangers have ever conceded in Europe. A Gladbach attack down the right came to nothing when Peter McCloy intercepted a cross from Rupp. The goalkeeper dropped the ball to his feet and dribbled it out with the intention of launching it forward. Unfortunately, just as he bent down to pick it up, Rupp, who was still lingering on the goal line, nipped in from behind and knocked the ball into the path of Heynckes, who had the simple task of stroking it into the empty net.

The look of surprise on McCloy's face as Rupp appeared from nowhere was matched only by the glares from his teammates as they stood in stunned disbelief at what they had just witnessed. Derek Johnstone made a half-hearted protest to the referee, although it's difficult to imagine what case he was making. 'That's no' fair!' might work in the playground but, sadly for McCloy, it has never been a defence in top-flight football. In reality the goal was a combination of slack defending and sheer cheek from Rupp and it was appropriate that the advertising board immediately behind McCloy's goal was promoting a brand of shoes called Gallus.

The goal inspired the Scots and minutes later they were almost back on level terms following an excellent passing move. Alex MacDonald chipped the ball forward to Alfie Conn, who laid it off first time to Doug Houston. He passed it on quickly to Parlane at the edge of the Gladbach penalty area, and he flicked it on in turn to Conn, who had continued his run on the outside. Conn slid in to beat the oncoming defender and fired a first-time shot that had to be well saved by goalkeeper Kleff.

For the next forty minutes Rangers kept Gladbach at bay, and to the delight of the small band of Rangers fans in the 33,000 crowd, managed to make a few chances of their own. Conn in particular had another great opportunity in the first half when he shot over following good build-up play by Willie Mathieson and Parlane down the right.

McCloy went some way to making amends for his first-half blunder when he made a good save from a Heynckes penalty in the fifty-eighth minute, awarded after a clumsy challenge on the same player by Tom Forsyth. But minutes later Heynckes scored his second, finishing clinically after finding himself on the end of a through ball in acres of space. With four minutes to go Borussia added a third, Rupp taking advantage of yet more slack defending.

The return match at a wet and windy Ibrox was always going to be difficult for Rangers, but they were given hope when Conn netted in the tenth minute to make the aggregate score 3–1, hitting home after a header by

Alex O'Hara rebounded off the crossbar. Jensen equalised for the Germans eighteen minutes later, before Colin Jackson put Rangers back in front with a header from a Houston cross. The Scots needed another three goals to go through and when MacDonald scored with a diving header, fifteen minutes into the second half, it seemed that an unlikely victory might just be a possibility. But Jensen scored his second goal midway through the half and any lingering hopes of a miracle were finally dashed. There was no further scoring and Gladbach were comfortably through to the next round on a 5–3 aggregate, leaving Rangers on the outside looking in once again.

For only the third time since 1956, Rangers failed to qualify for any of the three European trophies in 1974/75. But the long-suffering fans were more than compensated with their first league championship win for a decade, which, just as significantly, brought to an end a run of nine consecutive titles by Celtic. For the first time in eleven seasons, Rangers were in the European Cup in 1975.

When the first-round draw paired Rangers with Republic of Ireland champions Bohemians, much was made of the potential for violence when Rangers travelled to Dublin for the second leg. In the end, apart from a tense atmosphere inside the ground and a few skirmishes between rival fans, there was little trouble. A lot of that could be put down to the fact that the tie was virtually over as a contest after the first leg, Rangers having won 4–1 with goals from Graham Fyfe, Alex O'Hara, Derek Johnstone and an own goal. Johnstone scored again in 1–1 draw in Dublin.

Jock Wallace was always known for his plain speaking. So when he was asked to wax lyrical on the team Rangers had drawn in the next round, his answer was simple, but to the point. 'All I know is that we are not meeting a bunch of cowboys.' Funnily enough, the Western was all the rage at the cinema when Rangers had last met St Etienne in 1957. Back in the days of Ritchie, Caldow, Shearer, Scott and Hubbard, the Ibrox side won their European Cup tie 4–3 on aggregate. Wallace was well aware of the dangers facing the present day Rangers. The long-haired France international Dominique Rocheteau had great skill and pace and, in attack, brothers Patrick and Herve Revelli were a potent threat.

Rangers were dealt a blow before the first leg at the Guichard stadium on 22 October 1975 before the game even got underway. Goalkeeper Peter McCloy injured his wrist in the warm up and had to be replaced by Stewart Kennedy. As Wallace had predicted, St Etienne started the match like a whirlwind, and one of the danger brothers, Patrick, beat Kennedy in the twenty-fifth minute to open the scoring. Rangers fought their way back into the match and looked to have escaped with a reasonable 1–0 defeat, when they once again suffered from a self-inflicted wound. With only seconds to go, a slack pass across the penalty area by Alex MacDonald was intercepted by Dominique Bathenay, and he shot past Kennedy to double St Etienne's advantage.

The second leg was a disaster for Rangers, as they were played off the park by the French champions and then jeered off it by their own supporters. A crowd of 45,000 was inside Ibrox at kick-off, but when MacDonald scored in the last minute only a quarter of them were still there. The reason for the mass exodus and the disparaging chants from those who remained on the terracing was that St Etienne were already two in front, through Herve Revelli and Rocheteau, when MacDonald scored his consolation goal. The 4–1 aggregate defeat actually flattered Rangers who were totally outclassed over the two legs.

As is so often the case, St Etienne were a better team than many gave them credit for. After defeating Rangers they went on to eliminate Dynamo Kiev and PSV Eindhoven to reach the final at Hampden against holders Bayern Munich. In front of a 55,000 crowd, they were the more attack-minded team but lost a goal early in the second half to Franz Roth – whose goal had beaten Rangers in the 1967 Cup Winners Cup Final – and were unable to break the Bavarians down.

The matches against Rangers obviously meant a lot to St Etienne manager Roby Herbin. Shortly before facing Liverpool in the quarter-final of the following season's competition he said, 'The Rangers people are among the friendliest I have ever met in football.' He was so impressed with his visit to Scotland that he named his two cocker spaniels Glasgow and Rangers. The St Etienne fans who travelled to the match were also touched by the welcome they received, so much so that they called a city-centre hostelry in their home town The Glasgow Inn. The affection was mutual; Rangers granted *les Verts* the use of Ibrox as a training base for the European Cup final.

Losing to a team of St Etienne's calibre was nothing to be ashamed of but, during the following season, 1976/77, Rangers recorded one of their most disastrous results in Europe. Four years after winning the European Cup Winners Cup, they were dumped out of the European Cup by Swiss part-timers FC Zurich. Having won the domestic treble the previous season, Rangers supporters were entitled to expect that their team would have a significant run in Europe; an expectation that was enhanced when they were drawn against Zurich. But less than a minute into the first leg at Ibrox the Light Blues were a goal down, thanks to careless defending. Rangers launched wave after wave of attack but were lacking in subtlety, choosing instead to lump high, diagonal balls onto the heads of twin strikers Parlane and

Johnstone. Parlane did manage to snatch a goal, but Rangers failed to make any other inroads and the match finished in a dismal 1–1 draw.

Time-and-time again in Europe, Rangers have been punished by early and late goals and it was the same old story in the second leg. A goal from Marinelli in eight minutes left Rangers with the proverbial mountain to climb in Switzerland and despite a fighting performance they never looked like scoring. A miserable 1–0 defeat was capped by the sending-off of Derek Johnstone in the last minute for retaliation. He lashed out after being kicked once too often. The fact that Zurich made it all the way to the semi-final, before being knocked out by eventual winners Liverpool, was little consolation.

The match epitomised a dire season. After winning the treble the season before, they followed it up with a trophy-less campaign. Celtic finished nine points clear in the league and beat Rangers in the Scottish Cup final. A 5–1 defeat to Aberdeen in the semi-final of the League Cup was frankly embarrassing.

A place in the 1977/78 European Cup Winners Cup was 'gained' by virtue of their loss to the league winners in the Scottish Cup final. But once again Rangers were knocked out by what most would have considered an inferior team.

During the close season Rangers brought in three new signings to add much-needed creativity. Gordon Smith, an attacking midfielder, was captured from Kilmarnock and winger Davie Cooper arrived from Clydebank. The most unlikely signing of all was Robert Russell, a tremendously skilful midfielder, who came from Shettleston Juniors. The trio became great friends and were key figures in what turned out to be a glorious season, as Rangers swept all before them to win the domestic treble.

Smith made his Rangers debut in the first leg of the opening Cup Winners Cup tie against Young Boys of Berne. John Greig scored the only goal of the match at Ibrox, and the slender lead brought back memories of the previous season's debacle in Switzerland. Fears of a repeat performance in the return seemed to be allayed when Derek Johnstone scored just before half-time but, when Colin Jackson put into his own net just after the break and Young Boys added a second shortly after, the nerves began to rattle. Only when Gordon Smith got the equalizer on the night to put Rangers clear on aggregate did the tension ease. Johnstone's sending off for retaliation, for the second successive season in Switzerland, had no effect on the outcome although it did rule him out of the first game in the next round.

The continued success of Ajax and the national team ensured Dutch football was still riding on the crest of a wave in 1977, so no-one should have been surprised by the ability of Twente Enschede. The club had only been formed in 1965, but within a decade had progressed so far that they had reached the final of the UEFA Cup, come second in the Dutch league and won the Dutch cup. The team boasted two players who would become well known to British football fans, Arnold Muhren and Frans Thijssen. The midfield pair both joined Ipswich Town in the late seventies and enjoyed huge success in the English game, inspiring the sleepy East Anglian club to the best period in its history.

In the first leg at Ibrox, Jock Wallace took the difficult decision to leave club captain John Greig out, choosing to go with Alex Miller instead. Miller had filled in for Greig while the skipper had been out injured and the manager felt he had done little wrong. Goalkeeper Peter McCloy also got the Wallace seal of approval despite recent costly blunders. Rangers missed the goalscoring threat of the suspended Derek Johnstone and failed to break down the Dutch defence. The game ended goalless, leaving Rangers with a reasonable chance of progression.

However, in the second leg at the Diekman Stadion Rangers were outplayed by Twente who brushed the Scots aside with an easy 3–0 victory. The fact that Rangers had such a successful domestic season, yet were comprehensively outplayed by the fourth-best team in Holland, only served to highlight the growing chasm between Scottish football and the rest of Europe. Not only were Rangers apparently lagging behind the giants from the Big Four nations of England, Italy, Spain and West Germany, but they were also falling further behind the smaller countries.

The clean-sweep of domestic trophies was Jock Wallace's second treble in three seasons but in the close-season he shocked Rangers fans by abruptly handing in his resignation. The story of why he quit has never been fully revealed as Wallace maintained a dignified silence about his reasons until his death in 1996, although speculation has centred on disputes with the board over money. John Greig was immediately appointed to take over the reins, becoming the first Rangers player to go straight into the manager's job.

On the international stage, Scotland were depressingly bad, as evidenced by the disastrous World Cup campaign of the summer of 1978, when the Scots lost to Peru, drew with Iran and only salvaged some dignity with a victory over Holland when it was too late. However, the following season was to give a welcome, if unexpected, boost to the Scottish game and to the reputation of Rangers in Europe.

11

The Mugging of an Old Lady

It had all the ingredients of a Cold War spy thriller; a secluded bolthole on the outskirts of a beautiful Continental city, secret dossiers, the Iron Curtain, ruthless Italian hit men and a plot to bring down a European institution. At the Villa Sassi, a luxury hotel hidden away in twenty-two hectares of countryside on the edge of Turin, *Il Capo* was drawing up his plans to dispose of *La Vecchia Signora* (the Old Lady), also known as *i bianconeri*, *zebre* or *gobbi*. In the ornate rooms of the 280-year-old building, and in the secluded grounds that surrounded it, he issued his instructions to his foot soldiers. Every rival was examined in detail and a dossier was drawn up on each one. Such meticulous planning was essential if the boss was to succeed in his plan of European domination.

But this wasn't the work of John Le Carre or Frederick Forsyth, but rather the latest instalment of a longer running, and occasionally less believable, series entitled Rangers in Europe.

Few people had given Rangers much of a chance when they were drawn against Italian giants Juventus (the so-called Old Lady of Turin) in the first round of the European Cup in 1978/79. For a start they had never managed to knock out an Italian team in more than twenty years of European competition. Furthermore, Juve were undoubtedly one of the strongest teams on the Continent, in fact were among the favourites to win the European Cup. With the legendary Giovanni Trapattoni in charge, eight of their team had played for Italy in the World Cup a few months earlier and six would be in the *Azzurri* squad that won the competition four years later. Players like Zoff, Gentile, Cabrini, Scirea, Causio, Tardelli and Betegga were household names. But John Greig was convinced he could hatch a plot to overthrow these footballing superheroes.

For a relative youngster like Bobby Russell, who had been playing junior football for Shettleston only a year earlier, these were just names on a sheet of paper:

> The manager had made up dossiers on all the players on their strengths and weaknesses – although with Juve it was mostly strengths. Their players were household names, but for me I was only a kid, just starting out, so the names didn't really mean a lot to me. They were just people that you play against. Probably the older players looked at the names and thought 'we've got a big task here' but we still went about it in the right manner.

Defender Sandy Jardine recalls that he was asked to perform a new role, as Greig came up with an innovative way of blunting the threat of the strikers Roberto Betegga and Pietro Paolo Virdis:

> John was very good tactically and he looked closely at their team. He saw that they had two tremendous strikers, so he changed our whole system to combat that. Rather than our usual 4-4-2 or 4-3-3 he pushed me into sweeper and Tom Forsyth and Colin Jackson played as markers. The manager was relying on a defensive line that would have to be as strong as the famous Iron Curtain of the forties, and he wasn't let down. It was a completely new system that we'd never played before but we did very well.

After a frenetic opening spell in the Stadio Comunale when Virdis gave Juve the lead, Rangers settled down and were able to frustrate the Italians. Alex Miller and Kenny Watson played a deep midfield role that Juventus were unable to break down. The partisan fans in the 62,000 crowd were silenced, and out-sung by the small band of Rangers supporters crammed into a corner. The Scots offered up little as an attacking force, with their best chance being an over-hit back pass by Marco Tardelli, which Zoff couldn't hold. But Greig had been honest about his intentions before the match and the 1–0 defeat was considered to be a success. After the match, the manager was delighted.

Late in the game, Romeo Benetti, a tough midfielder and one of the Italy World Cup stars, committed a vicious, over-the-ball foul on Rangers midfielder Gordon Smith. Having already been booked, it seemed certain he would receive the red card that would rule him out of the second leg. But the Romanian referee chose to give him a lecture instead. In a highly unusual move, the UEFA observer declared after the match that he felt Benetti should not play in the return at Ibrox. The West German official Dr Hubert Claessen described the tackle as 'brutal' and claimed the referee had 'shirked his duties'. Smith for his part was left nursing a swollen knee on the flight home. He said,

'I honestly thought Benetti had done me a serious injury. If his boot had caught me just a little lower down then my leg could have been broken.' Greig said it was the worst tackle he'd seen in his time in Europe. Surprisingly Benetti was dropped for the second leg, which was probably just as well, because as he was substituted in the Stadio Comunale he appeared to gesture to Smith that he would complete the job in Glasgow.

In spite of the hostile surroundings, the few hundred Rangers fans in Turin behaved impeccably. This was in stark contrast to a section of the Celtic support that was making front-page headlines that morning thanks to a riot during an Anglo-Scottish Cup game in Burnley. Manager Billy McNeill argued they were not genuine Celtic supporters and was moved to brand those who had brought shame on the club – some of whom had also run amok in the Lancashire town earlier in the day – as 'scum'.

Although the first-leg result had been good, Rangers knew they would have to score at least twice to progress against Juventus. But, at the same time, an away goal could prove fatal, so discipline and patience would be essential in equal quantities. 'They had a large number of international players in their team,' said Bobby Russell, 'so it was still a tall order. We weren't really given a lot of hope that we would overturn their lead back at Ibrox but we did it. It was a great European night.'

An expectant crowd of 44,000 had packed into Ibrox for the return match on 27 September 1978. Rangers still hadn't won a league game, six matches into the season, but the European arena seemed to bring out the best in them. Greig pulled another tactical masterstroke by playing Tommy McLean on the left, rather than the right. It unsettled Juve and he was able to take advantage, and he was involved in Rangers' opening goal. McLean played a free kick to Alex Forsyth who drove the ball into the penalty area. Gordon Smith latched onto it and Zoff could only parry his shot onto the head of Alex MacDonald, who made no mistake with the rebound.

In the second half, Smith got the second goal, rising to head home a chipped cross from Russell. With twenty minutes to go, Rangers were forced to go on the defensive, knowing that a single goal from Juve would take them through on away goals. But it was a sterling performance, Alex MacDonald biting away at opposition ankles and Sandy Jardine majestic in the midfield role. Jardine said:

> Beating Juventus was probably one of my finest moments with Rangers because they had so many great Italian internationals and to go and beat a team of that quality was a tremendous result for us. We always knew the first leg was a good result because with the home record we had at Ibrox we knew we'd have a chance. We used the same system again and got the result.

By contrast with more recent times, when the club seemed to have money to throw away, the Rangers of the 1970s were a far more tight-fisted bunch. This was reflected in the bonus the players received for knocking Juventus out of the competition; a mere £200. It would have been the same payout no matter the opposition, but senior players felt this was unfair. Their pleas fell on deaf ears though, and they must have looked on enviously when they read years later how Rangers players were receiving bonuses of £30,000 and more for winning games against lesser opponents than Juve.

The victory, arguably the greatest ever achieved by the club in Europe, was a personal triumph for John Greig. The poor start to the domestic season had led some to question the wisdom of his appointment to the job at the age of thirty-five. He had gone straight from playing to the manager's chair and was renowned for his uncompromising style on the pitch, rather than his footballing skills. There were some raised eyebrows, therefore, when he proved himself to be so tactically astute in Europe. In fairness, having played so often in Europe himself, he must have known just about every potential pitfall. But a combination of his tactics, the determination of the players and the backing of the Ibrox crowd had brought Rangers a famous victory; it made the rest of Europe sit up and take notice and left bluenoses everywhere in raptures.

Like the blockbuster movie *Grease*, which was packing them in at the cinemas, Rangers were big box office all over the world, but few travelled as far as Hitoshi Sato to see his team. The 20-year-old had travelled seven thousand miles from Japan to see Rangers play Juventus, only to find himself robbed of £1,400 on the way to the match, the victim of a pickpocket. The economics student was left with just £2 to his name. But as he fretted in his hotel room the next day, two CID officers turned up with good news. The thieves had dumped a purchase slip for more than £1,000 of traveller's cheques and his air ticket in Govan's Harvey Street, not far from the stadium. The £50 in sterling and £300 in yen which he also had with him were nowhere to be seen, although quite what a Glasgow ned was going to do with such a large amount of Japanese currency was anyone's guess. 'Most of the people I met were so kind and I had been so happy that at long last I was seeing Rangers,' Hitoshi said later. 'It was such a fine victory. They are a very famous team you know, even in Japan.'

Greig said afterwards that he wanted to be drawn against another good side, and his wish was granted when they were paired with PSV Eindhoven. Surely, Rangers couldn't pull off another famous victory?

12

Eindhoven 78: 'You have created a bit of history'

If Rangers thought they had done the hard part by knocking Juventus out of the European Cup in 1978, they were in for a rude awakening when the draw paired them with Dutch champions PSV Eindhoven. With the financial backing of the Philips electrical company, PSV had risen to the upper echelons of Dutch football in the 1970s, forming a triumvirate with Ajax and Feyenoord that dominated the game throughout that decade and has continued to do so ever since.

PSV had had every reason to be confident going into the tie. The season before, they had won the UEFA Cup while their inferior compatriots, Twente Enschede, had knocked Rangers out of the Cup Winners Cup. Holland had reached the World Cup final in the summer of 1978, eventually losing to hosts Argentina. The national squad contained six PSV players, more than Ajax and Feyenoord combined, including twin brothers Rene and Willy Van der Kerkhof, Ernie Brandts, Harry Lubse, Adri Van Kraay and Jan Poortvliet. In addition, Jan Van Beveren, who did not travel to Argentina, was considered to be Holland's best goalkeeper, while Willy Van der Kuylen played in World Cup qualifying but did not appear in the final squad.

On a night of missed chances and excellent goalkeeping, Rangers failed to score in the first leg at Ibrox on 18 October 1978, although the disappointment was lessened as they had prevented PSV from securing a vital away goal. But the Dutch team was without three key players on the night and few pundits gave Rangers much of a chance for the return in Eindhoven.

The first leg was Rangers' one hundredth appearance in Europe and their fortieth in the European Cup. The overall record in all competitions was little more than passable; they had won forty-seven, lost thirty-six and drawn seventeen. In the European Cup the record was worse, with nineteen wins, seventeen losses and four draws. Despite this they were to return from the Netherlands with one of their best results of all time.

Rangers took a big support to Eindhoven, and they filled one end of the Philips stadium. Despite the optimism of the fans, Rangers knew they faced one of their most difficult European tests. They had to score at least once in Eindhoven, and somehow shackle the attacking threat from the Dutchmen. The fact that the home team were undefeated at home in Europe and had only ever lost two European Cup goals on their own ground – in two games in which they scored six and seven goals themselves – showed the magnitude of the task.

As in the Juve tie, John Greig had planned meticulously. He clearly identified PSV's strengths and weaknesses and drew up a game plan for the task in hand. Rather than the defensive approach that worked well against Juventus in Turin, Greig instructed his team to push up the field as much as possible and prevent the Dutch from taking the game to Rangers. Again the players were given all the information they needed about the opposition players. More than anything, an early goal was seen as vital to Rangers' chances.

What transpired was certainly not part of the game plan. With just thirty-four seconds gone, PSV took a stunning lead. Teenager Willy Jansen crossed from the right and Lubse sent a thundering drive past Peter McCloy. The blow of losing a goal after less than a minute could have destroyed Rangers, but they showed tremendous character to fight their way back into the game. Inspired by Bobby Russell, the Scots played superb, controlled football and repeatedly found gaps in the PSV defence.

'It was a tremendous goal they scored,' said Russell, 'a great strike. But I think if we had gifted them a goal through slack play then we would have been more down. We just accepted it and got on with it. We showed a bit of spirit and character.'

In ten minutes, Eindhoven's reserve goalkeeper Van Engelen made a brilliant save from a Derek Parlane diving header and four minutes later he threw himself across the goal to stop a thirty-yard drive from Kenny Watson. A header from Johnstone went just past the post and a shot from Alex Forsyth had to be scrambled away by the goalkeeper.

Still the vital goal would not come and when Gordon Smith had another shot saved by Van Engelen the Rangers fans began to doubt if they would make the breakthrough. Then, after fifty-eight minutes, Rangers finally got the goal their play deserved. Tommy McLean brought the ball down on the edge of the area and chipped it into the path of Alex MacDonald, who sent a diving header high into the net. Bobby Russell had missed a good chance with a header moments earlier and Doddy had given him some stick. Russell recalled, 'After he stuck his header away, he said to me: "That's the way you do it son," which was fair enough.'

The Rangers fans were still celebrating when PSV took the lead again within three minutes. The defence failed to clear and Deijkers stepped in to score with an overhead kick. It looked like it was going to be another Rangers hard-luck story, but there was a quiet confidence in the Rangers camp. In the sixty-sixth minute, the Scots were back level on the night and ahead on away goals. With the PSV defence awaiting a cross, Tommy McLean slipped a free kick to Kenny Watson who drove the ball into the penalty area for Derek Johnstone to head home and make it 2–2.

There was barely a break in the excitement. Two minutes later PSV had the ball in the net again, but it was disallowed for offside. Then with two minutes to go, the Scots secured their place in the quarter-final and sealed a historic win, with one of the best goals ever scored by a Rangers player in Europe.

The move started with a clearing header from Derek Johnstone to Smith on the edge of the penalty area. He laid it off to Tommy McLean, wide on the right, who spotted a run being made by Bobby Russell and, from inside the Rangers half, played a perfectly weighted ball into his path. Russell carried it forward towards the PSV area before coolly curling the ball round the onrushing goalkeeper into the corner of the net, sparking wild scenes among the travelling support. It was a superbly engineered goal and it was fitting that it secured a famous win, as Bobby Russell recalls:

> It was one of those situations where a manager would have been having kittens at me getting as far forward as that. Normally in those circumstances you would just sit back, not venture beyond the halfway line and concentrate on defence. But we broke their move down and it just happened. It was nice to see it go in.

Amid the celebrations, there was a moment that brought Russell crashing back to earth. His luggage had gone missing on the outward trip, leaving him without a change of clothes for his entire stay in Holland. As result, he was somewhat unkempt and as he savoured the adulation of his teammates and the Rangers fans, Alex MacDonald shouted over, 'Well done smelly!'

In those days, it wouldn't have been unusual for a Scottish team to celebrate such a victory by downing copious amounts of alcohol into the early hours of the morning. However, after the win in Eindhoven the players were so exhausted that they could only enjoy a couple of beers before retiring to bed.

For the one thousand Rangers fans, the celebrations continued long into the night as the supporters, used to seeing their team fall short, hailed one of the best performances by a Scottish team on foreign soil. John Greig went onto the pitch to receive his first – and, unfortunately, last – standing ovation as Rangers boss. He later revealed that he had taken a huge gamble in picking Peter McCloy, as the man nicknamed the Girvan Lighthouse had been ill for the twenty-four hours before kick-off. The gamble paid off, and the *Glasgow Herald* called it 'Rangers' Greatest Triumph'. Given the quality of the opposition and the way the game had unfolded there was certainly a strong case to be made. Sports reporter Jim Reynolds wrote, 'Rangers weren't just brave – they were courageous against a side rated one of the favourites for the tournament.' Bobby Russell revealed, 'It's only when you get home and people are waiting for you off the flight and you see the papers that it begins to sink in that you have created a bit of history.'

Having knocked out the two tournament favourites, Rangers fans now dared to entertain the possibility that they could lift the European Cup. An estimated four thousand travelled to Germany in the hope that they could get past Cologne and make it into the semi-final of the Champions Cup for the first time in almost thirty years.

It was an injury-hit Rangers team that took to the field in the Mungersdorfer stadium in March 1979. A severe winter meant that Rangers had only played three league games since the turn of the year and many players were lacking in match fitness. The much-maligned utility player Jim Denny – said to have been ironically nicknamed Pele by his teammates – was drafted in to replace the injured Derek Johnstone.

Cologne had won the West German league-and-cup double the season before under the leadership of coach Hennes Weisweiller, who had previously been in charge at Barcelona and Borussia Moenchengladbach. In fact he was in charge of Gladbach when they beat Rangers in 1973. His assistant at Cologne was Johannes Lohr, who had played for Cologne when they last took on Rangers in 1967. Also in that sixties team was youngster Heinz Flohe, who had developed into a fine international playmaker. The squad also contained promising young players like controversial goalkeeper Harald Schumacher, defender Bernd Schuster and dazzling winger Pierre Littbarski, all of whom would go on to star for West Germany at the 1982 World Cup.

Rangers put up a battling performance in the first leg, but went down to a single goal from international striker Dieter Muller. In the return leg at Ibrox, Muller scored again, and Tommy McLean's late goal for Rangers was no more than a consolation. What had begun as a spectacular European campaign had fizzled out like a damp squib, with Rangers again falling just short of what was needed. 'It was disappointing because we felt we could have beaten them and if we had the two or three injured players in the team I think we would have,' argued Bobby Russell.

Cologne went on to face Brian Clough's Nottingham Forest in the semi-final, and somehow managed to lose, despite drawing the first leg in England 3–3. Forest went on to beat Malmo of Sweden in the final. Russell is convinced Rangers could have beaten either of the finalists had they not failed to perform against Cologne. 'I know it's easy to say that, but having knocked out two of the best teams you have to think that was possible,' he said.

Rangers won the League Cup and the Scottish Cup, but failed to win the Premier League after losing a league decider by four goals to two against ten-man Celtic. It was a fine line between success and failure for John Greig in his first season as manager but the performances in Europe suggested a bright future.

The 1979/80 European Cup Winners Cup campaign started off in dreary style in the preliminary round against Norwegian club Lillestrom. The team from an Oslo suburb were strong and workmanlike and had enjoyed some good results in Europe. The season before, Lillestrom managed to draw their home leg with Austria Vienna, and a year earlier they secured their most famous victory of all time, a 2–0 triumph over Ajax. Star player Tom Lund was outstanding in that game, so good in fact that Ajax wanted to sign him. But, in a remarkable show of loyalty, he turned the offer down; just as he reputedly turned down Real Madrid and Bayern Munich, and went on to finish his career at Lillestrom. Fortunately for Rangers, Lund was injured and didn't play in either leg.

Ibrox was in the midst of the redevelopment announced in the wake of the 1971 disaster and at the start of season 1979/80 the new Copland Road stand had been completed. The players had already been taken aback by the sound created by the stand at a recent Old Firm derby and, before the Lillestrom game, John Greig urged the fans to generate an atmosphere that would faze the part-timers. Those who forked out £1.70 for one of the coloured seats in the gleaming new structure found themselves with little to shout about.

Lillestrom adopted an ultra-defensive approach that Inter Milan would have been proud of in their notorious *catenaccio* era. Despite almost constant, if uninspired, attacking from Rangers, the Scots only managed to breach the defences once, a thirteenth-minute hooked shot by Gordon Smith. The second leg at the Ulevaal stadium in Oslo was a more open affair, with Rangers winning 2–0 through goals by Alex MacDonald and Derek Johnstone.

Once again Rangers found themselves facing West German opposition in the next round, this time Fortuna Dusseldorf. The Rhineland club were enjoying their best spell since the 1930s, having won the German Cup in 1979 and reached the European Cup Winners Cup final the same season, losing a dramatic match 4–3 to Barcelona after extra time. On their way to the final they beat Aberdeen and manager Alex Ferguson supplied his old teammate John Greig with a dossier on the Germans.

The 22-year-old midfielder Klaus Allofs, whose younger brother Thomas was also in the team, was identified as the Fortuna danger man. He was the *Bundesliga*'s top scorer with twenty-two goals the previous season and scored in the Cup Winners Cup final. In the first leg at Ibrox, Rangers put on one of their better performances in what was a sorry season, winning 2–1. Alex MacDonald and Tommy McLean put Rangers two up but, as so often, there was sting in the tail, as Rudiger Wenzel scored a late goal after a good run by Klaus Allofs. Bobby Russell hit what he considers to be his European low point when he suffered a cruciate-ligament injury that kept him out of the team for weeks.

The second leg took place in the Rhinestadion, where Rangers had famously beaten Borussia Moenchengladbach in 1960, although it had changed beyond recognition after being rebuilt for the 1974 World Cup. Rangers spent most of the game under intense pressure but managed to hold Fortuna at bay to secure the no-score draw that was enough to take them through.

After the successes of the previous season, the victory over Fortuna further enhanced Rangers' reputation in Europe and this had not gone unnoticed by their next opponents in the Cup Winners Cup, Valencia. Argentina's World Cup-winner Mario Kempes was the undoubted star of the Spanish giants and in an article ahead of the first match in Spain, he told the *Daily Record*, 'Last season Fortuna might have won this tournament. And Rangers have beaten them already. That is indication enough. If not, we can look back to the games against Juventus and PSV and we have to give them respect.'

If he was saying all the right things about Rangers, Kempes was apparently less impressed by the Scotland international team, following their performances in the World Cup in his homeland the year before. He recalled how they were considered the 'joke' of the tournament, implying that the Scots spent most of the time during the tournament enjoying themselves off the pitch.

His comments may not have gone down too well with the Scotland players within the Rangers ranks, but if they had lost respect for Kempes then it did not show. As the teams lined up in the tunnel in the Luis Casanova stadium (the ground reverted to its original name of the Mestalla in the

1990s at the request of club president Senor Casanova himself), the Rangers players seemed to be in awe of the man who had lit up the World Cup final.

With his good looks and physique, his long, dark hair and olive skin Kempes looked more like a movie star than a footballer. And, like smitten schoolgirls, the Scots were transfixed by the presence of the charismatic Latin American. Almost to a man they stood staring at their famous opponent in the tunnel, having quickly to avert their gaze in embarrassment when their eyes met. Gordon Smith admitted that the charismatic Kempes fascinated the Scots.

The lucky Rangers player who would get up close and personal with Kempes on the night was 28-year-old midfielder Kenny Watson. On the Saturday before he was playing in the reserves, but John Greig gave him the biggest role of his career when he detailed him to a man-marking job on the Argentinian. Watson, who never managed to establish himself as a Rangers regular, had a superb game against the flamboyant Kempes but it was a foul he committed that led to the opening goal midway through the first half.

As another of Valencia's foreign superstars, Rainer Bonhof, lined up to take the free kick Kempes stepped in front of him and curled a superb shot past Peter McCloy. Although the Spaniards had another couple of chances in the first half, it was Rangers who scored next. Smith took advantage of disarray in the Valencia penalty area and robbed a defender of the ball, before rolling it to Davie Cooper. His cutback was shot home by Tommy McLean from about thirty yards.

With eleven minutes to go, Valencia had the chance to go back in front, when the referee awarded a penalty for a foul on Felman. Dead-ball expert Bonhof stepped up and thundered the kick towards goal, but McCloy leaped to his left and stopped the shot. There was no further scoring and Rangers secured a famous away result in Europe. The travelling Rangers supporters celebrated the 1–1 draw like a victory, but those who had gone round Europe with the team realised that the second leg was far from a formality.

After the match, Kempes approached the Rangers number ten Gordon Smith and gestured that they should swap jerseys, a great honour for the Scot. Astonishingly for a club of that size, Rangers only had three sets of strips so a shirt swap was banned. After Smith's attempts to explain a confused, and rather slighted, Kempes shuffled off empty handed. It was another example of the penny-pinching attitude at the time.

The events of Newcastle and Barcelona ensured that Rangers fans in the 1970s were more often than not portrayed in a negative light following their European excursions. A footnote to the first leg of the Valencia tie nicely sums up the attitude of the vast majority of bluenoses, who made friends all

In the beginning. The French newspaper headline points out that Nice had to beat 'Glasgow' in order to progress in the 1956/57 European Cup. It was Rangers' first tie in European football.

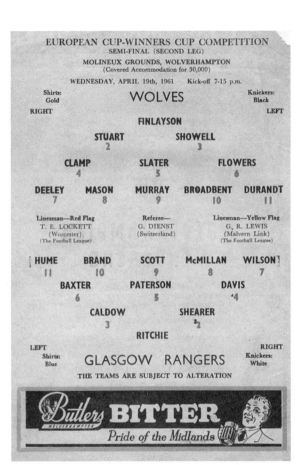

EUROPEAN CUP-WINNERS CUP COMPETITION

SEMI-FINAL (SECOND LEG)

MOLINEUX GROUNDS, WOLVERHAMPTON
(Covered Accommodation for 30,000)

WEDNESDAY, APRIL 19th, 1961   Kick-off 7-15 p.m.

Shirts: Knickers:
Gold   WOLVES   Black

RIGHT   LEFT

FINLAYSON

STUART   SHOWELL
2   3

CLAMP   SLATER   FLOWERS
4   5   6

DEELEY   MASON   MURRAY   BROADBENT   DURANDT
7   8   9   10   11

Linesman—Red Flag   Referee—   Linesman—Yellow Flag
T. E. LOCKETT   G. DIENST   G. R. LEWIS
(Worcester)   (Switzerland)   (Malvern Link)
(The Football League)   (The Football League)

HUME   BRAND   SCOTT   McMILLAN   WILSON
11   10   9   8   7

BAXTER   PATERSON   DAVIS
6   5   4

CALDOW   SHEARER
3   2

RITCHIE

LEFT   RIGHT

Shirts: Knickers:
Blue   GLASGOW RANGERS   White

THE TEAMS ARE SUBJECT TO ALTERATION

Butlers BITTER
Pride of the Midlands

The Wolves and Rangers line-ups for the semi-final, second leg, of the European Cup Winners Cup of 1960/61.

Follow, follow, FOLLOW!

ANTI-BOMB DEMONSTRATION? No—just wildly excited Rangers fans at Wolverhampton yesterday.

They followed on! Ranger fans march proudly through the streets of Wolverhampton.

The first final. Rangers take on Fiorentina at Ibrox in the
European Cup Winners Cup final of 1960/61.

(courtesy Mirrorpix)

Two great managers. Scot Symon and Bill Nicholson
shake hands before the Spurs–Rangers tie in the 1962/63
European Cup Winners Cup.

(courtesy Mirrorpix)

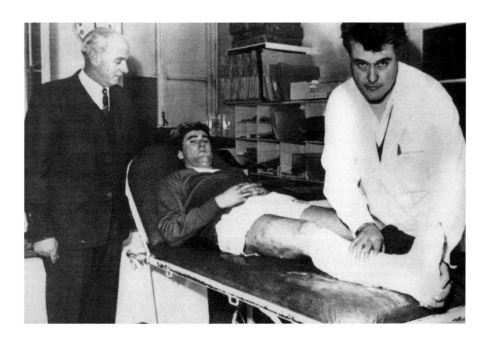

The late, great Jim Baxter gets treatment after breaking his
leg against Rapid Vienna in the European Cup of 1964/65.
Many Rangers fans felt that the Light Blues could have won the
European Cup that year but for Baxter's injury.

(courtesy Empics)

Main picture: Roger Hynd puts the ball in Bayern Munich's net in the 1967 European Cup Winners Cup final. Unfortunately, the referee decided not to award a goal.

(courtesy Mirrorpix)

Inset: the match programme.

'Pop' Robson of Newcastle United fires in a shot during the first leg of the 1968/69 Fairs Cup semi-final at Ibrox.

(courtesy Empics)

Derek Parlane and Sandy Jardine celebrate a famous victory.
Rangers had just knocked the mighty Bayern Munich
(Franz Beckenbauer and all) out of the European Cup Winners
Cup of 1971/72 at the semi-final stage.

(courtesy Mirrorpix)

One night in Barcelona! Colin Stein turns away after scoring
in the final of the European Cup Winners Cup in 1972.
Rangers went on to win the trophy.

(courtesy Newsquest)

Making history again. Rangers and Ajax contested the first
European Super Cup in 1973. Here, Derek Johnstone puts in a
strong challenge on the Ajax keeper, watched by John Greig.

(courtesy Empics)

Colin Jackson (right) in the thick of the action against
Juventus in the European Cup of 1978/79.
Rangers knocked the Italian giants out.

(courtesy Mirrorpix)

Ally McCoist is jubilant after scoring his team's second goal against
Leeds United at Elland Road in a European Cup tie in season 1992/93.

(courtesy Mirrorpix)

'The Hammer' strikes again! Jorg Albertz felt he had a point
to prove when he faced Bayern Munich in the group stages
of the 1999/2000 Champions League.

(courtesy Mirrorpix)

Michael Mols takes on the Parma defence in a
Champions League qualifier from 1999/2000
(courtesy Mirrorpix)

Peter Lovenkrands powers in a header at Ibrox in a
Champions League group-stage match against
Manchester United from 2003/04.

(courtesy Mirrorpix)

Dado Prso celebrates his Ibrox goal against Porto in the
Champions League of 2005/06.

(courtesy Newsquest)

over Europe during their trips. Journalist Maggie Vaughan was attacked and robbed at the airport as she arrived to cover the crowd scenes in Valencia. Left with no money after the bag-snatchers fled, two generous Bears loaned her £200.

Rangers continued to toil in the Premier League, but the different demands of Continental competition seemed to provide some relief. Having played in Europe for Rangers, Greig knew better than to go into the second leg with anything approaching complacency, although perhaps he was going a bit far when he said he hoped Kempes and Bonhof would play to the top of their game in the return leg. As the saying goes, 'be careful what you wish for'.

Sometimes teams have to hold their hands up and admit they were outplayed by the better team. In the second leg at Ibrox, Rangers were not beaten by the better team, but by one individual. After being shackled for most of the first leg, Kempes felt he had a point to prove and he set about doing just that in the worst way imaginable for Rangers. Quite simply, he single-handedly knocked Rangers out with a devastating two-goal performance.

Rangers, who had been struggling with injuries, had started the game brightly but went behind in fifteen minutes. Rainer Bonhof hit a powerful but speculative free kick from thirty yards, which appeared to take a deflection off a defender, and sailed past Peter McCloy into the net. The pressure was suddenly on the home team, but they responded superbly, equalizing nine minutes later through a Derek Johnstone header.

Three minutes before half-time, Mario Kempes started to play. With a strength that belied his lean frame, the Argentinian muscled past marker Kenny Watson before rifling the ball past McCloy. Bobby Russell was still injured, but watched admiringly from the sidelines:

> Kenny was told by John Greig to keep him on his right because he was so left-footed. So Kenny did just that. Kempes got the ball about twenty yards out and Kenny ushered him onto his right as he'd been told, and Kempes just hit it right into the postage stamp. He did everything the gaffer had said, but you just can't legislate for that sort of player. He was probably the best in the world at the time.

Rangers tried their best to get back into the game, but with twelve minutes to go Kempes ended the tie as a contest, with one of the best goals ever seen at Ibrox. Pablo crossed the ball from the left along the edge of the penalty area and into the path of Kempes. He stepped forward as if to hit it with his left foot, then fooled everyone by letting the ball run across his body, before lashing it first time into the net with his right.

The loss to the eventual tournament winners was a watershed in the management career of John Greig. A victory and continuing good progress in the Cup Winners Cup could have masked the domestic problems. But with Jardine, McCloy, Jackson, McLean and Miller all moving into the veteran category, his team was ageing and most of the younger players drafted in were simply not up to the job.

The fifth-place league finish in spring 1980 – behind champions Aberdeen, Celtic, St Mirren and Dundee United – meant Rangers had failed to qualify for Europe the following season. Rather than focusing on the league, Rangers made the ill-fated decision to enter the Anglo-Scottish Cup. A 1–1 draw at home against English third-division nobodies Chesterfield was bad enough, but the second leg at the Recreation Ground was an unmitigated disaster. Rangers were outplayed and outscored by three goals to nil. For many fans who suffered through the dark days of the early 1980s this remains the lowest point of their time following the club. It was nothing short of abject humiliation.

After a relatively positive start, the Chesterfield result coincided with the disintegration of Rangers' season. The only bright spot was a Scottish Cup-replay win over Dundee United in which Davie Cooper – dropped from the first game – was the undoubted man-of-the-match.

The cup victory ensured Rangers were back in Europe but it was to be a short-lived experience. Despite the addition of a number of new players, including Northern Ireland international defender John McClelland, midfielder Jim Bett, who was signed from Belgium, and striker Colin McAdam, Rangers suffered a crushing 3–0 defeat in the first leg away to Dukla Prague. Tommy McLean's sending-off did little to improve the mood, and a 2–1 victory in the second leg was meaningless.

Rangers had always attracted big crowds to Ibrox for European games and the atmosphere generated at these matches was something special. The dire fare being served up in the early eighties meant that the joy of these nights was being strangled, and the fans were voting with their feet. Just 20,000 bothered to turn up for the home leg against Dukla Prague, leaving the glistening new stands half empty.

The new stadium was the lasting legacy of the Ibrox disaster of 1971. As Rangers searched for a way forward in the aftermath of the tragedy, Willie Waddell toured Europe in search of a model for the new Ibrox. Deep in the heart of West Germany's industrial Ruhr district he found what he was looking for. The Westfalenstadion was the home of Borussia Dortmund. Rangers had played them in the Cup Winners Cup in 1966 but in those days the club's home was the far more compact Stadion Rote Erde.

The Westfalen was built for the 1974 World Cup and initially there were plans for an oval stadium with an athletic track surrounding the pitch. However, a limited budget meant the plans had to be redrawn and instead architects came up with a more straightforward design of four single stands, housing a total of 54,000 fans. It was on this simple concept that Waddell based the new Ibrox and it was fitting that Borussia should visit the new-look stadium on UEFA Cup business in 1982.

Having won the League Cup in 1981/82, Rangers were competing in the UEFA Cup for the first time since it replaced the Fairs Cup in 1971. Once again the Rangers fans were delighted with a draw that took them to Germany. The country has always been a favourite destination for the support, not least because its network of *autobahns* makes coach travel through the country easy. Rangers also have a large fan base in Germany thanks to the various British military bases and, since the early days of European competition, the travelling support has been swollen by hundreds of squaddies.

On the pitch in Dortmund, Rangers achieved an excellent goalless draw after a controlled and disciplined performance in the Westfalen. The new central-defensive partnership of John McClelland and Craig Paterson, a close-season signing from Hibs, were rock solid and in midfield Robert Prytz was superb in front of a capacity crowd. 'The stadium was beautiful, very like Ibrox, and the atmosphere was fantastic at that game,' recalled the Swede.

Prytz had been signed from Swedish club Malmo for £100,000. A stocky but skilful playmaker, he had already played in a European Cup final for Malmo against Nottingham Forest in 1978 at the age of nineteen and was an established Sweden international. His signing was an adventurous one for Rangers, and one that split the support; many thought he was a luxury they could not afford while others appreciated the cultured football he was capable of.

Prytz was a walking contradiction. On the one hand his somewhat languid style hardly fitted the stereotype of Scottish football, where brute strength and effort were considered to be more desirable than ability on the ball. He has since commented on how he would often barely touch the ball during a game, instead spending most of his time looking above his head as it was launched from back to front.

But on the other hand the same could be said for his midfield colleagues Bobby Russell, Jim Bett and Davie Cooper, all of whom were more renowned for their silky skills. In fact, Prytz believed that Rangers may have been succesful in that period if they had had a player in the image of manager Greig to do the hard work in midfield, thus allowing the creative players the opportunity to express themselves:

The first thing I noticed when I came to Scotland was that we didn't play much football on the deck, which would have suited me better. Actually, I would say that midfield had some of the best ball players the club has ever had. Davie Cooper was phenomenal, Bobby Russell and Jim Bett were exceptional passers of the ball and I could still pass a ball as well, but we just never saw the ball.

Prytz had another man-of-the-match performance against Dortmund in the second leg at Ibrox as Rangers progressed with an impressive 2–0 victory, the goals coming from Cooper and Derek Johnstone. Prytz believes he was able to flourish in Europe because his style better suited that arena.

Inevitably it was Germany calling yet again in the second round as Rangers were paired with Cologne. It was the third time the clubs had met in Europe, Rangers winning the first clash in 1967 and the West Germans getting their revenge twelve years later.

Legendary Dutchman Rinus Michels coached the Cologne team of 1982 and he was in charge of an impressive group of players, many of whom had played in the European Cup against Rangers in 1979. Klaus Allofs, the top scorer at the dreadful 1980 European Championships, was a key player and Rainer Bonhof had returned to Germany from Valencia. He had already faced Rangers twice in Europe: with the Spaniards in 1979 and with Borussia Moenchengladbach in 1973. Cologne also had several stars of the West Germany team which reached the 1982 World Cup final in Spain just a few months earlier, most notably winger Pierre Littbarski and Klaus Fischer.

But by far the best-known figure in the Cologne line-up was controversial goalkeeper Harald Schumacher, although his notoriety was down to one of the most unsavoury incidents ever to blight international football. With his mullet and moustache, Schumacher (nicknamed Toni after the West German World Cup-winning goalkeeper of 1954, Toni Turek) looked more like a heavy-metal star than a footballer, but he had talent. He played in two World Cup finals and won the 1980 European Championships as well as numerous domestic honours in his long career with Cologne.

But, whatever his achievements, he will always be known for the sickening assault he committed in the 1982 World Cup semi-final against the supremely talented French and for the arrogant way in which he refused to accept he had done anything wrong. Five minutes into the second half of a pulsating match Michel Platini played a perfect pass through to French substitute Patrick Battiston, who had only been on the pitch since half-time. As the midfielder ran onto the ball, Schumacher came charging out of his goal and leapt into Battiston at full force, catching him full on the head with his hipbone. The goalkeeper made no attempt to play the ball and clearly should have been sent off, but astonishingly the referee did not even award a foul. Battiston was knocked unconscious by the attack and for a few moments, his teammates actually thought he might be dead.

As medics attended to the Frenchman Schumacher enraged the spectators further with his arrogance, as he appeared more concerned more about restarting the game with a goal kick than the fate of his victim. The crime was compounded as Schumacher went on to help West Germany beat France in a penalty shoot-out to reach the final, which they lost to Italy. After the World Cup a French newspaper carried a poll to discover the most unpopular man in the country; Schumacher 'won', beating Adolf Hitler into second place.

In the face of universal condemnation, Schumacher remains unrepentant to this day, insisting that he never intended to maim Battiston and was only ever going for the ball. The incident reflected badly on German football and set the tone for a decade in which the country gained a reputation for a ruthless desire to win at all costs, a reputation that was largely justified. With Public Enemy Number One between the sticks, Cologne came to Ibrox expecting to win. They were defied by a battling Light Blues performance that ended in a 2–1 victory for the home team. Despite being subject to a torrent of abuse from the Rangers fans, inevitably Schumacher had a good game, and restricted Rangers to their precarious one-goal advantage with a string of saves.

Hopes of another victory over German opposition were high as Rangers travelled to the Mungersdorfer stadium for the second leg. But as so often is the case their optimism was wildly misplaced: the Germans destroyed the Scots with a deluge of first-half goals in front of 61,000 fans.

The night before, Rangers had been training at Mungersdorfer, as is common practice in European competition, when the stadium suddenly was plunged into darkness. The Cologne staff had switched the lights out, presumably in an attempt to unsettle the visitors. It's impossible to say if the tactic worked, but the lights certainly went out on Rangers' European hopes the following evening.

Rangers actually started the game quite well, with Derek Johnstone twice going close with headers early in the match. But within minutes Cologne had gone in front with a superb goal from Littbarski. He started the move on the right, beat one defender, completed a one-two with a teammate on the edge of the penalty area, then left two more Rangers defenders flailing as he drove the ball low past goalkeeper Jim Stewart.

Stefan Engel doubled the lead on the night soon after with a tremendous volley, which Stewart could only touch onto the underside of the crossbar on its way into the goal. Jim Bett then had a shot cleared off the line after he rounded Schumacher but normal service was soon resumed, with Klaus Fischer adding a third for Cologne. The Germans were scoring with virtually every attack and Engel got a second from the penalty spot before half-time. A fifth was added in the second half through Klaus Allofs.

'We got a thrashing,' said Robert Prytz. 'They were a really good side and they just took us apart. Littbarski was an exceptional football player and they were just too good for us. It's a game I remember well but for the wrong reasons.' Bobby Russell recollects looking up at the electronic scoreboard during the first half and seeing it displaying that Cologne were 4–0 up. 'We just thought, "My God this is going to end up in double figures," because everything they touched was ending up a goal.'

Despite the disastrous showing on the park, the 1,500-strong Rangers support were in a noisy mood and spent most of the match belting out trad-itional anthems like 'The Sash' with gusto. Anything that diverted attention from the action on the pitch had to be worthwhile. It's doubtful if the Germans would have known what the songs meant; however, those with a basic grasp of English would probably have got the gist of, 'We won the war, We won the war, E-I-adio, We won the war!' Unfortunately the battle on the pitch was going the way of the Germans. Thankfully for the Rangers fans, the scoring stopped at five, although there was some late drama, when Holger Willmer was inexplicably sent-off following a clash with Rangers substitute Colin McAdam.

As usual, Schumacher found himself the centre of attention. In the first half he collapsed dramatically after a goalmouth scramble, seemingly having been knocked cold by the boot of a Rangers attacker. His alarmed teammates slapped him around the face in a bid to bring him round as the German physio raced onto the pitch. But moments later he was back on his feet to take the resulting free kick, with no apparent ill-effects. Television pictures later showed there had been no contact.

Contact certainly was made near the end of the match when Schumacher was involved in another goalmouth incident, this time in his usual role of villain. A long-distance shot by Davie Cooper had beaten him but rebounded off the crossbar. Jim Bett was first to react and looked certain to put it into the unguarded net. Schumacher had other ideas. As Bett made contact with the ball, the goalkeeper leapt feet first into his chest, karate-style, leaving the Rangers player on the ground gasping for air. Just as in Spain, Schumacher was absolved of any blame by the referee and was able to continue without even a talking-to, let alone the red card the reckless challenge merited. 'It was a really silly tackle from Schumacher,' said Robert Prytz. 'He was a great goalkeeper, don't get me wrong, but there was something loose in his head.'

German football newspaper *Kicker* described the Cologne performance as *traumfussball,* or dream football. For Rangers it was a nightmare, an absolute thrashing from a team that was sitting fifth in the *Bundesliga.* It was the worst defeat they had suffered in Europe since the 6–0 loss to Real Madrid almost twenty years earlier and it summed up what was a deeply depressing era for Rangers fans. Robert Prytz agreed with the supporters:

It was the same for the players. I thought I had come to a side that was going to win championships but unfortunately it never happened. I think there was a lack of confidence in the team and if we had tried to play football in the league we could have had more success. We actually tried to play football in Europe and keep the ball but then when we came back to Scottish football we seemed to change the tactics and went back to the long-ball game.

13

Dublin 1984: In the Lion's Den

Like most football clichés, the one that holds there are no easy games in Europe doesn't bear close scrutiny. A quick scan of the one-sided results from the early rounds of the Champions League and the UEFA Cup is enough to put that particular myth to bed. In fact, on paper, there are lots of easy games. Unfortunately, to use another (rather more accurate) cliché, football is played on grass, not paper. Over the years, virtually every Scottish club has suffered an ignominious defeat at the hands of a European minnow they have been expected to beat easily. Even if it doesn't result in elimination, Scottish clubs always seem to make heavy weather of the most straightforward of ties.

That is why, on the rare occasion when a Scottish team *does* go to town on a weaker opponent, it is met with widespread disbelief. And when a lanky, teenage centre half playing in his European debut sets a new goalscoring record into the bargain then the shock is even more palpable.

David McPherson was just nineteen when he was called up for the Cup Winners Cup match against Valetta of Malta in September 1983. It would be something of an understatement to say the Mediterranean holiday island has never been renowned as a football hotbed, but the reputed improving standards of play on the island, the late-summer temperatures and the poor quality of pitch, were supposed to make the match a tricky one.

Fortunately, it seems no-one bothered to tell the Rangers players and, instead of going out in the usual cautious style, they tore the Maltese side apart. An early goal from Craig Paterson set them on the way before fellow centre half McPherson got in on the act. 'It was my first European tie and I couldn't believe it when I scored four goals,' he recalled. 'It was one of those days where everything felt to me and I was in the right place at the right time to stick a few away. I didn't have a bad scoring record for a centre half but I'd never had a performance like that in any of the club or school teams I had played for.'

Robert Prytz scored two in Malta as Rangers ran out winners by eight goals to nil although, as he pointed out, 'I think everybody got a goal, even Peter McCloy! You just don't get games like that nowadays.'

In the second leg it was another record-breaking performance from Rangers, as they reached double figures for the first time. The 10–0 win included a hat-trick from John MacDonald and doubles from the Australia international striker, Dave Mitchell, and Ian Redford.

Despite the feeble opposition, the 18–0 aggregate result was a significant achievement and remains a record scoreline for a Scottish club in Europe. However, by the time the next round was played Rangers were in crisis. After eight Premier League matches, they had won only three and lost four and were already languishing in sixth place, five points behind leaders Dundee United.

The weekend before the first-leg home match with Portuguese Cup winners FC Porto, Rangers had slumped to a 3–2 defeat to Dundee and this was followed by embarrassing losses to Motherwell and St Mirren. Therefore, it was not too much of a surprise when, on 28 October 1983, manager John Greig bowed to the increasing supporter pressure and quit, although the timing – shortly before a winnable second leg against Porto – was unexpected.

Rangers had actually played well in the first leg at Ibrox against a Porto team that would go on to reach the final of the competition, and would win the European Cup just three years later. Sandy Clark and Dave Mitchell scored a goal in each half to give Rangers a 2–0 lead but, with seconds remaining, a howler from goalkeeper Peter McCloy gifted Porto a goal.

Rangers travelled to the away leg in the city of Oporto with Greig's former assistant Tommy McLean in temporary charge. McCloy put in a good performance but the goal he conceded in the Ibrox clash proved to be crucial as Porto won the second leg 1–0 and went through on away goals.

Out of Europe and already out of the league, Rangers were now managerless and sinking fast. To add to the sense of crisis, the two top managers in Scotland rejected overtures from the Ibrox board. First, former Rangers striker Alex Ferguson knocked back the chance of leaving Aberdeen; and then Dundee United boss Jim McLean followed suit. In the end, Jock Wallace stepped back into the breach, returning to the job he loved.

His arrival rejuvenated the Rangers team and he took them on a four-month unbeaten run, which included a dramatic League Cup-final triumph over Celtic. Ally McCoist, a young striker signed from Sunderland in the summer, scored a hat-trick in a 3–2 extra-time victory. The cup triumph took Rangers to the following season's UEFA Cup, the first time Jock Wallace had been in Europe for seven years. Since leaving Ibrox he had served at Leicester and Motherwell, neither of whom had made it into European competition.

On two previous visits to the Republic of Ireland, Rangers and their fans had emerged relatively unscathed. But when the draw paired them with Bohemians of Dublin in the first round of the UEFA Cup in September 1984, the authorities once again feared the worst. And this time they were right.

Wallace's last game on the European stage was the Cup Winners Cup defeat to Twente Enschede, and there were only two survivors from that team remaining at Ibrox, Bobby Russell and Davie Cooper. Cooper in particular had developed into a fine player and, after years of being ignored by his country, was finally receiving international recognition for his performances. A few days before the Bohemians tie he scored the opening goal and played superbly in a 6–1 rout of Yugoslavia by Scotland; his performance in that game had struck fear into the Irish.

But it was always likely that matters on the pitch were going to take second place to the behaviour of the supporters and a massive security operation was planned to prevent an outbreak of violence. Unfortunately, the police failed to keep the peace and shameful scenes followed involving fans of both sides.

Perhaps inevitably, the outrage that followed focused almost exclusively on the actions of the Rangers supporters and there is no doubt that there was some appalling behaviour by followers of the Glasgow team. However, in the rush to condemn, the role of local hooligans and the sheer incompetence of the Irish police were largely ignored.

The first sign of trouble had come the day before the match as the skipper of the ferry *MV Leinster*, which was carrying around 175 Rangers fans from Liverpool to Dublin, turned it around because of fights on board. Several arrests were made at the city's Canada Dock and a number of Rangers fans pleaded guilty to being drunk and disorderly when they appeared in court.

Many fans set off from Glasgow early on the morning of the game. Gordon Semple was among a group who gathered in what appeared to be an unused building at eight in the morning – so he was rather bemused to find a bar going full swing with people milling around and drinking as though it was early evening. The party then set off on a bus to Stranraer and caught a ferry to Larne before meandering through Ulster towards the heavily guarded border-crossing at Newry. Semple recalled: 'We had the RUC to pass at the first checkpoint, and then the Garda at the second. As the bus pulled away from the Republic's checkpoint, there was a powerful sensation that we were on foreign turf now, and on our own.'

Soon after crossing into the Republic the bus entered Dundalk, an IRA stronghold. Gordon Semple remembered the stir the Rangers fans created:

> The locals appeared to be interested in us, a Rangers bus in Dundalk was a rarity after all, and the onboard troops launched into some well-known ditties. Some of the locals were making the odd rude sign, but a few of the women were smiling at us. I actually thought that Dundalk appeared to be a homely wee town but my thoughts were soon interrupted as one of the bus windows was smashed after being hit by a missile thrown by one of the locals.

Another of the travelling supporters, John White, flew to Dublin with two workmates for the game and, unlike those who travelled by coach, spent some time in the city during the day. He said:

> We got into the city at lunchtime and went for a beer and something to eat and met up with another few Bears. Everything was very relaxed during the day and we decided to explore the city. As it was, we ended up walking past the Sinn Fein office and were stared at menacingly by the two heavies on the door.

By teatime Dublin was full of Rangers supporters and White believes some of the behaviour was out of order. 'It's OK shouting and swearing at rival supporters, but when I saw grown men, top-to-toe in Rangers colours, shouting anti-Catholic insults at passers-by on the street, I felt ashamed. It marked the end of the pleasant atmosphere and, from then on, a menace filled the air.'

Inside Dalymount Park, the atmosphere was even more poisonous. Hate poured from the terraces as chants were spat across the fences between the rival groups of fans in the 10,000 crowd. Amid chants of 'IRA', a Union flag was set alight in the Bohemians end, while an Irish flag was torched in retaliation at the opposite end.

In one incident at half-time, a lone Bohemians fan, wearing a Celtic strip and brandishing an Irish tricolour, was allowed to run almost the full length of the pitch to taunt the Rangers supporters and apparently make to attack the substitutes as they warmed up. By the time he was finally apprehended, several Rangers fans had managed to scale the fence and raced onto the pitch to meet him. At the other end, Bohemians fans did likewise. Police, who had clearly lost control and were in a state of panic, waded into the crowd with batons flailing. Twice Jock Wallace came out to appeal for an end to the violence on the terraces but his pleas had little effect.

Gordon Semple remembers the atmosphere inside the ground as 'venomous':

> There was a real hatred flowing from each side to the other. A variety of incidents occurred which would have been nipped in the bud had the match been properly policed, but the local Garda had no experience of handling high-profile, volatile football contests, and it showed. Individuals were invading the park at will and being attacked by rival supporters. The police didn't know how to respond to the pitch invaders, and at least one guy was reputed to have been thrown out of the ground once, only for him to re-invade a second time.

At half-time, Semple watched with growing concern as events unfolded:

> The Irish police had decided to charge the Rangers support, but were soon rebuffed. Yet again the police mounted a charge, and once more the Rangers support sent them back down below terracing level to the launching point of their assault. I noticed what appeared to be a railway sleeper being positioned by our supporters near the edge of a wall above the tunnel from where the police had emerged, ready to be dropped on the next police charge. As the only sober person in the place, it was clear to me that the next police onslaught was going to take casualties . . . serious casualties. Fortunately for all concerned, that next charge never came, possibly because it would have been a futile act, or perhaps someone had noticed that carnage was the certain outcome.

John White was in the heart of the Rangers end as the Garda moved in. He recalled:

> The police were soon beaten into a retreat with some boys grabbing the police caps and setting fire to them. In the middle of it all stood one Rangers fan, probably in his fifties, with his hands up in the air begging everyone to calm down. He got pelted as well. Soon the riot police arrived and another rammy ensued as fans went toe to toe with police in riot gear.

After the game, the Rangers fans were shepherded out of the ground past a line of police kitted out in riot gear and with batons drawn. Semple said, 'As we shuffled along, the police began beating their shields with their batons, and it was evident that a confrontation of sorts was on the cards. As my pal and I walked away from the ground, the crowd behind us stirred and then began to rush past us. The charge had begun.' According to Semple, the advancing police moved amongst the Rangers support lashing out wildly with their batons.

John White and his pals were also caught up in the crush outside the ground as they attempted to get away from the stadium and make their way to the airport. As the police began their first charge, they attempted to make their escape to somewhere they could catch a bus to the airport:

> All we did was run into the next wave of riot police, who then charged into us. I remember being hit across the back as I ran and feeling as if all the wind had been knocked out of me as I continued to run. We got back to the main road where the Rangers fans were and witnessed the police charge the supporters two or three more times.

The supporters travelling by road finally made it to their bus relatively unscathed. 'As the bus engine fired up and we moved off, I informed the driver that we wouldn't be stopping at red lights,' recalled Gordon Semple. The driver didn't need much persuading. As the convoy of coaches sped through Dublin, many of those on board put their seatbacks flat against the window to protect them from missiles.

The journey through the Irish countryside was incident-free but tensions began to rise as the buses approached Dundalk, as Gordon Semple explained:

> As we neared this Republican stronghold, a voice from the back of the bus piped up, 'Watch out chaps, bandits at six o`clock.' Amid much laughter, we prepared ourselves for the next assault and defensive positions were adopted. Sure enough, hiding behind parked cars, a variety of bandits were lying in wait, and yet again several buses were struck.

The bus immediately in front of Semple's was hit by a petrol bomb, but fortunately it bounced off the vehicle and onto the road where flames spewed over a length of tarmac, safely away from the supporters.

There was some retaliation from the Rangers supporters. Semple recalled:

> From my seat at the front, I had a clear view of some of the incidents, and the next one will long live in the memory. As one of the 'bandits' rose from behind a parked car to launch an attack on the bus in front of ours, a Rangers fan appeared through one of the bus's skylight windows and fired a full can of beer at his target. His aim was sound and the bandit collapsed in a heap, unable to launch his missile after taking a can of Tennent's full in the face.

As they approached the border at Newry, the Rangers coaches were waved through without fuss, and the relief was tangible. The sight of gun-toting RUC officers was a reassuring sight.

At Dublin airport, the Rangers team and officials bumped into fans who were flying back. John White said, 'Rangers secretary Campbell Ogilvie asked us what had happened as they were all enjoying half-time drinks when it all kicked off. I remember as we told him, the chairman John Paton saying that none of this would come back on the club, security was not Rangers' problem.' The UEFA observer at the match, Antoine Queudeville from Luxembourg, was also in the dark about events at half-time. He was apparently in the referee's dressing room enjoying a cup of tea as the mayhem raged.

On the pitch, things were just as bad for Rangers, despite taking an early lead through Ally McCoist, his first European goal, and going 2–1 up through Dave McPherson midway through the first half. Understandably, the chaos on the terracing unsettled the Scots and they lost concentration. Goalkeeper Nicky Walker, who was making his European debut, spent most of his time thirty yards or so from his own goal-line to avoid the missiles aimed in his direction. He was at fault every time as Bohemians twice equalized then scored an unlikely winner in the second half, but it would be harsh to criticise in the circumstances, as Dave McPherson argues:

> Nicky was getting darts thrown at him throughout the game. He got a bit of stick for not looking too sharp in goal, but when you're dodging darts that's understandable. There was no understanding of what the players went through. As a player you try to ignore it and remain as professional as possible but it can be difficult. Any time you went to defend a corner you were thinking you were going to be hit with something.

Bobby Russell was in the Rangers squad that night, although he didn't make it onto the pitch and watched with growing alarm at the events:

> It was a bit intimidating. At the end of the day it's a game of football but because of the history of the club and the history of the events over there it was a little bit tense. When you're playing in a match like that, the incidents in the crowd definitely affect you. You sense things could happen but you try to put it to the back of your mind and get on with the football. And they weren't that bad a side, so they made it tough for us.

The second leg at Ibrox was, thankfully, a tame affair with very few Bohemians fans making the trip from Dublin. However, it was a far from convincing Rangers performance and, with just six minutes to go, they were on the verge of a humiliating defeat. Finally, to the relief of the 30,000 crowd, Craig Paterson and Ian Redford scored to give Rangers their victory.

Both on and off the pitch the tie had been a thoroughly sordid experience for Rangers.

14

'It is just a special club'

It says something when an international player who appeared in a European Cup final at the age of nineteen and went on to star in *Serie A* and the *Bundesliga* names his career highlight as a UEFA Cup second-round match that saw his team knocked out.

Robert Prytz is that player. In 1979 he collected a European Cup runners-up medal for Malmo after losing to Nottingham Forest in front of 57,000 at the Olympic stadium in Munich. Three years later he joined Rangers, before going on to play for Verona and Atalanta in Italy and Uerdingen in West Germany. He also appeared fifty-six times for the Swedish national team between 1980 and 1989.

But he was never happier than when he played for Rangers, even though his time at Ibrox coincided with one of the worst periods in the club's history. And the game he regards as his greatest is a European clash with Inter Milan; the Italian superstars came to Glasgow in the autumn of 1984 and were handed a beating. At a time when there were few highlights for Rangers fans, that match stands almost alone. The sad thing is that it was a tainted triumph, because, despite the victory on the night, the Light Blues were knocked out on aggregate.

Having come through the trials of Bohemians in the previous round, a glamorous tie against one of the greatest names in European football was exactly what was needed, not that many thought Rangers would have much chance of going through. Inter's squad was packed with international stars like goalkeeper Walter Zenga, Irish midfielder Liam Brady and German forward Karl-Heinz Rummenigge.

The annual salary of just one of those players wouldn't have been much less than the total paid to the entire Rangers first eleven. Former Arsenal and

Juventus star Brady was reputedly on £250,000 a year and he was by no means alone. They were also on a bonus of £8,000 per man to get through to the next round. These were riches beyond avarice for the Rangers players.

The first leg took place at the San Siro and Rangers warmed up at Ibrox on the Saturday beforehand with a drab goalless draw in the Premier League to part-time Dumbarton. The attendance was a paltry 16,000. It was hardly the ideal preparation to face one of the world's leading clubs in front of 66,000 screaming *tifosi*.

Jock Wallace picked a defensive-minded team, similar to that which had worked so well for John Greig against Juventus six years earlier. But the quality of player Wallace had at his disposal was nowhere near the standard his predecessor had enjoyed. Peter McCloy, now in the twilight of his career at the age of thirty-eight, was still in the team as were Davie Cooper and Robert Russell. Being brutally honest, of the rest, only Prytz, John McClelland and Ally McCoist had the ability to perform at the highest level.

The smothering tactics seemed to be working until Inter scored in the seventeenth minute. Rummenigge crossed to the back post, where Alessandro Altobelli headed it back across goal for Antonio Sabato to knock it in. Rangers regrouped and managed to keep Inter at bay until the sixty-sixth minute when substitute Franco Causio shot home after being set up by Altobelli. Two goals behind and Rangers were struggling. Scotland manager Jock Stein had warned before the match that Italian teams considered they had already qualified if they went into the second leg with a two-goal lead, such was their defensive prowess.

With fifteen minutes to go Rangers made a rare foray up the park and created their one real chance. A shot from Ian Redford rebounded back off the crossbar and seemed to fall perfectly for Ally McCoist, unmarked and just six yards out. But agonisingly the ball seemed to take forever to drop and the striker may have mistimed his jump. Either way he failed to get any power on the header and it dropped harmlessly into the arms of Walter Zenga. Robert Prytz watched in agony as the chance slipped away. 'The ball was hanging up in the air, but unfortunately it hung too long for Coisty,' he recalled. 'Really he should have scored.' The impact of the miss was magnified, as BBC One was showing live coverage of the game.

This squandered opportunity woke Inter up and with two minutes to go £2 million striker Rummenigge headed home the crucial third goal. It was a cruel blow and appeared to end Rangers' already slim hopes of progressing. Bobby Russell said, 'I think if Ally's chance had gone in we would have had a lifeline for the second leg. But realistically 3–0 down against an Italian team was going to be a big, big task.'

Flying in the face of logic, Jock Wallace refused to accept defeat and in the run-up to the second leg predicted that Rangers would beat the *nerazzuri*. Speaking at the team's Ayrshire base, he declared, 'It might sound like a kamikaze pilot to say we will win, but maybe I'm nuts and I'll be certified on Thursday after the match.' Wallace vowed to 'go for the jugular'.

Inter arrived in Glasgow promising to shut-up shop and so ensure a comfortable passage into the third round. Only a handful of fans came over with the team but they did have their own chef in tow to prepare meals – much to the disgruntlement of the upmarket Grosvenor hotel, where they were staying.

It was a patched-up Rangers team that lined-up in front of a 30,000 crowd. Ibrox may not have been full but the atmosphere was electric, as noisy as anything heard at the ground in recent years, including Old Firm matches. The most bizarre sight of the night was defender John McClelland starting the game with number three on his back and playing as a striker. It was to be his final game for Rangers and he had some success as a makeshift forward. In the fifth minute Ibrox erupted: McClelland headed a cross into the path of Cammy Fraser and although his shot was saved the ball spun to Australia international Dave Mitchell, who headed home.

Hopes were dashed again just ten minutes later: Altobelli scored after being set up by Liam Brady, a future Celtic manager, who was booed all night. It should have killed Rangers off, but the goal had the Scots fighting back almost immediately. Within two minutes, record signing Iain Ferguson, who had been recalled after missing the first game, pounced on a pass from Cammy Fraser and hammered home a stunning twenty-yard shot. Inspired by the raucous Ibrox crowd, Rangers were magnificent and shortly after half-time went further in front. Prytz sent a free kick into a packed penalty area and Ferguson dived bravely to give Rangers a third.

Suddenly, with more than half an hour to go, the impossible seemed within reach. Rangers piled forward but the Inter defence stood firm and somehow there was no more scoring. The 3–1 win on the night was a tremendous effort, but once again it was glorious failure from Rangers in Europe.

Unfortunately the cameras weren't present to record the match so all that remains are grainy still-photographs. But for Robert Prytz the night will be forever etched on his memory:

> The games against Inter Milan are the ones I remember most in Europe, especially the home match. I have never experienced an atmosphere like there was in the stadium that night. You felt that they were going to lift you

up off the park – it was absolutely incredible. We went out and had a go at them at Ibrox. We played exceptional football that night and you could see how scared they were. A lot of that was down to the crowd. The fans were unbelievable and, to this day, I honestly remember that game as one of my best in Europe; it even surpasses the European Cup final. You have to consider the players they had on the park, like Rummenigge and Brady, and so many good Italians as well. After the game at Ibrox they admitted to us they thought they were going to be out.

Prytz believes the team had the ability to do better in Europe in the eighties and may have been more successful at home if they had practised a passing game in the Premier League: 'It just showed you that we could have been a force in Europe if we played like that in every game.'

Prytz has settled in Scotland and is still involved in coaching Rangers youngsters. 'I go to as many games as I can and Rangers are always going to be in my heart,' he said. 'I don't know what it is but there is something about the club that always stays with anyone who goes there. It is just a special club.'

15

April 1986: The Ibrox Revolution

The excitement of the glorious failure against Inter was a distant memory by the time European football came around again. Season 1984/85 was a depressing experience; the League Cup had been won in October 1984 but, after Christmas, Rangers' form in the league under Jock Wallace slumped alarmingly.

To make matters worse it was announced on 8 November 1984 that captain John McClelland – a Northern Ireland international with World Cup experience – had been sold to Watford after a fall out over money. He had been a key figure in the Rangers team and his loss was met with anger from the support and was keenly felt on the pitch. From January, Rangers won only four matches out of sixteen, were knocked out of the Scottish Cup by Dundee and finished in fourth place – twenty-one points behind champions Aberdeen.

The 1985/86 season started brightly enough, but by September there were signs that all was not well. Dundee and Aberdeen both won at Ibrox and Hibernian knocked Rangers out of the League Cup. In Europe, Rangers were drawn against Club Atletico Osasuna in the first round of the UEFA Cup.

The club from the Basque country were little known outside of Spain, where they had spent most of their existence in the lower leagues. The previous season had been successful enough to see them qualify for Europe for the first time in their history.

European football was in a dark place in 1985. A few months earlier, millions of television viewers around the world had watched in horror as Liverpool and Juventus fans battled on the crumbling terraces of the Heysel stadium before the European Cup final. The violence resulted in the death of thirty-nine, mostly Italian, supporters when a wall collapsed as they fled from charging hooligans.

English clubs were banned indefinitely from European competition and there were fears that hooligans from south of the border could attach themselves to Scottish clubs to cause trouble. A climate of fear was created and Rangers pleaded with fans not to travel to Spain. Chairman John Paton said at the time, 'UEFA are waiting for the first sign of trouble and we don't want to suffer.'

The ban on English clubs meant there was more interest than usual from the London-based media when Rangers went into action against Osasuna in the first round. They were met with a day of torrential rain in Glasgow and by the time kick-off came around the pitch was a mud bath and should have been declared unplayable. The match went ahead despite the dreadful conditions and Rangers managed to secure a 1–0 win through a headed goal from Craig Paterson.

In the second leg there were no such weather problems and Osasuna gave a better account of themselves in the more pleasant conditions in Pamplona. A goal in each half was enough for Rangers to be knocked-out once again. The Spaniards were themselves knocked out of the competition in the next round by Belgians KSV Waregem.

The season dragged on in similar fashion, with Rangers also eliminated from the Scottish Cup by Hearts at the first hurdle. In March 1986, Rangers and Celtic played out one of the most exciting Old Firm derbies ever, drawing 4–4 at Ibrox, but by that time Rangers had dropped to fifth place in the league and that was where they ended up.

With no trophies won, a mediocre team on the pitch and a manager who had lost his inspirational qualities, the future looked grim for Rangers. Although average attendances compared favourably with other clubs, Ibrox was rarely anywhere near full. In short, it was a club in terminal decline. Younger fans had known nothing but failure and it was a sad indication of how things had deteriorated that results like the 4–4 draw with Celtic were celebrated like league-championship wins.

New Rangers chairman David Holmes felt exactly the same way. Appointed by the John Lawrence organisation, which had taken a controlling interest in the club, Holmes was given the unenviable task of turning the ship around. After years of aimless drifting a firm hand was required.

On Monday, 7 April 1986 monumental changes were made that were to have a profound impact not only on Rangers but also Scottish football as a whole. The night before, Wallace called his lawyer, Jock Brown, the football commentator, to reveal that he was being sacked. The next day,

Graeme Souness was revealed as the new player-manager. The football world was stunned.

Like everyone else on the staff at Ibrox, Bobby Russell was shocked. 'Nobody would believe it until he was actually there,' he said. 'But he transformed not just Rangers, but the whole of Scottish football.' Souness, who appointed Dundee United assistant manager Walter Smith as his number two, immediately declared his intention to bring success to the club and he set about doing so by luring some of the biggest names in English football north of the border. First came goalkeeper Chris Woods, followed by the ultimate coup: England captain Terry Butcher.

Scotland had never seen anything like it. For decades the best Scottish football talent had made the journey south. Now England's leading players were reversing the trend. Undoubtedly money was a factor, but Rangers had more to offer than pounds, shillings and pence.

The attraction of working under such a renowned figure as Souness was crucial. It's doubtful whether Jock Wallace could have persuaded Woods and Butcher north, even if he had had the same budget as his successor. The sheer size of the club and the worldwide support it commanded was also a vital factor in bringing in the big names. Anyone who helped resurrect this sleeping giant was guaranteed a place in the history books.

Another attraction was European football. With the ban on English clubs still in place, Rangers could offer something that their rivals south of the border could not; the chance for players to pit their talents against the best on the Continent.

As a player, Souness had already proved his European pedigree. He had won the European Cup three times with Liverpool and one of his principal aims at Rangers was to restore the club's reputation in that arena. Generally, the performances of the last decade had been woeful and it was yet another aspect of the club that needed an entirely new approach. The new management team's first venture into Europe came in the 1986/87 UEFA Cup against Ilves Tampere of Finland, the first time Rangers had come up against a club from that country.

By the time of the first leg in the middle of September, the revolution was already well under way, albeit after a stuttering start. Souness was sent off as Rangers lost their opening league match against Hibernian. Four days later, Rangers only managed to beat Falkirk by a single Ally McCoist penalty at Ibrox and the following Saturday they lost 3–2 at home to Dundee United.

It was hardly what the Rangers fans, who were already turning up in droves, had expected. But by the end of August a 1–0 victory over Celtic at

Ibrox, in a match shown live on television, indicated that the new team was beginning to gel.

Summer signing Colin West was injured early in the season, giving young Scottish striker Robert Fleck a chance to show what he was capable of. He grasped the opportunity with both hands, scoring a hat-trick in his first start of the season against Clydebank. Four days later he repeated the scoring feat against Tampere, with a considerable helping hand from Davie Cooper, who put in a magnificent performance. The first came from a Cooper corner, which was nodded back across goal by Butcher for Fleck to head home from the edge of the six-yard box. He scored again shortly before half-time, pouncing on a loose ball after the goalkeeper spilled a ferocious Cooper shot.

Fleck completed his treble in the second half after a piece of typically sublime skill from Cooper. The winger collected the ball on the left, halfway inside the Tampere half. He shimmied inside past one defender and cut inside, heading towards a line of yellow-shirted Finns. As he stumbled into the next defender it seemed that he had lost control of the ball, but he managed to turn away and somehow took the ball with him. A third defender lunged in, but Cooper danced past him and, with amazing close control, evaded another desperate tackle before driving into the penalty area. As he approached a fourth defender he unselfishly cut it back to Fleck who finished clinically from virtually on the penalty spot. As *Scotsport* commentator Arthur Montford put it: 'Oh, Davie Cooper brilliance. Fleck hat-trick. What. A goal.'

'Davie Cooper was brilliant in that game and to be honest wee Robert Fleck will have to put his hat-trick down to the magic of Davie Cooper,' said Bobby Russell. Ally McCoist completed the scoring after brilliant build-up play down the right. The move was started by Ted McMinn, who beat one man before playing it inside to Cammy Fraser. He knocked it on first time to Durrant at the edge of the penalty area and his back-heel flick deceived the defenders, allowing McCoist to fire home. The 4–0 victory was enough to guarantee Rangers' progress although they suffered a scare in the second leg, losing 2–0, as complacency crept in.

That match in Finland was the last game Bobby Russell played for Rangers before he was moved on to Motherwell. It was a disappointing end for a player whose vision and passing skills had helped Rangers to some of their greatest triumphs at home and abroad, and who provided some of the few bright spots during a dark period. He never got the chance to play for his country, a scandalous omission, but his goal against PSV will be long remembered by Rangers fans.

The aggregate win over Ilves set Rangers on their way to an unbeaten month of October, which culminated in a Skol Cup-final victory over Celtic at Hampden. The final came a few days after Rangers had beaten Boavista 2–1 at Ibrox in the first leg of the UEFA Cup second round. McCoist and McPherson had scored but the Boavista goal in the first minute of the match meant Rangers would travel to Portugal for the second leg with a slim advantage. Rangers produced a fine performance in Oporto, frustrating the home team before snatching a late goal through Derek Ferguson to give Rangers a 3–1 aggregate victory. The highlight of the match was a remarkable fingertip-save by Chris Woods from a swerving eighteen-yard shot by Jose Augusto. With the ball seemingly headed for the back of the net, Woods threw himself backwards, twisting in mid-air to touch the ball onto the bar.

The win in the Bessa stadium was a triumph for Souness's tactics and demonstrated a maturity Rangers hadn't shown in Europe for many years. However, in the next round they showed an astonishing level of naivety.

For the third time in their history, Rangers were drawn against Borussia Moenchengladbach. The West Germans' glory days were now a distant memory and they were a shadow of the team Rangers had faced in 1973. However, like most German teams, they were well-drilled and ruthless in their pursuit of a result. In the first leg at a sold-out Ibrox, the Light Blues took an early lead through Ian Durrant and appeared to be in full control. But, as half-time approached, Rangers conceded a soft goal. Ferguson lost the ball in midfield and Gladbach immediately moved it out to the wing. The cross from Winkhold evaded the static Rangers defence and Uwe Rahn had the easy task of knocking the ball in at the back post. The match finished 1-1.

As always for matches in Germany, Rangers took a large contingent of fans to the second leg and much was done in advance between the two clubs to ensure the supporters were going to be treated well at the Bokelberg stadium. Rangers had actually taken part in the match officially to open the stadium in 1962, but any warm feelings evaporated when the match got underway.

In an ill-tempered game, Rangers became increasingly frustrated at the cynical tactics of the home team. Either they were diving into fouls on Rangers players, or they were simply diving. It was the beginning of a shameful era in German football; one in which the nation's footballers gained a reputation for play-acting, reaching a peak in the early nineties with the antics of Jurgen Klinsmann.

Rangers had a number of good chances to win the game in the first half, most notably a superb, dipping twenty-five-yard shot from McCoist, which hit the bar with the goalkeeper beaten. But it wasn't to be. Terry Butcher was denied a good penalty claim when he was hauled down at the back post and it was by no means the only decision by Belgian referee Alexis Ponnet that infuriated the Scots. He threw yellow cards around like confetti, mostly in the direction of Rangers players, and did his best to break up any sort of momentum the Ibrox club managed to generate.

Ponnet also chose to send-off two of the most placid players in the Rangers team – Davie Cooper and Stuart Munro – for retaliation. Both reacted in a manner totally out of character after falling victim to one foul too many and, while Monsieur Ponnet hardly needed any encouragement to brandish his card, the players should have known better.

The game ended goalless and Rangers went out once again to German opposition, albeit on the away-goals rule. But the aftermath highlighted the togetherness that had been forged in the few short months since Souness had arrived. Captain Terry Butcher had to be physically restrained by the manager and goalkeeping coach Peter McCloy as he tried to confront the referee at the end. As the players saluted the Rangers support, who had been tremendous throughout, many were in tears. The flight home was also a subdued affair as the players moped over the match. Butcher said later, 'The emotion of it all got to me. The tears I wept were first anger, then frustration. It all seemed so unfair.'

Borussia progressed to the semi-final, where Dundee United knocked them out. Ironically, Iain Ferguson and Ian Redford, both former Rangers forwards, scored United's winning goals. Rangers chairman David Holmes was as disappointed as anyone at the exit to Gladbach, but he recognised that progress was being made, insisting after the match: 'The defeat doesn't change a thing. I saw plenty in West Germany that convinced me we were heading in the right direction.'

In November 1986, the final piece of the jigsaw fell into place with the signing of Tottenham Hotspur defender Graham Roberts. He was a player with little finesse, but he was tremendously passionate and a ferocious tackler. His presence alongside Terry Butcher in the heart of the Rangers defence coincided with a nineteen-match unbeaten run in the league, which swept them to the top of the table.

On 2 May 1987, more than 22,000 crammed into Aberdeen's Pittodrie stadium to witness Rangers clinch their first title in nine years with a 1–1 draw. Fittingly, it was Terry Butcher who scored the goal that took Rangers back into the European Cup for the first time since 1979.

16

Back in the USSR

The goalposts are moved in football all the time, metaphorically at least. But until Graeme Souness came up against the Soviet Union's finest, no-one had thought of moving the touchlines.

If there is one thing Souness knows all about, it's getting under the skin of his opponents. Narrowing the pitch by twelve feet hours before an important European Cup tie shouldn't really have much impact on the playing style of your opponent. But it is a clear message of intent, a two-finger salute: 'We are going to do everything in our power to beat you and there's nothing you can do to stop us,' it says. 'If we are capable of pushing the rules to the limit by changing the size of the pitch, what else will we do?'

Critics would call it gamesmanship, some might even describe it as cheating, but that's to miss the point. Football had long since ditched its Corinthian ideals and now it was survival of the fittest, in both senses. Rangers had a man who was capable of returning some of the low blows that had come their way from Continental opponents over the years.

The championship win under Souness had brought Rangers back into the European Cup for the first time since the 1978/79 season, when they had claimed the notable scalps of tournament favourites Juventus and PSV Eindhoven, before being beaten in the quarter-final by Cologne. Nine years later, in 1987/88, they were again drawn against one of the favourites: the champions of the USSR, Dynamo Kiev.

The Ukrainian club – usually referred to as Russian by British sports writers whose knowledge of the internal structure of the Soviet Union left something to be desired – were arguably the best team in Europe at the time. They had broken the Moscow domination of Soviet football and had won the European Cup Winners Cup in 1986. Coach Valeri Lobanovsky was also in charge of the USSR national team and his players made up more than half of their 1986 World Cup squad, normally supplying at least eight of the starting line-up. Forward Igor Belanov was the current European player of the year and legendary winger Oleg Blokhin had won the honour twice in the past. Other star names included Sergei Baltacha, Oleg Kuznetzov, Vladimir Bessanov, Vasily Rats and promising midfielder Alexei Mikhailichenko.

Perennial contenders Kiev were being strongly tipped finally to land the Continent's top prize, but there were signs that the constant demands of domestic, European and international football were taking their toll. As they prepared for the game against Rangers, they were a lowly seventh in the Soviet league, which ran from spring to autumn. Lobanovsky himself admitted, 'We are tired of football.'

Despite these concerns, everyone at Rangers knew this would be a very difficult hurdle. Souness admitted to having been 'frightened' by the draw and after seeing Dynamo on a spying trip added, 'I came here to be more frightened.'

The logistics of trips behind the Iron Curtain during the Cold War were a nightmare and it required all the skills of the Rangers backroom team to ensure they went smoothly. Prior to the Kiev match, Rangers secretary Campbell Ogilvie and security chief Alistair Hood travelled east to reconnoitre the Ukraine and returned with a bulky dossier. Every one of the travellers was issued with a ten-page document detailing everything from potential problems at customs to meal times. The club took their own chef and their own food and even hired the services of an interpreter to overcome language barriers. The whole trip was planned with military precision, right down to working out exactly how long the party would be held up at Kiev airport on the way in. The dossier predicted two to three hours and in reality it worked out at two hours and ten minutes.

A vast crowd of 100,000 packed into the Ukrainian Republic's central stadium, although with many in military uniform it appeared that a large proportion of them were conscripts rather than genuine fans. The same couldn't be said about the Rangers fans in the ground. The story goes that hundreds of bluenoses joined the Communist Party in Scotland to circumvent the red tape that denied them entry visas to the Soviet Union. Having signed up, they immediately set about applying to make a pilgrimage to Kiev. The ploy apparently worked and the Soviets, presumably delighted at this upsurge in socialism in the west of Scotland, granted entry for their new membership.

Whether the story is true or not, there was definitely a larger-than-expected contingent of Rangers fans in the stadium and they made themselves heard. Ally McCoist later said the Scottish supporters made 'a spectacular racket' and, for most of the match, they had plenty to sing about as Rangers tactics paid off. McCoist was deployed as a lone striker in a 4-5-1 formation, with Ian Durrant moving out of midfield to support him when required. Rangers spent most of their time defending but McCoist did create one golden opportunity when he burst through from the halfway line, beating Bessanov and Baltacha, before the ball ran away from him and was collected by goalkeeper Viktor Chanov.

Midway through the second half, with Rangers seemingly in control, Kiev got a penalty when Mikhailichenko went down easily under a challenge from Graham Roberts. Despite the protestations of the Rangers players, who claimed the Ukrainian had dived, the Austrian referee gave a penalty, which Mikhailichenko gratefully converted. After the game, Rangers assistant manager Walter Smith diplomatically described the award as 'rather soft'. Smith obviously wasn't one to bear a grudge because he signed the player for Rangers four years later. Mikhailichenko himself probably didn't think twice about the incident again, until he turned up for his first training session in Glasgow and discovered that Scottish players have long memories when they believe they've been cheated.

While the match was going on in Kiev, more than 12,000 fans had turned out at Ibrox to watch the game on big screens. It was the first time since the Fairs Cup tie with Leeds more than twenty years earlier that the club had tried such a venture. With so few supporters able to make the trip, it was considered the next best thing. It was also thought that the big screens might be a way of discouraging fans from travelling to games with the potential for trouble. The daytime kick-off meant there were some problems with sunshine on the screens but overall it was a success and a further demonstration of Rangers' pulling power under Graeme Souness. Among the fans watching the action from Kiev in the stands at Ibrox were Davie Cooper and Stuart Munro, who were both suspended after being sent-off against Cologne the previous season.

The pair would also miss out on the second leg at Ibrox, which turned out to be one of the greatest European occasions the stadium has ever seen. In the run-up to the match, Kiev officials registered their concerns about the dual threat of Rangers' passionate support and tough-tackling players. The Soviet newspaper *Izvestia* reported a club spokesman as saying, 'We will have to contend with a particularly fanatical and hostile crowd. Furthermore we can expect intimidation on the field as well. If our players can survive the cauldron of Ibrox they will have done Soviet football proud.' In the event the club official was right to be worried on both counts, although he should also have mentioned the physical menace from his own side.

The first thing the Rangers supporters noticed as they took their seats at Ibrox was the pitch. There was definitely something different about it but it took a while to register. Then the penny dropped. The gap between the edge of the track and the touchline was wider than normal, and the pitch appeared to be narrower. Closer inspection confirmed that the old markings had been covered up and replaced with new white lines about six-feet further in. If the fans were confused that was nothing compared to the Rangers players, whose first knowledge of the move came when they ran out for the warm-up. As they stood scratching their heads, wondering if the groundsman had taken leave of his senses, it became apparent that this was a deliberate ruse by Graeme Souness to unsettle the Soviets.

If it left him open to allegations of gamesmanship, then Souness had been around long enough not to let it bother him. He felt he had the right to take advantage of anything that would improve Rangers' chances and if narrowing the pitch adversely affected the Ukrainians then that's what had to be done. Not surprisingly, Kiev were furious, accusing Rangers of underhand tactics, and lodged an official complaint with UEFA.

'The first thing we noticed when we got to Ibrox was the size of the pitch,' former Kiev defender Sergei Baltacha remembered. 'This was a big surprise to us. Our strength was the pace and mobility of our players and we were now going to be a little bit limited. We complained but there was nothing you could do.'

An hour after the match there was the comical sight of burly former referee Tom 'Tiny' Wharton, a FIFA official, crawling around on his hands and knees with a one-hundred-feet-long measuring tape, surrounded by excitable Soviets. Kiev were convinced they had been cheated, but their protests were in vain. The minimum width of a pitch for an international match is seventy yards, and the Ibrox field beat that by ten-and-a-half inches. As long as it was within the permitted dimensions, Rangers had no obligation to disclose any changes in advance. The pitch had been slimmed down by more than two yards on each wing, not exactly a vast difference, but enough to rattle the Ukrainians. 'There are clearly no gentlemen at Glasgow Rangers,' stated Dynamo's disgruntled secretary Mikhail Oshenkov.

Ibrox was a 44,500 sell-out for Rangers' return to the European Cup and the atmosphere was electric as the home team attempted to impose their will. Just as the Kiev official had feared, Ibrox was a cauldron of noise and the Rangers players used every means at their disposal, fair and occasionally foul, to put pressure on Kiev. The narrower pitch meant the game was condensed more into the middle of the park, curbing Dynamo's efforts to spray the ball into space and utilise the pace of their front men. Souness and

McGregor both put in heavy challenges on Kiev forwards, with the latter's foul on Belanov resulting in Europe's player of the year being substituted.

Souness had appealed for patience from the Rangers fans, urging them not to expect the team to charge forward looking for a goal in the early minutes. The Rangers play would need to be 'sensible and patient' and if successful the goals would come. That's exactly how it turned out, although the opening goal at least was of the comic-cuts variety.

A Rangers attack in the twenty-third minute broke down and the moustachioed Kiev goalkeeper, Viktor Chanov, collected the ball safely. With several players from both teams milling around the penalty area in front of him, Chanov decided to throw the ball out. Unfortunately for Kiev, he threw it straight against the backside of Baltacha who was standing a few feet in front of him. The ball broke to a disbelieving Ally McCoist, who, as Chanov desperately tried to retrieve the situation, prodded it back to Mark Falco. From the edge of the penalty area, the former Tottenham player rolled it left-footed into the empty net and sent the stadium into a frenzy.

Baltacha – who now teaches physical education at a college in London – remembers the moment well. 'We were a little unfortunate to lose that funny goal,' he said. 'I was just walking out of the penalty area when I felt the ball hit me on the back. I could not understand what was going on then I turned around and saw the ball rolling into the net.'

The assumption at the time was that Chanov had started to throw the ball out but halfway through the motion had changed his mind. The momentum was too great and he involuntarily let the ball go. But watching the pictures in slow motion now it's difficult to come to that conclusion. The throwing motion is perfectly smooth and Chanov's face doesn't show any sign of panic as the ball leaves his hand. It's only when the ball hits Baltacha that he reacts, almost as if he's just realised the consequences of his actions. It would obviously be going too far to say he deliberately threw the ball at the defender, but he certainly appeared to be in control of what he was doing, no matter the consequences. Whatever the reason for this moment of madness, it left Kiev rattled and inspired Rangers.

The winner came in the fiftieth minute from McCoist, but it was a goal created by former England international Trevor Francis. The veteran – who had been signed from Italian club Atalanta on a one-year deal – had already shown, in the few games he had played, glimpses of the genius that had made him Britain's first £1 million player in the late seventies. His cross in from the right was perfectly weighted and Falco rose majestically to head it back across goal and into the path of McCoist. From eight yards, the striker sclaffed it with his head, leaving Chanov flat-footed and unable to do anything to stop the ball going into the net. As the scorer wheeled away to celebrate, Chanov stood rooted to the spot before slumping backwards to the ground and looking up to the heavens. As he sought guidance from above, Ibrox was in tumult and the shock on the faces of the Dynamo players showed they were a beaten team. Even with most of the second half remaining, Kiev were never going to retrieve the situation.

Sergei Baltacha is convinced his team should have done better:

It was a really good game, both teams played very well and that's what made it worse to lose. We knew it would be very tough and that is how it turned out. There was a very noisy atmosphere in the stadium but we were used to playing in front of 100,000 in Kiev and they could make a lot of noise.

The defender also recounted a tale that will cast a shadow on a certain Rangers striker's Mr Nice Guy image:

I was marking Ally McCoist in the second leg and I just remember at the start he elbowed me right in the nose! I could not believe it. Then three years later I signed for St Johnstone, and I came up against him again. He was saying, 'I didn't mean to hit you, honest!' He was a great guy though even though he scored the winner against us. We couldn't have predicted on that night that we would face each other again in Scotland three years later.

The roar when McCoist's header went in was earth-shattering and many fans and players, including *Serie A* veterans Souness and Francis, reckoned the noise generated for the rest of match was the loudest the stadium had ever known, certainly since its modern redevelopment. The atmosphere that night has probably never been surpassed, even during the many Old Firm and Champions League clashes that have followed. It was understandable. After nine years of frustration in Europe, finally Rangers had achieved something they could be proud of.

17

Success at Home; Disappointment Abroad

Having knocked out Dynamo Kiev a chill wind blew through the Ibrox corridors when the draw for the second round of the 1987/88 European Cup was made. It threw up a notorious name from the past: Polish champions Gornik Zabrze.

The Poles had inflicted one of Rangers' most devastating European defeats in 1969, and were directly responsible for the sacking of manager Davie White. This time there was no danger of Graeme Souness losing his job, no matter the result against Gornik, but in any event Rangers went through comfortably. Mark Falco, Ally McCoist and Ian Durrant scored as Rangers won the first leg at Ibrox 3–1 on 21 October 1987 and McCoist struck again in Poland to complete a comprehensive victory.

After the exhilaration of the previous season's title win, the 1987/88 campaign was proving to be something of a letdown, on the domestic front at least. Rangers had got off to a poor start and never recovered. Although a number of quality players were signed during the season – including Trevor Francis, Ray Wilkins, Richard Gough and Mark Walters – this was offset by a crippling injury list. The most notable long-term absentee was the captain, Terry Butcher, who suffered a broken leg in a challenge with Aberdeen defender Alex McLeish.

The surprising sale of strikers Robert Fleck and Mark Falco in mid-season also seemed foolhardy when Ally McCoist was forced to undergo a cartilage operation ten days before the first leg of the European Cup quarter-final against Romanian champions Steaua Bucharest. To everyone's surprise, McCoist started the match, but was clearly not fully fit, and against a quality team like Steaua, nothing less than 100 per cent was good enough.

The army side, the favoured team of brutal dictator Nicolae Ceauacescu, had won the European Cup two years earlier and boasted two world-class players in Gheorghe Hagi and Marius Lacatus. They were also in the middle of a three-year unbeaten run in the league, which eventually stretched to 104 games, when they faced Rangers.

The under-strength Rangers team faced a difficult task in Bucharest, but their mission became almost impossible when Piturca scored in just two minutes. Chris Woods played superbly, pulling off a string of saves, but he could do nothing when Stefan Iovan's free kick was cruelly deflected past him to make the final score 2–0.

Rangers still harboured hopes of reaching the semi-final, but their chances were effectively killed off in the opening minute of the second leg at a packed Ibrox. Lacatus lobbed Woods from twenty-five yards to put the Romanians three clear, with a vital away goal. The 44,000 crowd was stunned. Just as the noise generated by the Ibrox crowd on European nights is unique, so too is the eerie silence that instantly envelopes the stadium when the away team scores. The silence seems to be amplified, if that is possible, when the opposition has a handful of supporters; only the jubilant shouts of players and officials break the sudden peace.

Rangers fought back and by half-time were leading 2–1 thanks to goals by Gough and McCoist, but Steaua stood firm in the second half and prevented any further breaches of their defence. Once again the European dream was over.

Rangers ended the season in third place, some distance behind champions Celtic. It would be some eighteen years before Rangers would again finish so far down the table, but even more significantly it was to be the last time for almost a decade that the Light Blues would not win the league. The following season marked the beginning of a period of domination, the first of nine title-winning campaigns in a row.

In the UEFA Cup of 1988/89, Rangers found themselves travelling to Eastern Europe for the fourth tie in succession, after being drawn against GKS Katowice of Poland. GKS were the local rivals of Gornik Zabrze and the second leg of the tie would take place at the same Slaski stadium where Gornik thrashed Rangers in 1969.

Rangers went into the first leg at Ibrox on a high, after crushing Celtic 5–1 in the opening Old Firm clash of the season, ten days earlier. It was a masterful performance, one of the best of the Souness era, and fittingly it was marked by one of the best Glasgow derby goals of all-time: a stunning volley from Ray Wilkins. Despite the mauling, some fans saw the match as a missed opportunity, believing Rangers had the chance to better Celtic's 7–1 League Cup final victory of 1958. In the end Rangers went on to win the league comfortably from nearest challengers Aberdeen. Celtic finished a distant fifth – seventeen points behind in an era when it was only two points for a win.

However, far from being overawed by the reputation of Rangers' international stars, the Poles were inspired to play above themselves and came at Rangers. A Mark Walters goal gave Rangers a lead that looked precarious to say the least. GKS also did a good job of frustrating Rangers, with fiery defender John Brown boiling over at one point. Suspecting the Poles of play-acting, he tossed the Katowice physio's bag off the pitch in a bid to get the match restarted during another stoppage for treatment to an 'injured' player. Unfortunately, the bag burst open on impact, sending assorted bandages and sprays spilling over the track and gaining Brown a yellow card.

In the return match, Rangers went behind early, as was becoming customary, but they went on to produce an excellent performance. Terry Butcher scored twice, along with goals from Ian Durrant and Ian Ferguson, to secure a 4–2 victory.

They were far from the most illustrious team to have graced the Ibrox pitch, but GKS left a memento of their visit that always gets a positive reaction. In the magnificent trophy room at Ibrox, among the glistening silverware collected in more than 130 years of football, there sits a somewhat odd-looking, shiny black vase. So striking is the piece, that virtually every visitor to the stadium asks where it came from. The answer is that it was a gift from the Katowice club to mark the meeting between the two teams in 1988. The vase, seventeen-inches tall, was carved out of a single piece of coal and features intricate patterns and a carving of a helmet-wearing miner.

Rangers have collected dozens such mementoes of their European travels and many are on display in the trophy room. The room, opened in 1959, was the brainchild of Scot Symon after he was inspired by a visit to Real Madrid. He ordered the conversion of the players' billiard room and filled it with trophies, gifts and mementoes that had been amassed over the years but were stored out of view. Today the panelled wooden walls – said to have been intended for the liner *Queen Mary* – are covered from ceiling to floor with pennants, pictures and silverware presented by clubs from all over the globe.

But apart from the glorious trophy cabinets and the portrait of Bill Struth, which dominate the room, it is the unusual gifts from European adversaries that catch the eye. These priceless gifts range from the sublime (an intricate trophy encrusted in multi-coloured jewels from Ankaragucu of Turkey) to the slightly ridiculous (a silver cake-stand from Glentoran) but all are treasured. The season before, Borussia Moenchengladbach had presented the club with an elegant clock-tower, while Dynamo Kiev gave a unique silver samovar (a traditional tea-urn). Most unusual of all is a racing bike gifted by old rivals St Etienne, which is incongruously propped up against a wall, below the portrait of Struth.

Having defeated GKS, the second-round draw paired Rangers with Cologne for a fourth time, their third clash in less than ten years. The Mungersdorfer stadium was beginning to seem like a home-from-home for the Scots. It was far from a happy hunting ground, with Rangers losing on all three visits, scoring just one goal and conceding nine in the process. Cologne captain Pierre Littbarski had been involved in the two previous clashes in 1979 and 1982.

With Rangers expected to bring their usual large and noisy travelling support, fears of crowd trouble were high on the agenda. The violence that had marred the European Championship finals in Germany a few months earlier meant the police were on alert for any troublemakers. But, as so often happens, the fears proved unfounded. A lot of drink was consumed and a lot of songs were sung, but the authorities declared themselves delighted by the behaviour of the Rangers supporters. Both the British Consulate in West Germany and Cologne's chief of police heaped praise on the 'Follow, Follow' brigade.

On the pitch it looked as though Rangers were heading for a highly creditable goalless draw, as they were in control for the majority of the match. However, they tired towards the end and lost two late goals. Ally McCoist was also sent off for a needless, and reckless, challenge on defender Paul Steiner.

Derek Ferguson had been one of Rangers' outstanding players and his performance was all the more remarkable as he had suffered an agonising injury after just ten minutes. He dislocated his shoulder after an awkward fall but, as Jimmy Nicholl stripped down and prepared to come on, club doctor Donald Cruickshank popped the shoulder back into position and Ferguson played on. In the second leg, Rangers piled on the pressure but it took until the seventy-fifth minute to get the breakthrough, courtesy of a Kevin Drinkell goal. Unfortunately, a late equalizer killed off any hopes of taking the tie to extra time.

Once again, Rangers were overcome by German opponents. It was becoming a habit. The Cologne tie was the seventeenth time Rangers had come up against a team from Germany, east or west, and the eighth time they had been eliminated. More significantly, Rangers had been knocked out on seven of the previous ten meetings since the beginning of the seventies.

So when the draw for the first round of the 1989/90 European Cup paired the Scottish champions with Bundesliga winners Bayern Munich there was a sense of disbelief, even trepidation. Bayern were still the top club in West Germany and their team was packed with internationals. However, in common with many of Europe's biggest clubs at that time, they were often an uninspiring lot to watch.

The days of Maier, Beckenbauer and Muller were long gone and their replacements Sven Scheuer, Olaf Thon and Alan McInally were hardly in the same class. McInally in particular was a lumbering Scottish centre forward who had played for Celtic before going south to Aston Villa. Football historian Ulrich Hesse-Lichtenberger – in his book *Tor!* – described the Bayern of that era as 'a strikers' graveyard'. McInally was just one in a long line of forwards who failed to fill the gap left by Karl-Heinz Rummenigge when he left for Inter. In fairness, McInally was a better footballer than pundit. After his career ended, he moved into broadcasting and became notorious for a string of 'Colemanballs' gaffes.

If it was a surprise to see Alan McInally turning out for Bayern Munich, it was even more of a shock that another former Celtic player was to turn out against him for Rangers. That it was Maurice Johnston, who had announced he was returning to Celtic weeks before he signed for Rangers, was even more unbelievable.

Two weeks after the exit to Cologne, Rangers had undergone another dramatic change, when Edinburgh-based steel magnate David Murray took control of the club from the Lawrence organisation. Murray had been thwarted in an earlier attempt to take over Ayr United but was introduced to the idea of buying Rangers by his friend Graeme Souness. When the sale went through, the manager also became a director by taking up a significant shareholding.

Murray finally took over as chairman from David Holmes the following June and, a few weeks later, he made his mark. On 10 July 1989, Rangers signed Maurice Johnston – a Roman Catholic from the West of Scotland – from under the noses of Old Firm rivals Celtic. The story of how Johnston went from the verge of rejoining the team he supported as a boy to signing for Rangers, and the reaction it provoked on both sides, has been well documented. Suffice to say, some Rangers fans were opposed to his signing on religious grounds, but most of the opposition was based on his disdainful attitude towards the club when he was with Celtic. And, in reality, most of the hostility he faced on his return to Glasgow came from Celtic supporters.

Johnston scored his first competitive goal in a 1–0 victory over Aberdeen at Ibrox the weekend before the Bayern first leg, but in the run-up to the European tie most of the headlines focused on Alan McInally and the welcome he would get from the Rangers support as a former Celtic player.

Rangers started the home leg brightly, going ahead through an early Mark

Walters penalty after Johnston was fouled. But the lead was short lived, as Bayern equalised through Wiggerl Kogl three minutes later, after a mistake by young Rangers defender Scott Nisbet. After half-time Thon scored with a penalty before skipper Klaus Augenthaler blasted a stunning thirty-five yard shot past Chris Woods to complete the scoring. Rangers were overwhelmed, with Graeme Souness later admitting they had been taught a football lesson.

In the second leg, with Israeli goalkeeper Bonni Ginzburg playing in place of Chris Woods and McCoist still suspended, Rangers put up a decent fight but were never likely to overturn the 3–1 deficit. In stereotypical German style, Bayern played the game out for a goalless draw, much to the frustration of the 40,000 crowd in the Olympic stadium, who booed the teams off the park.

Although Bayern reached the semi-final of the European Cup that season, they were by no means the legends of old. The success of Steaua Bucharest showed that the traditional power base was shifting, if only temporarily. Unfortunately for Rangers, the next Eastern European team to rise to prominence was their opponents in the second round of the following season's European Cup, Red Star Belgrade.

Rangers disposed of old whipping boys Valetta 10–0 on aggregate in the first round, even enjoying the luxury of a penalty miss by goalkeeper Chris Woods at Ibrox. Although not one of Europe's biggest names, Red Star were a very different proposition. Assistant manager Walter Smith was sent to Yugoslavia to spy on their opponents during a local derby with Partizan. His report to Graeme Souness of the task facing Rangers is said to have been simple and to the point: 'We're fucked.' In public, Smith was slightly more circumspect, although the message probably amounted to the same thing. He described Red Star as being 'as strong as Bayern in attack'. Given the demolition job inflicted by the Germans twelve months earlier, this was not what the Rangers fans wanted to hear.

Red Star played with a flair not often associated with Europe's Communist states, with 21-year-old playmaker Robert Prosinecki pulling the strings in the middle of the pitch. The chain-smoking Croatian, who was born in Germany, went on to play for Real Madrid, Barcelona, Seville and Standard Liege before a somewhat unlikely spell at Portsmouth. Alongside him in midfield was Dejan Savecevic, who later signed for AC Milan and helped inspire them to a European Cup win in 1994.

In defence, they had Miodrag Belodedic, who had won the European Cup with Steaua in 1986, while in attack the main forward was Darko Pancev, who was coveted by several top European teams and eventually went to Internazionale.

In the face of the expected Red Star onslaught, Rangers adopted a defensive 4-5-1 formation in front of an 80,000 crowd in the first leg in Belgrade, but were unable to prevent Prosinecki from controlling the match. He was involved in the opening goal after just eight minutes, his wonderful cross-field pass leading to a cross from Dusko Radinovic that was deflected into the net by defender John Brown. Somehow Rangers managed to make it to half-time just one goal behind, but any hopes of taking anything from the game were extinguished after an hour, when Prosinecki's curling twenty-yard free kick went in off a post.

Pancev added a third with a volley on seventy-two minutes, but in reality the score could and should have been even more embarrassing for Rangers. As Souness put it afterwards, 'I thought we were lucky to get away with conceding just three.'

Even with Savecevic missing through injury, Red Star were a class above Rangers, a fact that Souness glumly accepted. In the aftermath of the first leg he conceded, 'We are a long way from being a top European team. As yet we do not have the balance that we need to compete at that level.'

Before the return match, club captain Terry Butcher was put on the transfer list after a fall out with Souness, but his presence in the team would have made little difference to the outcome. A dismal attendance of 23,000 at Ibrox showed that few Rangers fans believed that the home team could overcome the three-goal deficit and sadly they were correct.

Rangers, with veteran reserve coach Davie Dodds playing up front in place of Maurice Johnston, huffed and puffed but rarely looked like breaching Red Star's defence and, shortly after half-time, Red Star scored the inevitable away goal through Pancev. Fourteen minutes from the end, Ally McCoist scored for Rangers, but it was far too little, far too late.

Red Star went on to win the tournament that year, defeating Marseille on penalties in what was widely considered to be one of the worst European Cup finals of all time. However, their victory was little consolation to Rangers fans.

Yet again, Rangers had failed on the European stage. For all that Souness had transformed the club's domestic fortunes, the much talked-about Holy Grail of the European Cup was no closer than it had been under previous managers. In five European campaigns Souness had achieved just one major result and – as impressive as the victory over Dynamo Kiev had been – it was scant reward for the money he had spent. By reaching the quarter-final in 1988 Souness had achieved no more than John Greig, nine years earlier.

Red Star was to be Souness's last crack at Europe for Rangers. With four league games remaining, and Rangers in danger of throwing their title away, he left to become manager of Liverpool. At his final press conference on 16 April 1991, David Murray warned his friend that he was making the biggest mistake of his life. After a nightmare four years with the Anfield club, Souness realised what Murray had meant.

While he may not have been every fan's choice, Walter Smith was promoted to manager and took charge for the dramatic climax to the season, which culminated in Rangers retaining their title after defeating Aberdeen in a match they had to win. Smith's first venture into Europe in season 1991/92 took Rangers to Prague to face Czech champions Sparta and hopes were high that they could reverse the depressing trend for early exits in recent seasons.

An extra incentive for Rangers was the tempting prospect of competing in a new group stage of the competition that was being tried as an experiment by UEFA. After the normal first-and-second-round knockout stages, the remaining eight teams would be split into two groups, with the guarantee of a further six matches. The group winners would then play each other in the final. The new format was an attempt to appease powerful chairmen like Bernard Tapie of Marseille, Silvio Berlusconi of AC Milan and Real Madrid's Ramon Mendoza. It was all about maximising revenues, with increased gate receipts and television stations clamouring to cover the expanded tournament.

Another change enforced by UEFA that season was the three-foreigner rule. This prevented clubs from playing more than three overseas players in European competitions and for a club like Rangers that had successfully plundered the English market, and was also scouring Europe for players, this was a serious setback. Foreigners who had played for a certain length of time in Scotland were considered, in UEFA's *Star Trek*-style language, to be assimilated. Two were allowed to play in addition to the three foreigners. However, the rule meant that Rangers had to change their transfer policy and to focus on recruiting the best Scottish players. From being criticised for ignoring Scottish talent, Rangers were now under fire for 'stealing' all the good Scots. It seemed that only a return to the days of signing mediocre players, of whatever nationality, would keep certain commentators happy.

Despite the three-foreigner rule (or the eight-diddy rule as it was cruelly dubbed in Scotland), on paper Rangers were far superior to the Czechs. The team that turned out in the first leg at the Letna stadium included Scotland internationals Andy Goram, David Robertson, Richard Gough, Stuart McCall and Ally McCoist as well as Dutch winger Pieter Huistra and England stars Gary Stevens and Mark Hateley.

Goram was signed from Hibernian for £1 million in the summer as successor to Chris Woods, one of the first victims of the new UEFA quota system. A Scotland international at both football and cricket, he went on to have a spectacular career at Ibrox and was a key figure in the attainment of nine-in-a-row, despite numerous off-field tribulations. His performances in Old Firm matches in particular led former Celtic boss Tommy Burns famously to declare that his headstone would be carved with the words 'Andy Goram Broke My Heart'. But there were doubts in those first few weeks that he was the man to replace Woods and the fans' concerns came to a head in the tie with Sparta.

In the first leg, Rangers lost 1–0 to a freak goal scored by Czech international Jiri Nemec. His speculative cross in the nineteenth minute caught Goram off his line and the ball sailed over the goalkeeper's head into the net. Rangers had a couple of chances to equalise but, overall, Sparta were deserving of their lead. In the dying seconds, Goram pulled off a superb save from Pavel Cerny but it was his first-half blunder that was remembered.

Defeat to Hibernian in the League Cup semi-final followed by a 2–0 home loss to Aberdeen was hardly the ideal preparation for the return leg at Ibrox. Rangers went into the match missing the injured Gough and Hateley but, despite a few scares, they seemed to have done enough to progress. Stuart McCall scored the equalizer shortly after half-time to take the tie into extra time, before adding a second with a brilliant volley in the ninety-fourth minute to put the Scots in the lead.

Then, in age-old fashion, Rangers pressed the self-destruct button. Five minutes after McCall's goal, Sparta broke down the right, although there seemed little danger when Mistr's cross came into the area. Defender Scott Nisbet stuck out a leg in a bid to clear the ball, but instead diverted it towards his own goal. Some reports of the time state that Siegl managed to flick it on, while others said that Nisbet got the last touch. Everyone, though, agreed that Goram was at fault as the ball squirmed out of his grasp, under his body and into the net.

Smith insisted that Rangers didn't deserve to lose over the two legs, declaring in his post-match interviews, 'We lost one goal in Prague, which was a fluke, and some particularly bad defending tonight means we are out.'

In fairness, he had a point. Rangers probably were the better team over the two legs, but the hard-luck stories were beginning to grate with the fans. The Premier League was secured for the fourth season in a row with 101 goals scored and a nine-point advantage over nearest challengers Hearts. Ally McCoist finished top scorer with forty-one goals; this achievement secured him Europe's coveted Golden Boot, awarded to the Continent's top striker. And Rangers finally won the Scottish Cup for the first time in eleven years.

But the greater the domestic dominance, the more pressure grew for a good European run. The draw for the first round of the 1992/93 European

Cup was the sort of banana skin that had caused Rangers to slip up on many previous occasions. Danish champions Lyngby may not have been the toughest opponents but, a few weeks earlier, Denmark had won the European Championship and the country had been producing quality players for almost a decade. Lyngby had few players who would go on to bigger things, although midfielder Morten Wieghorst went on to play for Dundee, then Celtic.

In front of an expectant crowd of more than 40,000 at Ibrox, Ally McCoist was presented before kick-off with his Golden Boot for the previous season's exploits. As hard as he tried, he failed to get on the score sheet that night, but Rangers gained a useful 2–0 lead, with goals from Mark Hateley and Pieter Huistra.

Lyngby chose to play the second leg in Copenhagen's Parken stadium in the mistaken belief that their own ground, which held 12,000, would not be big enough to cope with demand. The decision backfired as just over 4,000 turned up to the national stadium, around three-quarters of them Rangers fans.

The crowd was missing one coach-load of travelling supporters after they were caught up in a bizarre incident on their way to Copenhagen. Following reports of an incident on board a ferry carrying fans from Germany to Denmark, police were waiting at the port of Rodbyhavn to greet the Rangers followers. Claims were made that perfume and champagne had been stolen from the duty-free shop.

Donnie, from Dunoon, was on one of the buses. He recalled:

> Every bus was searched as we got off the ferry and when they got to ours we had to get off and open our bags in front off the customs men. After all the bags were taken off, there was one suitcase left that nobody would claim. We were put back on the bus and the police came out with sniffer dogs who went berserk at this case. It turned out there was a huge quantity of hash inside.

The suitcase actually contained eighty-eight pounds of the drug, said to have a street value of £250,000. The forty-nine fans on board were questioned over the find and, not surprisingly, they all denied owning the case. Donnie added, 'Everyone was taken off the bus, arrested and had their fingerprints taken, we were then allowed to carry on into Copenhagen, about two hours' drive away. We just got into the stadium with about three minutes to go.' The source of the drugs was never discovered but one theory was that they may have been planted on the coach during a stop in Holland and no-one on board knew anything about it.

The thousands who did make it to the match enjoyed an exciting game.

Although they had one or two chances, which were well saved by Andy Goram, the Danes never looked like seriously troubling Rangers and with five minutes to go Ian Durrant latched onto a pass from Trevor Steven and went round the goalkeeper, before knocking it into the net.

Having successfully negotiated a tricky tie, Rangers moved into the second round hoping for a draw that would ease their passage into the newly formed group stage of the Champions League. Instead they were thrust into one of the most-hyped football matches this country has ever experienced. With Leeds United the opponents, once again Rangers were to take part in a Battle of Britain.

18

Leeds 1992: 'You wonder how Scotland could ever lose a football match'

Archie Knox strode into the Ibrox dressing room and threw a pile of newspaper cuttings on the floor. He gave no explanation to the gathered players other than to say: 'If that isn't inspiration for you, then nothing is.'

No other words were needed. The articles were from newspapers south of the border and each reported how Rangers were about to be put in their place by English champions Leeds United. Fleet Street, to a man, was convinced that the best Scotland had to offer would be no match in their Champions League qualifier for the winners of the self-proclaimed greatest league in the world.

Knox knew exactly what he was doing when he lobbed the cuttings onto the floor. Just as he expected, the Rangers players were incensed at the lack of respect. A column in the London edition of *The Sun* provoked the biggest response. The cutting, which found its way onto the dressing-room notice board, read: 'Rangers are no great side at all.' It went on to argue that the Scots would struggle to finish in the top half of a British league.

The Rangers players were desperate to shove the disparaging words of the pundits back in their faces. 'The papers were just full of how easy it was going to be for Leeds and what the score was going to be,' said defender Dave McPherson. 'Archie used that to good effect – not that he needed to right enough. I think the players were more than capable of going down there and winning the game anyway.'

At stake was a place in the first UEFA Champions League group stages and unprecedented riches. Rangers had already convincingly beaten the Danes of Lyngby while the English champions had a somewhat fortuitous route to the second qualifier. Having lost the first leg away to Stuttgart 3–0, the

Yorkshire side faced an uphill task at Elland Road. They managed to beat Stuttgart 4–1 but went out on away goals. It then emerged that Stuttgart had fielded four foreign players instead of three, the maximum allowed, and so UEFA awarded the game to Leeds 3–0. With the aggregate scores now level, the match went to a replay in Barcelona where a tiny crowd of 7,000 rattled around the vast Camp Nou and saw Leeds triumph 2–1.

By that time Rangers already knew they would be facing the winner of the play-off and when Leeds came out on top the hype really kicked-off. Predictably, the match was billed as the Battle of Britain. Although Scottish teams, including Rangers, had faced English rivals on many occasions in Europe, this was only the third clash in the European Cup. In 1970 Celtic had defeated Leeds 3–1 on aggregate in the semi-final and, in 1980, Aberdeen were hammered 5–0 over two legs by Liverpool in the second round.

But with Rangers having so many Englishmen in their squad, not to mention the Leeds tartan contingent of Gordon Strachan and Gary McAllister, interest was greater than ever. Fears of crowd trouble led the clubs to impose a ban on away fans at both legs, although live television coverage ensured that twenty-million viewers would see both legs.

Leeds travelled north for the first leg in confident mood, despite an indifferent start to the league season. Their strike partnership of Lee Chapman and Eric Cantona was highly rated and, in midfield, Strachan, McAllister and Gary Speed provided attacking flair while David Batty was the muscle. However, there were question marks over how Leeds would cope with the Rangers attack. In the previous round they had been vulnerable at the back and the Ibrox strikers Hateley and McCoist were in irresistible form. Leeds goalkeeper John Lukic, the former Arsenal back-up, was also considered a weak link.

The general view, south of the border at least, was that Rangers would suffer from the lack of quality in the Scottish league. Leeds were installed as firm favourites because they faced 'intense competition' every week in the newly created Premiership. Such simplistic analysis failed to take account of the sheer will to win in this Rangers team. Players like Hateley, Richard Gough, Gary Stevens, Stuart McCall and Trevor Steven had already proved themselves in more powerful leagues and characters like McCoist, Andy Goram, John Brown, Ian Durrant and Ian Ferguson were born winners.

'It was a massive game for Rangers,' said McPherson. 'The European Cup hadn't been kind to us but we knew we had a good squad of players and we were keen to get a good run. We knew Leeds were starting favourites, even at Ibrox everyone expected them to actually win the game.'

The stage was set for a classic. And when the evening of 21 October

1992 came around, the first match lived up to expectations. The teams emerged from the Ibrox tunnel to a tidal wave of noise. The lack of an away support did nothing to dampen the atmosphere as 44,000 Rangers fans sang themselves hoarse. The songs continued as Leeds kicked-off and immediately went on the attack, winning a corner off John Brown after just thirty seconds. Strachan guided the kick to the near post where Robertson headed it clear under pressure from an attacker. The ball dropped to McAllister on the edge of the penalty area and he volleyed it right-footed into the top-left-hand corner. It was the perfect strike and, as the net rippled, a stunned silence fell over Ibrox. For a few seconds, the only sounds that could be heard were the shouts of delight from the Leeds players. 'It was one of the best atmospheres I'd ever played in and Gary McAllister silenced it pretty quickly!' said McPherson.

Rangers were stunned; going behind after less than a minute was not in the script. But as the players looked at each other in disbelief, the noise from the stands slowly started to rise again and so too did the players, as McPherson explains: 'When they scored such a fantastic goal early on everyone probably expected them to go on and win the game. But on the park we just decided to roll up our sleeves and get on with it and ignore it. We had another eighty-nine minutes to pull it out of the bag.'

Rangers put the nightmare start behind them and set about looking for an equalizer. When they eventually got the breakthrough, it came in bizarre fashion. A corner from Ian Durrant on the left seemed harmless enough but Lukic flapped and punched the ball into his own net. He later claimed to have been blinded by the Ibrox floodlights. The goal in the twentieth minute inspired Rangers to their best spell and they had numerous chances before Ally McCoist put them in the lead. Again, there were question marks over Lukic as he failed to hold a powerful McPherson header and the unmarked McCoist pounced to scramble the ball over the line.

Leeds, who seemed on the verge of collapse at points in the first half, recovered after the break and held Rangers at bay. There was no more scoring and the Scottish champions went into the second leg with a narrow 2–1 lead. However, after the bad start the players were pleased with the result. 'It was testament to that squad that we came back in that game,' said Dave McPherson. 'We had a fantastic bunch of players and guys, and every game we went into that season, especially in Europe, we believed we were going to win it.'

Despite all the talk of Leeds being favourites to go through, Rangers fans were desperate to beat the ban and get into Elland Road for the second leg. Pre-match predictions that up to a thousand would travel may have been an exaggeration but there is no doubt that there was a good number inside once the game got underway. The Elland Road capacity was reduced to 25,000 because of construction work and the £18 tickets were being sold for up to £150 on the black market. A major police operation was launched to prevent touts operating and seek out those Rangers fans trying to sneak in. Had the police held off until three minutes into the game, they would have had no trouble identifying the bluenoses.

Just as at Ibrox, Leeds started the game well and had an early opportunity to score when Cantona broke free, only to be thwarted by Goram and Brown. A penalty claim for handball was waved away by the Russian referee. A minute later, Goram launched a long kick downfield that was flicked into the path of Hateley and he lashed a brilliant volley from outside the penalty area into the back of the net. Again, just like at Ibrox, the noise from the home fans ceased, the only difference being that Elland Road wasn't quite silent, as Dave McPherson explains:

> When the goal went in I don't think it was as quiet as it was when they scored at Ibrox. A few Rangers supporters appeared out of nowhere and jumped when we scored! In any game you play, you've got to get the goals at the right time. In that game, Mark struck early and they were shell-shocked, I think. First we beat them at Ibrox then went down there and scored early on yet they had a lot of quality players in their side and were expected to win easily. They failed to show the mettle we showed when we went behind at Ibrox. It was now a completely different ball game. At that point we knew we were going to win it and they realised there was a good chance they were going to lose it. You could feel that when you were on the park.

The cheers of the Rangers fans were soon stifled as police moved in; mostly for their own safety. Later it emerged that twelve fans were ejected, although that was a fraction of the number inside the ground. Stories of Rangers fans who beat the ban are legion; they include the wealthy businessman who spent a fortune on an executive box and then filled it to overflowing with supporters. Others weren't so lucky. Bob Anderson had arranged to pick up a ticket from an acquaintance in Leeds but, on arriving in the city, he realised that the rendezvous point was actually behind the police cordon. In the days before the mobile phone it was impossible to get the message through to his pal. 'With my accent, I could hardly go and ask a policeman for help,' said Bob. He ended up watching in a pub with dozens of other disappointed Bears.

Leeds tried to get back into it but they never looked likely to make the breakthrough and Rangers were always menacing on the break. Lukic made up for his previous blunders by saving twice from McCoist. At the other end, Goram was also on top form, ably assisted by his back four. Cantona was the only Leeds player who seemed capable of breaching the defences, but even he found it impossible to get past Goram.

Then, on the hour mark, Rangers killed the game stone dead with a brilliant breakaway that ended in a clinical finish. The move started in defence as Hateley flicked the ball on to Durrant and continued his forward run. The Scotland international sent Hateley clear down the left and, as the Leeds defenders frantically tried to get back, he launched a superb cross to the back post, where McCoist dived in to plant a glorious header past Lukic.

From then on there was no doubting the outcome. Leeds were frantic in their attempts to get back into the match, but they needed four goals to go through and that was never going to happen. Cantona finally got a consolation in the closing minutes but by that time many Leeds fans had gone. Those who remained were generous in their applause for Rangers at full time. It had been a performance marked by determination, spirit and character – and no little skill.

Leeds manager Howard Wilkinson lavished praise on his conquerors, saying: 'You wonder how Scotland could ever lose a football match.' The English media, who had been so dismissive of Rangers before the tie, were also forced to eat their words. In *The Independent*, Joe Lovejoy summed it up. 'Once the best in Europe, [the English] are no longer the best in Britain.'

Rangers marched on into the Champions League as Britain's only remaining European survivors. They ruled Britannia, now it was time to take on the Continent.

19

A Glorious Run in the Champions League

'Rangers have proved themselves to be not only the biggest club in Britain, but also the best.'

Few observers would have argued with the words of Stuart Jones in *The Times* after the Scottish champions knocked Leeds United out of the Champions League. By comprehensively beating the best England had to offer, Rangers had won the right to compete alongside Europe's elite and, in doing so, also won the admiration and support of the football public south of the border. Rangers were flying the flag for Britain in the Champions League and were suddenly given unprecedented coverage in the national media.

For players like Trevor Steven and Mark Hateley, this was a vindication of their decision to come to what many of their fellow countrymen saw as a backwater. And, for the Scottish players in the team it was a two-finger salute to those pundits who derided the Scottish game.

The ITV network cleared its schedules for Rangers in the Champions League, while the national newspapers sent their top football correspondents to chart the progress of the Scots. But after an hour of the opening game of the group stage they may have been wondering what all the fuss was about.

The first official Champions League featured eight teams, split into two mini-leagues, guaranteeing each competitor a minimum of six games. The draw in Geneva put Rangers into Group A alongside French champions Olympique Marseille, FC Bruges of Belgium and Russian champions CSKA Moscow. The new-style competition brought a completely different look to European football, with UEFA regulating everything from pitch-side advertising to the format of match programmes to television graphics. The now famous Champions League music – a specially commissioned arrangement of Handel's 'Zadok the Priest' by British composer Tony Britten – was also introduced and played in the stadiums before every game.

It was a gold mine for the clubs. UEFA guaranteed each club that qualified for the group stage a minimum of £500,000, and £200,000 was paid for each point gained. The three home games would also rake in more than £1 million from ticket sales and television.

The eyes of Britain were on Rangers as they lined up in torrential rain for their opening match against Marseille at Ibrox. The stadium was a virtual sell-out and the noise from the home fans as the two teams stood for the traditional presentation was deafening. Rangers were under-strength, through a combination of the three-foreigner rule, injury and suspension. UEFA regulations deprived Walter Smith of Pieter Huistra, Gary Stevens, Dale Gordon and Oleg Kuznetzov, while Ally McCoist had a calf injury and Ian Ferguson was suspended. Teenager Neil Murray – until recently a Glasgow University accountancy student – was drafted into the team from the start and Ian Durrant was deployed in a more attacking role in the absence of McCoist. On the bench Rangers had to rely on youngsters Steven Pressley, David Hagen and Gary McSwegan, while at the other end of the age scale, reserve-team coach Davie Dodds was also listed, even though he was supposed to be retired.

Marseille had quality in all departments, from goalkeeper Fabien Barthez, who at the age of twenty-one still had a full head of hair, through to German centre forward Rudi Voller. A quick scan through the rest of the line-up shows what Rangers were up against; international stars like Angloma, Boli, Sauzee, Desailly, Boksic, Abedi Pele and Deschamps were household names, and among the most highly regarded players in Europe.

Marseille lived up to their fearsome reputation and totally dominated the match for the first eighty minutes. Even as the weather conditions worsened, and the Ibrox pitch turned into a quagmire, they managed to maintain their poise and it was no surprise when they took the lead in thirty minutes, Alen Boksic side-footing past Goram after a pass from Voller. The German himself doubled the Marseille lead in the fifty-seventh minute, capitalising on a horrendous mistake by 19-year-old Pressley, who had come on to replace the injured Richard Gough at half-time.

The French champions continued to press for more goals and it seemed that Rangers might suffer one of their most crushing European defeats of all time. Then, in the seventy-seventh minute, Walter Smith made one of those rare substitutions that can instantly turn a manager into a tactical genius. Steven, who had not been enjoying one of his better games, was withdrawn from the midfield and replaced by young striker Gary McSwegan. A minute later McSwegan met a cross from Mikhailichenko and directed a powerful looping header over Barthez and into the top corner of the net. It was his first-ever touch of the ball in European competition.

The goal inspired the Rangers players and driven on by the reinvigorated crowd they piled forward. Four minutes later, Mikhailichenko, a player not renowned for his tackling ability, gamely won the ball on the left. He released Durrant, whose cross was diverted towards Hateley, who stooped low to head past the goalkeeper. Ibrox erupted. It was an astonishing comeback from the Scots, who had seemed dead and buried moments earlier. Marseille were stunned and ended up hanging on for a 2–2 draw.

Basile Boli, who joined Rangers two years later, believes the noise from the stands inspired the Scots to their recovery, as he told the *Sunday Herald* in 2006:

> We went 2–0 up and thought we had the win wrapped up. But that was without counting for the Rangers fans! They made such a hullabaloo, such a huge wall of noise, that Rangers were spurred on and came back to draw 2–2. And I can tell you that in those days we were not the sort of team to let teams recover from 2–0 down! I still get goose bumps just thinking about the atmosphere in the stadium. That was the night that convinced me to join Rangers.

Marseille had played the superior football on a pitch that eventually resembled a farmer's field, but their superior skills were matched in the end by the spirit and determination shown by Rangers. 'We played the best football,' said Marseille's veteran coach Raymond Goethals, 'but Rangers showed the quality and character of Scottish football.' Character was a word that would be used frequently to describe Rangers' performances during the campaign as they battled to cope with injuries and suspensions.

The Marseille game gave the Rangers team a lesson in how to play European football, according to Dave McPherson:

> In that game we managed to defend really well and worked hard to shut them down as much as possible. But they were a fantastic team with lots of world-renowned names. It's really important in any game that even if you are not on top and teams are playing well against you, you still maintain that belief that you're going to score. With that squad we always had the belief that we were going to score.

Next Rangers had an away game against CSKA, which had been moved to Germany because of the severity of the Russian weather in December. Although it was theoretically a home game for the Russians, they were hugely outnumbered in the crowd of 9,000 inside the Ruhrstadion in Bochum. Around 5,000 Rangers fans were present, and they flew hundreds of banners and flags (including one proclaiming Brady Must Stay – a reference to hapless Celtic boss Liam Brady). The only indication that this was a home match for CSKA was the entertainment provided by a Russian army band, whose bizarre repertoire included a selection of Glenn Miller tunes.

Injuries meant that Walter Smith had to change the team again. Gough and Gary Stevens were both out, and Trevor Steven was played at right back. In the opening minutes the makeshift defence was all over the place, as the Russians were denied what seemed a certain goal by a desperate last-ditch tackle. Bouchmanov went clear through to face Goram, who made a good save, but the ball broke loose and bobbled dangerously close to the unguarded net. Two CSKA forwards moved in for the kill, but from nowhere David Robertson slid in to clear. Meanwhile four or five forwards and attackers were entangled in a heap on the goal line.

CSKA had started the game well, but it was Rangers who drew first blood with a goal that typified their Champions League campaign. The move started on the left with a cross from Robertson. Hateley won an aerial challenge with goalkeeper Gouteev and knocked the ball down towards Ian Ferguson on the edge of the penalty area. He managed to get his shot in but it took a deflection off Fokine and spun past the goalie into the net.

Rangers had a number of chances to increase their lead, most notably through Ally McCoist; he had three good efforts, two were saved and one went narrowly wide from a tight angle. But despite good play from both teams there were no further goals and, to the delight of the travelling bluenoses, Rangers had secured a vital away win.

The victory put Rangers level at the top of the group with Marseille. The French team had beaten Bruges at the Stade Velodrome 3–0, but the match was marred by crowd disturbances and resulted in UEFA ordering Bruges to play their next European home game behind closed doors. Unfortunately for the three thousand Rangers fans who had already booked up for Belgium, that match was against the Ibrox men. FC Bruges appealed against the decision on the grounds that Marseille fans had infiltrated their section of the stadium and were responsible for the trouble. In typical UEFA style, the supporters' ban was lifted, meaning Rangers did not face the prospect of a hefty bill to compensate fans for their aborted travel plans.

It was three months since the last Champions League game, but Rangers' injury woes had not improved. Gough, Stevens, Ferguson, Steven and Gordon were all missing, while Durrant, who was struggling for fitness, remained an unused substitute. But on a bitterly cold night, it was another defiant performance from Walter Smith's team, one that deserved a victory. In the end the match ended 1–1, but only an outstanding performance by FC Bruges goalkeeper Dany Verlinden denied Rangers two points.

The first half had been open, with both teams having chances to score but, just as it seemed Rangers would go in level at the break, Bruges took advantage of a botched chested clearance by Mikhailichenko and Tomasz Dziubinski finished clinically. In an exhilarating second half, Rangers bombarded the Belgians' goal. First Hateley had a close-range header brilliantly saved, and then Huistra's rebound was blocked. Brown and McCall both went close with shots before Huistra crossed for McPherson, and his downward header was touched away spectacularly by Verlinden, diving down to his left. The pressure from Rangers was incessant and when Huistra finally got the equalizer with sixteen minutes to go, it was no more than they deserved. Rangers had stretched their unbeaten run to an astonishing forty games by playing some of their best football of the season.

The equalizer effectively knocked FC Bruges out of the reckoning but its value became even more apparent when news came through that CSKA had held Marseille to a draw in Germany. The champions of Scotland and France were going head-to-head for a place in the European Cup final.

Some goals are never forgotten. Some are remembered for their dazzling skill, like Archie Gemmell's famous solo run against Holland in the 1978 World Cup. Others stick in the mind for their sheer power, such as Bert Konterman's League Cup semi-final strike against Celtic. Some, like Ole Gunner Solskjaer's last-minute winner for Manchester United in the Champions League final of 1999 are famous for their stunning timing. And some are remembered because of their controversy, like Maradona's 'Hand of God'. Then there are some goals that go down in history just because they are plain daft.

Scott Nisbet was never the greatest player to pull on a light-blue jersey; he was a defender who joined the club as a 17-year-old and, over the next eight years, made sporadic appearances in defence, usually covering for a more illustrious colleague. But thanks to one special goal his name will be remembered for generations to come, long after some of his teammates are a distant memory. His moment of glory came midway through the second half of Rangers' fourth group match, at home to Bruges.

The game was poised at 1–1 after Lorenzo Staelens had cancelled out Durrant's excellent opener. In terrible conditions, Rangers were reduced to ten men when Hateley was unjustly sent off, but were pressing the Belgians further and further back. An attack down the right petered out, and the ball broke to Nisbet thirty yards from goal. There seemed to be little danger when the young defender swung his right boot and sent the ball looping into the FC Bruges penalty area. But then something extraordinary happened. The ball dropped in front of Verlinden, then bounced off the turf at a bizarre angle over the goalkeeper's head and landed in the net. The 40,000 Rangers fans went berserk as Nisbet charged towards the Rangers dugout, with his teammates in close pursuit. His expression suggested he couldn't quite believe what had just happened, and he certainly wasn't alone. As the ITV commentator put it, 'It might be the biggest fluke in Europe this year, but who cares!'

Fellow defender Dave McPherson says Nisbet maintains to this day that he meant it. On first viewing, the shot appears to have taken a deflection off defender Stephane van der Heyden, with the resulting spin causing the ball to loop into the air and bounce over the keeper. But closer examination of the video, although inconclusive, suggests that there was no deflection. So what was it that caused the ball to bounce into the net in such a freakish way? Well, it may seem fanciful, but there were some Rangers supporters who thought that fate was on their side, and decided to intervene at the crucial moment, drawing the ball into the net as part of a pre-ordained plan. Another, more prosaic, view is that the ball hit a divot in the dreadfully churned-up pitch as Nisbet let fly, then hit another when it bounced in the penalty area. Either way, it was a goal that gave Rangers a vital 2–1 win, and set up a thrilling decider against Marseille for a place in the final.

'You know that if you work hard to get a result, even if you're not playing as well as you can, you are liable to get the breaks and that happened that night,' said Dave McPherson. 'It added to the belief we already had.'

For Scott Nisbet the joy of the goal was short-lived. Three days later, he started against Celtic, but had to come off early with a groin strain. It was the last professional game he ever played. At the age of twenty-five, he developed a pelvic injury that, if he had continued to play, could have left him crippled for life. Doctors said he had no choice but to retire. If fate had a hand in his famous goal, it had delivered a painful blow in return, physically and metaphorically.

Ian Durrant was another player whose career was blighted by serious injury, although in his case it was caused by an act of malice rather than bad luck. He had fought back to fitness after a brutal tackle by Aberdeen's Neil Simpson shattered his knee in 1989, and although he was never the same player again, he was a vital figure in the Champions League run.

Having scored the opener against Bruges, Durrant was handed an attacking role alongside Ally McCoist in the next game in Marseille because of Mark Hateley's suspension. The match had become a virtual European Cup semi-final, with the winner certain to finish top of Group A and qualify for the final. Both teams were level on points after the French side had exploited some dubious goalkeeping and secured an unlikely 6–0 victory over CSKA. It was more than thirty years since Rangers had been so close to a European Cup final but, although they were within touching distance, it was going to be difficult. No team had gone to Marseille and won in Europe since 1988.

Marseille's fans, renowned as the most passionate in France, had gathered in the Velodrome more than an hour before kick-off and along with the one thousand Rangers supporters generated a tremendous atmosphere. The noise when the teams appeared was deafening and the atmosphere continued to crackle throughout the opening exchanges. Neither team stamped their authority on the match, until Marseille pounced on a defensive error in the sixteenth minute. Franck Sauzee picked up a slack clearance by David Robertson and played it wide to Voller. Sauzee continued his run and when the German played the ball into his path, he shot first-time past Goram.

With Marseille piling on the pressure, and the atmosphere in the stadium reaching boiling point, it seemed inevitable that the French champions would add a second. But the resilience of this Rangers team could not be underestimated and slowly they worked their way back into the game. In thirty-one minutes, Durrant set up a good chance for McCoist who shot over the bar, but Rangers maintained the initiative for the rest of the first half, and whenever Marseille looked dangerous Gough and Brown were rock solid in the centre of defence.

Five minutes after the break, Sauzee hit the crossbar with a dipping free-kick from twenty-five yards but, within a minute, Rangers got the vital breakthrough with a stunning strike. Trevor Steven's corner from the left was headed out by a defender, but it only went as far as Durrant on the corner of the penalty area. With a technique that Scottish players are not supposed to possess, he volleyed it with the outside of his right foot, curling the ball in at the back post. The ball travelled all the way at waist height, leaving Barthez with no chance.

The goal shocked the Marseille fans, who were not used to conceding on their own territory. They had seen their team score nine goals in the Champions League, without letting any in, and expected Rangers to be swept away. But they reckoned without the determination of Richard Gough and his team. Rangers held on for a 1–1 draw, surviving a nervous four minutes of injury time. Rangers supporters, who had been enclosed by a net to protect them from missiles, celebrated long after the final whistle had blown.

'I remember it was a really muggy night,' said Dave McPherson, who started at right back. 'We definitely had more of a belief that we could beat

Marseille than we did when we played them at Ibrox. It wasn't a massive squad we had. If there was an injury, somebody would come in and do a good job and that was important as well.'

When the dust finally settled, the reality of what was required became apparent. If both teams won, they would finish level on seven points, but because Marseille had scored two goals at Ibrox, compared to one from Rangers in the south of France, they held the advantage. Quite simply, on the final match-day, Rangers had to go one better than Marseille.

The Scots knew they had to rely on help from FC Bruges to qualify, but the problem was that the Belgians had nothing to play for. Richard Gough quipped that they should send the Bruges captain Franky van der Elst a case of champagne if he helped Rangers go through. The Belgian star replied, 'I'd be happy to drink it and I expect to hear from Gough on the morning after the match.'

However, as the vital games approached, it became clear that Bruges would not be treating the game quite as seriously as Rangers hoped. The Belgians went into the clash with Marseille without *seven* first-choice players, including van der Elst and Lorenzo Staelens, two of their star performers. Both could have played but were rested by coach Hugo Broos ahead of a league game against Waregem the following Sunday.

Mark Hateley was still suspended but, apart from his absence, Rangers faced CSKA with a full-strength side. Confidence was high among the players that they could make history and this was transmitted to the supporters, who turned Ibrox into a cauldron of noise as the teams lined up. The roars of the crowd when the match kicked off lifted the hairs on the back of the neck. If Rangers were going to fail, it would not be down to a lack of backing.

Chance after chance came Rangers' way, but none found the net. Ally McCoist, normally lethal, somehow contrived to scorn five excellent chances. On another night he could have broken all European scoring records but on this night it simply wasn't to be. As the game wore on there was a sense that Rangers could play all night and never score. They were denied by a combination of poor finishing and brilliant goalkeeping from Yevgeny Plotnikov. A save in the dying moments from a rasping volley by John Brown was truly world class. 'Our luck ran out that night, we needed another Scott Nisbet goal,' said Dave McPherson. Despite having absolutely nothing to play for, CSKA defended as if their lives depended on it, and even came close to scoring themselves during two late breakaways.

Throughout it all, the Rangers fans willed on their heroes. But the Ibrox crowd could not affect what was going on hundreds of miles away in FC Bruges's Olympia stadium, where Alen Boksic took advantage of static defending after just two minutes to give Marseille the lead. It was the only goal of an insipid game and, in the end, it didn't matter what Rangers did in Glasgow – the French champions were in the final.

The final whistle at Ibrox was met by silence. Physically and emotionally, the Rangers players were drained. Blood poured from an open wound on Richard Gough's head and the rest of the team stood on the pitch, heads bowed, awaiting confirmation that Marseille had done enough. As news finally came through from Belgium that the dream was over, the tears began to flow, McCoist in particular breaking down. Then as the players took a bow, Ibrox began to reverberate with the sound of more than 43,000 fans paying tribute to the efforts of their heroes. The English media, which had avidly followed the Scots throughout their unbeaten run, were suitably impressed by the defiant stance of the Rangers fans. Jeff Powell wrote in the *Daily Mail*: 'Television transmission enabled the Scots to offer an object lesson to the English in how to fail graciously.'

Dignity in defeat, and the knowledge that they had made many new friends south of the border, meant little to Rangers when they watched Marseille take on AC Milan in the final. And the French club's unexpected 1–0 victory was scant consolation.

In France, Marseille's win, the first by a club from the country that invented the European Cup, was celebrated as a national triumph. The morning after the victory, *L'Equipe*'s headline was, '*Le jour de gloire!*' (glory day). But four weeks later, the celebrations turned sour. Police dug up £30,000 from the garden of the parents of Christophe Robert, a forward with French first-division club Valenciennes. The discovery set in motion a chain of events that was to result in the dramatic fall from grace of France's biggest club and its flamboyant owner Bernard Tapie.

Robert claimed he and several teammates had been offered money by Marseille to play badly in a game that the southern giants needed to win to secure a fifth successive title. Marseille subsequently triumphed and won the league, relegating Valenciennes in the process. Marseille were eventually relegated to the French second division because of the allegations and Bernard Tapie ended up in jail.

As the French authorities launched their investigations, there was a new, and potentially disturbing, development. CSKA's coach Gennady Kostylev, told Russian magazine *Sport Express* that Marseille had tried to bribe his players before their Champions League match in France. Then he suggested the player's drinks were spiked at half-time in the game they lost 6–0.

Kostylev claimed that a number of calls were made to players and officials at the team hotel in Marseille, offering them money to lose the match. The coach insisted they refused to countenance the idea of accepting cash. Later, according to Kostylev, the CSKA captain Oleg Kolotokvine had a visitor to his hotel room from a man speaking fluent Russian, who offered the equivalent of almost £20,000 for each player to throw the match. In comments that were widely reported in France and Britain, the coach then claimed several of his players reported feeling sick after the half-time break. Kostylev said, 'Something happened during the break. There must have been something wrong with the players' tea.'

Kostylev admitted he could not say for sure that the mystery callers were representatives of Marseille or hoaxers, but his comments seemed unequivocal enough. Which made it all the more surprising when, a few weeks later, UEFA announced they had been faxed a signed statement from Kostylev retracting his allegations that CSKA had been offered a bribe. Without the prime witness, the UEFA investigation came to nothing and, contrary to what many people think, Marseille were allowed to keep their European Cup. However, the following September, European football's governing body banned them from defending their title and from taking part in the Super Cup.

If Marseille *had* been stripped of their European title, runners-up AC Milan wanted to play the final again, this time against Rangers. Club president Silvio Berlusconi – a future Italian prime minister and himself no stranger to controversy – said they would rather contest a play-off than simply be handed the trophy. The idea generated great excitement among Rangers fans, but the club was less excited, choosing to wait until the final outcome before commenting.

Coincidentally CSKA had a recent history of being embroiled in a match-fixing scandal. On 24 November 1992, days before the Champions League campaign started, the club took out a full-page advert in a national newspaper to apologise for their part in a conspiracy to bribe. Former coach Pavel Sadyrine had lifted the lid on the corruption, after quitting the army club to take over as national coach. He was quoted as saying, 'When I was coach with CSKA, matches were fixed. The outcome was known before the first whistle.'

None of this proves that anything untoward happened in the Champions League matches but, to this day, many Rangers supporters believe there was something distinctly dodgy about the competition. The players prefer to reflect on how well they did rather than dwell on what might have been, as Dave McPherson explains:

Rather than looking back saying 'that should have been us in the final' because Marseille were cheats, I prefer to reflect on it fondly. Marseille had some quality players; we had a fantastic run and came very close to having a brilliant season on top of winning the treble. You could also look at it and say: even if they were cheating we came so close to toppling them.

The season was hugely successful domestically. It saw a fifth consecutive title delivered as part of the club's fifth treble. The league was won by a nine-point margin from Aberdeen and Rangers' unbeaten run in all competitions eventually stretched to forty-four games. Ibrox was a fortress, with Walter Smith's team going undefeated at home all season. Both the Scottish Cup and the League Cup were won with 2–1 wins over Aberdeen. Once again the Light Blues had proved too strong for the rest of Scottish football and their performance in the European Cup showed they were also the best in Britain. Now Smith hoped to build on the success in Europe by landing the ultimate prize.

20

October 1995: Torture in Turin

After the previous season's heroics, hopes were high that Rangers could go even further in the Champions League of 1993/94, and perhaps even win it. But as so often with Rangers in Europe, reality soon reared its ugly head. A first-round draw against Bulgarian champions Levski Sofia should have posed few problems for a team that had been strengthened over the summer with the £3.75 million purchase of Dundee United striker Duncan Ferguson, one of the most promising Scottish talents of his generation, although a player who seemed to be a magnet for trouble on and off the field.

At Ibrox, Rangers swept into a two-goal lead through Dave McPherson and Mark Hateley and looked comfortable until a dramatic closing spell when the roof fell in. With eleven minutes to go Levski substitute Georgi Ivanov sent in a near-post cross which Borimirov managed to head past Rangers goalkeeper Ally Maxwell, who had replaced the injured Goram. A minute later, Rangers extended their lead through a Mark Hateley header and that should have been that but Rangers contrived to lose another goal with five minutes left. The narrow win, and the loss of two home goals, meant what should have been a routine second leg was now fraught with danger, for the players and the fans.

Stevie Tyrie and four pals from Ayrshire set off in high spirits at 10 p.m. on the Saturday before the match, which was on the Wednesday night. They were booked with the Kinning Park Loyal, one of only two buses that were running to the game. The privations they endured in getting to Sofia shows the lengths to which Rangers fans will go to support the team they love:

I don't think anybody fully appreciated just how far it was we had to travel to be honest. Nothing of any great note happened until we arrived in Vienna early on the Monday morning. That was when a few of us began to question the wisdom of undertaking so long a bus journey. Anxious to get a wash and something substantial to eat, the company I was with decided to get off the bus. So, at five o'clock on a Monday morning, five of us were traipsing the streets of the Austrian capital without a word of German between us. Unsurprisingly, no shops were open. We then decided – getting desperate to get cleaned up – to offer to pay a hotel for the use of a room for one night if we could use the shower in a room for the length of time it would take the five of us to get a wash. Three hours of trying this at every hotel we came to got us nowhere.

By this time desperation was kicking in:

It was rush hour so the subway stations were open and we ended up in one of them looking for the toilet. With them having sinks and the like we all began to strip, desperate to be rid of the clothes we'd been wearing on a smelly bus for thirty hours. Then, as best we could, we began to wash using the sinks, beginning to feel a wee bit human again. But then in stormed a massive woman – a Mutha Bacon type – and threw our bags out into the platform and chased us all out of the toilet. What a sight! Five semi-naked Scots covered in soap in full view of the Viennese rush hour! Not my shining moment. Trying to walk away with what dignity we could muster we got sort of dressed and ended up at about nine in the morning on the streets again. The bus wasn't due to leave till three.

However, the problems were only just beginning for the intrepid travellers. After a day spent downing schnapps in a bar, they made it back to their bus and set off for Sofia:

At that time the borders in Eastern Europe were a nightmare to get through and we got held up at the border between Hungary and Romania for ages before we were allowed to pass thanks to bribes of warm Tennent's Lager and a couple of Rangers scarves. The journey through Romania was a real eye-opener with folk using horses and carts on the motorways and so on. On the bus it was becoming unbearable. It was now early Tuesday morning and we had spent over forty-eight hours on board. Imagine what that was like with fifty drunks on it.

Tuesday morning brought another border crossing, between Romania and Bulgaria:

The mood began to lighten a wee bit as we could see signs for the place we were travelling to. As we got to the border a few folk got off the bus for a bit of fresh air. My wee mate said: 'There's no point getting off; we'll be moving in five minutes.' Those five minutes developed into nine hours before we were allowed to move. There were no shops, pubs or anything to fill the time in. Nobody had any Romanian money anyway. One guy – who had begun the journey with twelve bottles of QC sherry for his carry-out – did a big of haggling and swapped one of them for a bottle of coke with some wee street trader. Come the time we eventually got through to say the mood was a bit tense doesn't really do it justice. Bar a few hours in Vienna we'd been on the bus since ten on Saturday night and, to be frank, I was feeling on the verge of suicidal. It's a feeling I can't do justice to in words. I've never felt as uncomfortable in my life. Can you imagine what the bus was like?

On the day of the game they quaffed thirty-pence bottles of wine while trying to avoid the attentions of the Sofia police, who were on a knife-edge throughout the day. They then got a taxi to the ground, three hours before kick-off, but even that brought problems: 'Some of our crowd got a crook who drove them around for three hours before getting them to the stadium just in time for kick-off and demanding an exorbitant fare.'

The dividing line between success and failure in football can be ridiculously fine at times. In Sofia, Rangers were seconds away from progressing to the next round of the European Cup only to see their hopes dashed in the most extraordinary fashion. The Scots had controlled the first half, even though Levski scored in the thirty-sixth minute through their captain Nasko Sirakov. Seven minutes later, European specialist Ian Durrant equalized, heading home a long diagonal cross from Gary Stevens, before crashing into the advertising boards behind the goal.

Having been in control throughout the first half, Rangers seemed to go into their shell after the interval, inviting the Bulgarians to come at them. For all that they had to rely on desperate defending, and at times superb goalkeeping from Ally Maxwell, Rangers seemed to have weathered the storm and almost scored a clincher when a McPherson header was saved with fifteen minutes to go.

As the clock ticked down, Rangers were content to knock the ball around and the fans were already celebrating. Then, in injury time, Nikolai Todorov picked the ball up thirty yards from goal. With the referee poised to blow for full time, it was obvious that Todorov's only thought was to unleash a last, desperate shot. Ian Ferguson recalled in his autobiography how he said to himself, 'Go on shoot!' as the Levski player lined it up, so confident was he that the effort would come to nothing. Unfortunately for Rangers, it was a once-in-a-lifetime shot that rocketed past Maxwell and into the net.

The devastated Rangers players sank to their knees in anguish. There was no time to come back and after going so close to reaching the European Cup final the season before, this time they had stumbled at the first hurdle. Ferguson described the defeat on away goals as 'a nasty blow'. This was a serious understatement. The official flight back to Glasgow in the early hours of the morning resembled a wake as the players came to terms with what had happened.

For the fans, there was the depressing prospect of a two-thousand-mile coach trip. Stevie Tyrie vividly summed up their mood:

> We stood in the pissing rain watching Rangers go out to a last-minute fluke. The thought of the bus journey home on top of that was possibly the most depressing moment of my time as a Rangers supporter. With regard to the police being on a knife-edge, one of the guys came back on the bus covered in blood. He'd been battered senseless and he had to fly home. He spent ages in a hospital and I think he almost lost the sight in one eye because of it.

If it was possible the journey home was even worse than the outward trip because of the result. After more border delays and a minor road crash in Romania they finally arrived back in Glasgow at eleven on the Saturday morning, a full week after they'd left.

Walter Smith blamed the defeat squarely on the two sloppy goals that had been conceded in the later stages of the first leg at Ibrox. 'You always know that away goals in Europe can kill you, and that's what happened,' he said. As well as the loss of prestige that followed an early exit, the defeat was costly in financial terms. The Champions League format was already proving lucrative and Rangers had raked in an estimated £5 million from their ten-game unbeaten run in 1992/93.

Despite a horrendous injury list that lasted throughout the season, Rangers once again dominated domestically, winning the title by three points from Aberdeen. Motherwell were the unexpected challengers and they finished third ahead of Celtic. The Parkhead club hadn't finished in the top two since their title win in 1988 and were going through a period of turmoil that made Rangers' dark days of the early eighties pale into insignificance.

Although it hadn't been a vintage season in terms of the quality of football, the delivery of the sixth consecutive title to Ibrox was warmly welcomed, and thoughts were beginning to turn to Celtic's record of nine titles in a row.

The only black spot on the 1993/94 season was the Scottish Cup final, when Rangers could have won a second consecutive treble, only to lose to Dundee United through a farcical goal scored by Craig Brewster after calamitous defending.

Smith strengthened the squad again in the summer, bringing in brilliant Danish winger Brian Laudrup and Marseille's European Cup winner Basile Boli for a total of more than £5 million. While Laudrup would go on to achieve legendary status at Ibrox, Boli lasted only one season.

The following season, 1994/95, saw the Champions Cup undergoing another change of format; it was yet again designed by UEFA to quell a breakaway threat by the Continent's richest clubs. The new system would see the holders and the top seven seeds automatically qualify for the group stage, with those ranked between eight and twenty-three taking part in a preliminary round to establish the other eight qualifiers.

The immediate impact of these changes on Rangers was a preliminary-round tie with Greek champions AEK Athens on 10 August, three days *before* the opening Premier League fixture. Yet with the arrival of Laudrup and Boli the Rangers fans felt they had every chance of making a mark. It was the first time Rangers had faced a Greek team in a competitive match and it was an experience that they would not want to repeat in a hurry . . . for a host of reasons.

The trip got off to a bad start when the official charter flight was held up. After a three-hour delay at Glasgow airport the squad finally departed for Athens, but were kept on the tarmac for twenty minutes after landing because of a power failure in the terminal building. When they eventually passed through the airport the players were met by a hysterical local media pack, thrusting cameras and microphones in their faces.

It was an exhausted Rangers party that finally checked in to their hotel in the Greek capital at 11 p.m. local time. Temperatures in Athens in early August were soaring into the nineties and even late at night the heat was incredibly uncomfortable, a fact that didn't improve the players' mood.

On the night of the match, the Rangers players were greeted at the Nikos Goumas stadium by the sight of forty riot police trying to hold back a baying mob of AEK fans. Missiles were hurled at the team bus as it pulled up outside and one bottle smashed on the windscreen. More bottles were thrown at the players as they entered the stadium, with one narrowly missing Ian Durrant.

The hostile welcome was not unusual. AEK fans had a long history of such behaviour and they revelled in their intimidating image. The club had been banned from Europe for a year following trouble in a home tie against

Marseille in 1989 but the punishment apparently had little effect. Inside the ground, extra riot police were drafted in to keep the Greeks away from the one thousand travelling supporters but they did little to prevent the hail of missiles that rained on the bluenoses throughout the match. Shortly before kick-off, a lit firecracker was thrown toward the Rangers section, missing the fans but setting a banner on fire. Then, during the first half, more flares were launched at the Rangers end. A bottle thrown by a Greek fan also struck Scottish Television reporter Jim Delahunt and a cameraman and press photographer were also hit. The £25,000 fine that was later imposed hardly seemed to fit the crime.

After the game the Rangers supporters were held in the stadium for more than an hour in a bid to allow the AEK hooligans to disperse but when the Scots were eventually allowed to leave they found that there were gangs lying in wait. At least one group of fans was set upon and suffered serious injuries, with one Scot receiving stitches for a leg wound after being stabbed with a broken bottle.

Another supporter who was in the ground recalled:

> For the whole ninety minutes we were coming under fire with all sorts of missiles and flares and frankly the police did nothing to prevent it. If this had happened in Scotland you can be sure that there would be parliamentary inquiries and demands for stadiums to be closed down but over there it just seemed to be tolerated. I've been all over Europe with Rangers to some scary places but I'd never go back there. In fact I'd never even go to Greece on holiday.

If the Rangers travelling supporters were having a hard time of it, so to were the players. Having watched his team struggle through the pre-season, Walter Smith surprised everyone, including the players, by adopting what was billed as a 3-5-2 formation but in reality was more 5-3-2. Richard Gough, Gary Stevens and youngster Steven Pressley were deployed as a three-man central defence, with Neil Murray and David Robertson pushing into wide midfield roles.

The fact that the tactic had never been deployed before showed, and Rangers were in disarray as the Greeks ripped them apart. Finally, their pressure paid off in injury time at the end of the first half, when Murray was caught in possession and the ball was worked through to Dimitrios Saravakos who hit an unstoppable shot past Andy Goram. The veteran Greek international scored a second in the seventieth minute. Rangers were played off the park, and in the end, it was amazing that the game ended only 2–0.

Walter Smith accepted the blame for the performance in Athens, which was at times shambolic. He admitted he had taken a chance with the new formation and conceded it had not worked out, the change in tactics contributing to several mix-ups, especially in the first half. Undoubtedly, the fact that the domestic season had not yet kicked-off also contributed to the ragged performance, but the same applied to AEK.

To cap a depressing trip, the Rangers party suffered more delays on the way home. Having switched companies following the delays on the outward journey, a starting motor on their Boeing 737 failed and after a three-hour wait at Athens, the team was forced to change planes, eventually arriving home at 6.35 in the morning. Ally McCoist, a substitute in Athens, told anyone who would listen, 'I'm officially knackered.'

A minor miracle would be required at Ibrox if Rangers were to make it through to the Champions League group stages alongside AC Milan, Ajax and Salzburg of Austria. Smith again threw up a surprise when he played Basile Boli at right back and in attack he deployed Mark Hateley and Duncan Ferguson, both target men with a similar style. As a result, Rangers resorted to booting high balls to the pair for most of the match. Brian Laudrup, in only his fourth game, was a major disappointment, with many of his passes and crosses going astray.

Rangers suffered the inevitable killer blow shortly before half-time, when Toni Savevski met a cross and swept the ball past Andy Goram. Four goals were now required, but Rangers never looked likely to score even one, and so it turned out.

The AEK fans voted the victory as their best match of the season, but for Rangers it meant an exit in one of the early rounds of the European Cup for the fifth time in six seasons. It was also the first of three consecutive home defeats, which some Rangers fans to this day believe should have led to the dismissal of Smith. The following weekend, Celtic, led by new manager Tommy Burns, won 2–0 at Ibrox, then in midweek, Rangers were knocked out of the League Cup by Premier League newcomers Falkirk.

A troubled week culminated in a French newspaper interview with Basile Boli, in which he appeared to criticise the professionalism of his teammates and Walter Smith. Boli seemed certain to be fired after the comments were widely reported in Scottish newspapers. His criticism centred on the decision to play Hateley and Ferguson together and he also appeared to condemn his teammates for their attitude.

'You cannot go about winning such an important game when you are having a laugh in the dressing room half an hour before the match,' he was reported as saying. Such comments were sure to go down like a lead balloon among his colleagues, as Smith had cultivated a squad that was renowned for exactly such behaviour. In many people's eyes, it was the togetherness of that team rather than technical ability that drove them to success, at least on the home front.

Predictably, following showdown talks, Boli was cleared of any wrong-doing and the blame was shifted onto a mistranslation of the original interview. As more foreigners came into the Scottish game, this pattern would be repeated on umpteen occasions. Whether Boli was misquoted or not, elements of what he was reputed to have said struck a chord with the fans. The 1992/93 season apart, Rangers had failed to achieve anywhere near the level of performance expected in Europe during the previous decade given the amount of money invested.

In fact, since the arrival of Graeme Souness in the spring of 1986, Borussia Moenchengladbach, Steaua Bucharest, Cologne, Bayern Munich, Red Star Belgrade, Sparta Prague, Levski Sofia and AEK had eliminated Rangers from Europe in the knockout stages. Despite the mounting pressure for action, David Murray gave his firm backing to Smith and his support soon appeared to be well placed. Rangers managed to recover from the disastrous start to the season and went on to secure another league title. Brian Laudrup was outstanding; his close control, pace and vision helped drive Rangers to a fifteen-game unbeaten run that laid the groundwork for the championship. In the end, Rangers finished fifteen points ahead of Motherwell, who were managed by former Aberdeen defender Alex McLeish.

The domestic dominance only served to highlight Rangers' poor European record. For all Murray's support, the general view was that another failure in the European Cup could not be tolerated. The investment in the summer of 1995 was once again significant, with the signing of Russian striker Oleg Salenko, Serbian defender Gordan Petric and Scotland right back Stephen Wright. However, it was the spectacular £4 million capture of Paul Gascoigne from Italian club Lazio that captured the imagination of the support.

Gazza, the most talented English player of his generation, arrived in a blaze of publicity and was greeted by thousands of fans outside Ibrox. Scottish football had never seen anything like it. Ever since his rise to super-stardom during the 1990 World Cup, Gascoigne's every move had been splashed all over the English newspapers, and not just the tabloids. His arrival back in Britain after an ill-fated and injury-blighted spell in Italy sparked media hysteria and brought Rangers Britain-wide coverage that they hadn't enjoyed since the arrival of Souness and Butcher almost ten years earlier.

But for all the stories about Gazza's haircuts and suits, his worth would be judged by his performances on the pitch, particularly on the European stage. In the final analysis, the verdict must be that he never scaled the heights expected of him in the Champions League. His first test was a European Cup preliminary-round tie with Cypriot champions Anorthosis Famagusta. On the surface it was a favourable draw, but closer analysis revealed the tie to be another potential banana skin. Like the previous season, the games would be played in early August when Mediterranean temperatures are at their highest and the Ibrox men were certain to get a hostile reception from the Anorthosis fans. The ties would take place before the start of the league season, meaning Rangers' new players would have little time to gel.

Perhaps just as worrying for Walter Smith was the fact that Georghi Vassiliev, who had led Levski Sofia to their unexpected victory over Rangers in 1993, was now the coach at Anorthosis. And to complete the bad omens, Nicolai Todorov, who scored the 'once-in-a-lifetime' goal that eliminated the Scots in the dying seconds of that game, was one of three Bulgarians in the Famagusta midfield.

A Gordon Durie goal gave Rangers a 1–0 victory at Ibrox in the first leg after a less than impressive display, in which Gascoigne's threat was largely nullified by the tough-tackling Bulgarian, Ilian Kiriakov. Nevertheless, Rangers had survived without conceding an away goal, something that hadn't looked certain at points during the match. In the second leg at the Antonis Papadopolous stadium in Larnaca, the 'Welcome to Hell' banners were out in force. The ground's official capacity was only 9,000 but Rangers fans estimated there must have been at least another 3,000 inside and they generated a tremendous, if intimidating, atmosphere.

With Laudrup missing through injury, an injury to Gascoigne in the twenty-fifth minute was a blow, and the player himself took it badly, bursting into tears in typical Gazza fashion as he left the pitch. But on a tense night, his teammates did enough to get a no-score draw, which took them into the group stages for the second time. Gazza's tears were a distant memory as he joined the rest of the team on the park to celebrate at full time in front of the 1,500 jubilant Rangers fans. The players were reportedly on a bonus of £25,000 each to qualify, but that would have been far from their thoughts as they saluted the supporters.

In financial terms the group stage of the 1995/96 Champions League was the promised land, but it was anything but utopia for Rangers. Drawn in Group C along with tournament favourites Juventus, German champions Borussia Dortmund and old adversaries Steaua Bucharest, it was always going to be a tough prospect to qualify for the quarter-final. Juve, with players like Paulo Sousa, Didier Deschamps, Fabrizio Ravanelli, Gianluca

Vialli and Alessandro Del Piero, were the obvious favourites to win the group. Dortmund coach Ottmar Hitzfeld had moulded an impressive team with a host of familiar names that included Jurgen Kohler, Patrik Berger, Andreas Moller, Steffen Freund, Stefen Reuter, Matthias Sammer, Stepahne Chapuisat, Karl-Heinz Riedle and Ruben Sosa. In goal was Stefan Klos, a player who would soon become very familiar to Rangers fans.

The Romanians also had a future Ibrox employee in their ranks, although central defender Daniel Prodan could hardly be classed as a Rangers player. Signed by Dick Advocaat in 1998, he never played a competitive game for the club, one of many expensive signings in the 1990s whose time at Ibrox was blighted by injury. The Romanians saw Rangers as the weakest team in the group, while the Scots held a similar view of Steaua. The two met in the opening game in Bucharest and Rangers needed at least a draw if they were to have a realistic chance of progressing. Walter Smith adopted a cautious, some say negative, approach, clearly setting out to achieve that single point. Despite the dismissal of Alan McLaren for an off-the-ball incident midway through the second half, the approach seemed to have worked. But playing for a draw is always a risky tactic and with eight minutes to go Prodan proved the point, sending a left-foot volley rocketing past Goram. It was too late for Rangers to come back, and the 1–0 defeat meant they were immediately under pressure in the group.

Rangers were unlucky to lose in Bucharest, but the defeat meant victory was imperative against Borussia Dortmund at Ibrox. The Germans had been beaten by Juventus at home in their opener and had never beaten the Scots in their four previous meetings. Rangers took the game to Dortmund but, in typical fashion, went behind to a counter-attack in the eighteenth minute when Herrlich headed home a cross from Reuter. Gascoigne was having one of his best games since joining Rangers and provided the cross for Richard Gough's headed equalizer seventeen minutes into the second half. By this time Rangers had already lost Brian Laudrup to injury and he was to miss the next two months as a result. The Germans went back in front seven minutes later through Martin Kree, but Rangers levelled again when substitute Ian Ferguson diverted a Gascoigne shot past Klos. It was an exciting game; one which Rangers might easily have won.

Disappointingly only 33,000 turned out, 10,000 less than had been at the qualifier against Famagusta. The poor attendance was due to a controversial ticketing policy, which saw the cheapest three-match packages being sold for more than £80. At approaching £30 per game, many Rangers fans felt they were being fleeced and simply refused to fork out. The banks of empty blue seats told their own story and forced a rethink in future competitions.

If Rangers felt unlucky to have taken only one point from their first two games, they had few complaints after the third match against Juventus in the Stadio delle Alpi on 18 October 1995. The Italians tore Rangers apart, and raced into a three-goal lead after just twenty-three minutes. The goals came from Ravanelli, Conte and Del Piero, the latter marking a phenomenal individual performance with a thirty-yard free kick. Had Juve not eased up it could easily have turned into a humiliation on a par with those suffered in the 1960s against Eintracht Frankfurt and Real Madrid. In the end, the Italians scored just once more through Ravanelli, and Richard Gough got a late consolation.

For the Rangers fans who had travelled to Turin – and endured the shower of coins and bottles of urine that were hurled on them in the stadium – the 4–1 loss was painful viewing, particularly the contest between Del Piero and Rangers defender Alex Cleland. The Italian forward tormented the young Scot, including one turn that left a baffled Cleland swinging at mid-air as Del Piero headed off in the opposite direction. Later, in a fit of pique, an embarrassed Cleland made a wild lunge at Del Piero and, although no contact was made, he was rightly shown a straight red card. As he left the field, Ravanelli approached Cleland and patted him on the head, apparently in sympathy. But the gesture wasn't quite what it seemed to the 50,000 in the stadium and the millions watching at home. Rather than offering support, the Italian was actually trying to rile the player into lashing out again by nipping him in the back of the neck.

The game haunted Cleland – a Glasgow lad who attended Bannerman High School in the east of the city – for the rest of his career and even today he suffers jibes about the night he was skinned by Del Piero. In his new life as a coach, he still has young players coming up to him saying, 'My dad told me to ask you about Del Piero.' As irritating as it must be, he can at least point to the fact that his career allowed him to face one of the greatest players in the world on the biggest stage of them all.

In the return match, Rangers gave a better account of themselves but the outcome was the same; a comprehensive defeat. Juve were a goal up at half-time and added a second after the break. Billy Thomson had been brought on at the interval to replace the injured Andy Goram but he could do little to prevent the Turin giants scoring another two goals late on. The four-goal margin was misleading, but Rangers were well beaten in both games against Juventus, and it highlighted just how far behind the big guns the Scottish champions were.

The chances of Rangers progressing were already distant and after the fourth game they disappeared completely. A 1–1 home draw against Steaua

– featuring a brilliant solo goal from Paul Gascoigne in which he ran half the length of the pitch – coupled with a Dortmund victory over an under-strength Juventus in Turin, meant Rangers were out.

The final fixture against Borussia in the Westfalen was meaningless, but Rangers put on a good performance in Germany, extending their unbeaten run against the hosts to six games. In bitter, sub-zero temperatures Rangers took the lead in the tenth minute through Brian Laudrup and although Moller and Riedle gave Dortmund the lead, Gordon Durie equalized near the end. The game was marred by a pointless red card for Paul Gascoigne who was given a second yellow for arguing with the referee over a penalty claim.

His sending-off ensured he would be missing for the first two European matches of the 1996/97 season and, with Rangers having seen off the challenge of Celtic in the Premier League again, this meant Gascoigne would be unavailable for the Champions League qualifiers.

One piece of good news for Walter Smith later in the season came in the unlikely form of a ruling in the European Court of Justice. A previously unheralded Belgian player by the name of Jean-Marc Bosman had taken action against his club Liege for preventing him from moving to another team at the end of his contract. The court ruled that the existing transfer system was a restriction of the free movement of workers within the European Union. The main effect was that players would be allowed to move to any club they chose at the end of their contract, with no transfer fee being paid. But the ruling also ended UEFA's controls on the nationality of players in European competition, bringing to an end the three-foreigner rule. As a result, Rangers were no longer restricted in their transfer dealings and were able to pick their strongest team, regardless of nationality.

The question was whether this would improve the chances of Rangers fulfilling their European potential.

21

Agony in Amsterdam

It is one of the joys of football that every so often it can throw up something so unlikely that it takes everyone by surprise. Few Rangers fans would have been particularly confident of progression after being drawn against the Russian league winners in the qualifying round of the 1996/97 European Cup. Halfway through the first leg at Ibrox, Rangers were a goal behind to a team in the middle of their league season and staring an early exit in the face. At that stage, the riches of the Champions League could not have been further away. Yet by the end of the second leg, not only had Rangers qualified but also they had achieved one of their biggest victories in Europe.

Alania Vladikavkaz were obscure even within their own borders before the break-up of the Soviet Union in the early 1990s. But the creation of the Russian Premier League brought the team from the tiny, remote republic of Northern Ossetia to national prominence. Former Dynamo Moscow coach Valeri Gazzaev took the club, then known as Spartak Vladikavkaz, into Europe for the first time in 1994 and they competed well, losing by a single goal to Borussia Dortmund. The following season they were knocked out of the UEFA Cup by Liverpool as they pipped Spartak Moscow to the title.

Once again the first leg was played before the start of the Scottish season and Rangers looked ill-prepared in a nervy opening period. Alania had a string of first-half chances and forced Andy Goram into a number of saves before finally getting the opening goal. At half-time the prospects for Rangers looked bleak, but they managed a rousing comeback in the second half, inspired by Brian Laudrup.

Derek McInnes, a fringe player signed from Greenock Morton during the previous season, scored the equalizer with a drive from the edge of the penalty area. After constant pressure and a string of missed chances, Ally

McCoist added a second. He had finally managed to beat the long-standing European scoring record of twelve goals he jointly held with Ralph Brand and Jimmy Millar. Surprisingly, McCoist had not found the net in Europe since the second leg of the Leeds United game in 1992.

Gordan Petric celebrated scoring the third goal – a powerful header after a cross from Derek McInnes – by sprinting towards the centre circle and swinging his top round his head. Predictably he was shown a yellow card for his troubles. In the closing moments Alania were handed a glorious chance to narrow the gap when Andy Goram inexplicably charged out of his goal and floored an attacker who was heading nowhere. The goalkeeper dived the wrong way for the penalty, but, thankfully, Yanovski's shot went wide. As it was, a 3–1 lead was hardly comfortable and most observers felt Rangers would struggle to qualify.

The city of Vladikavkaz is more than a thousand miles from Moscow and is not the sort of place that receives many Western visitors. Nestling in the foothills of the Caucasus mountains, the city lies just over sixty miles from the war-ravaged Chechen capital of Grozny. Known as Ordzhonikidze during the Soviet era, it reverted to its original name after the fall of the communist regime. It was the most easterly point reached by the Nazis during the war before they were defeated trying to seize the city. Rangers had to make their trip by a small, chartered jet in two stages, stopping overnight in Vienna before a four-hour final leg to Ossetia. The Rangers plane, loaded with supplies of food and drink, landed on a bumpy runway at a remote military airstrip. When they arrived in Vladikavkaz they found themselves in a hotel with no toilet seats and water that ran only intermittently. The players had even been advised to bring their own bed linen.

For the fans the journey was even more troublesome. A party of around forty paid upwards of £1,000 each to fly to Vladikavkaz. A few other hardy souls made a two-day journey by train across Europe. The British travellers were advised by their doctors to have a course of inoculations for diptheria, tetanus and polio and they set off in the knowledge that nightlife in the city was 'virtually non-existent' and with the chilling words of the Foreign Office ringing in their ears. 'Violent mugging, theft and pick-pocketing occur. Do not accept food or drink from strangers, as it may be drugged. Use officially marked taxis and do not share them with strangers.'

With only one hotel in town, the Rangers supporters mingled with the players before the match and shared tales of their journey before being nourished with hot food by Rangers catering boss Peter Kingstone. Midfielder Derek McInnes said later, 'More than anything you felt you had to get a result for diehards like that.'

Given the conditions, Rangers would have been happy to scrape through with a no-score draw or even a 1–0 defeat, but no-one expected what followed. With just thirty-six seconds on the clock, Rangers took the lead through Ally McCoist. He followed that up with a quick-fire double to secure his first European hat-trick. It wasn't all one-way traffic in the first half, though. Alania scored between McCoist's second and third goals and they pulled another back in the twenty-third minute from the penalty spot. But any doubts over the outcome were quickly dispelled as Dutch winger Peter Van Vossen rounded the keeper and added a fourth before half-time.

In the second half, Brian Laudrup broke down the left onto a pass from Van Vossen and ignored the screams from an unmarked Ally McCoist in the centre; the Dane then lashed the ball into the net. Laudrup added a sixth and could have claimed a hat-trick of his own near the end but unselfishly fed Charlie Miller, who finished off a remarkable 7–2 win. Walter Smith described the second half of the first leg and the first half of the second leg as the best ninety minutes of his time at Ibrox. A 10–3 aggregate victory over the Russian champions was quite stunning, and when it is considered that seven of those goals were scored in one of football's most inhospitable outposts the performance was all the more impressive.

It was hoped that the result in Russia would make the rest of Europe sit up and take notice, but even more importantly the support was hoping it would pave the way for real progress in the Champions League. The draw for the group stages could have been much worse. Rangers were drawn against the previous season's runners-up Ajax, who were the clear favourites to go through. Most expected Rangers and French champions Auxerre to fight it out for second place, with Swiss side Grasshoppers Zurich the predicted whipping boys.

Having added German midfielder Jorg Albertz and Sweden international defender Joachim Bjorklund to their star-studded roster Rangers fans believed they had a squad capable of progressing from this group, one of the weakest in the competition. In the end, the campaign was another embarrassment. The opening game saw Rangers travel to Zurich to face the Swiss champions. It was a game that Rangers were capable of winning but they were comprehensively thrashed, and then ridiculed, by their opponents.

Before the game, Grasshoppers coach Christian Gross had described Rangers as 'one of the best sides in Europe' and tipped them to finish top of the group. But after seeing his team beat the Scots 3–0 he said he knew that the Ibrox side were not up for the match a full twenty-four hours before kick-off: 'I saw Rangers train on Tuesday and left feeling sure they had come here on their holiday. They believed they would leave Zurich with the three points without any problems.' Swiss international striker Kubilay Turkyilmaz, who scored twice and made the first goal for Murat Yakin, joined in the gloating. 'I think Rangers underestimated us and came here for a holiday.' And Grasshoppers captain Mats Gren added, 'They didn't take us seriously. In the Champions League you cannot underestimate any of the opposition. But Rangers came here thinking they would get the three points and then head home to Glasgow without any problems.'

It had been a woefully inept performance by Rangers, who started the game poorly and never recovered. Big-name players like Laudrup and Gascoigne came in for severe criticism, with only Andy Goram emerging with any credit after making two saves to keep the score close to respectable. Walter Smith was clearly stung by what he called 'smart-arse' comments from the Swiss and he immediately banned his squad from making any media appearances for a month in a bid to concentrate their minds. Unsurprisingly, Gascoigne was the first to be affected when he was prevented from appearing on the terminally unfunny television show, *They Think It's All Over*. Instead he asked his best friend Jimmy 'Five Bellies' Gardner to take his place. After his performance in Zurich, some Rangers fans might have suggested Gardner could have taken his place in the Ibrox midfield.

French champions Auxerre, who had been coached by the eccentric Guy Roux for thirty-five years, were the next opponents at Ibrox. Although prices had been reduced by an average of 14 per cent from the previous year, the dismal start against Grasshoppers, coupled with live television coverage, meant that ticket sales were still slow. In the end just 37,000 tickets were sold, although it was a trend that was repeated across Europe and perhaps an indication that the Champions League format was not as popular with the fans as UEFA liked to think.

As usual the pre-match focus was on whether Laudrup and Gascoigne would perform to the level expected of them. The England international was making his fiftieth appearance for Rangers, but although he had been named Scotland's player of the year, and had secured the championship with a virtuoso performance on the last day of his first season, he had not proved his worth in Europe. Both Gascoigne and Laudrup actually played quite well against Auxerre, but were let down by their defensive colleagues. Two headed goals from stand-in striker Thomas Deniaud meant Gazza's late header from a Laudrup cross was no more than a consolation. Deniaud, a 25-year-old who was brought in at the last minute for the injured Lilian Laslandes, had never scored for Auxerre before and had been farmed out on loan to a second-division club. He confessed afterwards, 'When I stepped out at Ibrox I was trembling because I have never played in a stadium like that before.' Rangers had dominated the game but failed to capitalise on their possession and were caught napping twice at set pieces. It was the tenth Champions League game in row that Rangers had failed to win, their last victory coming in 1993 against Bruges.

Only victories over Ajax in their next two games would give Rangers any chance of qualifying from the group. The Dutch giants had not enjoyed the best of starts to their domestic season, and had unexpectedly lost to Grasshoppers in Amsterdam, so a Rangers win was by no means impossible. Ajax also had injury problems and were missing striker Patrick Kluivert. Nevertheless, the team still included names like Edwin Van Der Sar, Frank and Ronald De Boer, Winston Bogarde, Marc Overmars and Dani and, in the event, Rangers were embarrassed once again. In a match that at times resembled the previous season's hammering by Juventus, the Scots were soundly beaten 4–1.

It was another devastating European defeat, but it was overshadowed by yet more unsavoury twists in the Paul Gascoigne soap opera. With the original James Bond, Sean Connery, watching from the stands as a guest of Rangers chairman David Murray, Gascoigne was red-carded in the twenty-eighth minute for petulantly kicking out at Ajax midfielder Bogarde.

Thanks to a lengthy injury list, Rangers were already under-strength and a goal behind when the red mist descended and the rest of the team did not appreciate his actions. Interviewed on television shortly after the match, Richard Gough revealed how Gascoigne had incurred the wrath of his teammates. 'We are disappointed with Gazza because the same thing happened in Dortmund last season,' he said. 'A few of us had a word with him and he knows himself – he's very upset.'

What his colleagues did not know was that Gascoigne was in the midst of turmoil in his personal life. However, like the rest of the country they were soon to find out. As the Rangers squad flew back from Amsterdam, the first editions of the *Daily Mirror* were hitting the news-stands with allegations that a drunken Gazza had beaten up his wife Sheryl at Gleneagles hotel in Perthshire.

The story had an instant impact, and brought huge amounts of bad publicity to the club. The allegations, coupled with the sending-off in the Amsterdam Arena and growing concerns over his drinking, put enormous pressure on Rangers to get rid of the player. The attack was said to have taken place on the Sunday night, the day before Rangers began their preparations for Amsterdam, and apart from the moral outrage at Gascoigne's actions there were concerns about his alcohol consumption. One senior Rangers official told the author the morning after the Ajax game, 'His future must be in serious doubt if the allegations are true. Domestic violence is unacceptable and apart from anything else a professional athlete should not have been drinking so much before a match of this importance.'

In the end Rangers weathered the storm and gave Gascoigne another chance. He was clearly a troubled individual and casting him into the wilderness at that stage could have had tragic consequences. On the other hand, his increasingly erratic behaviour was having a serious impact on the team. The player himself came out publicly and admitted he was 'a disgrace' and at an Ibrox press conference apologised to his manager and teammates for his red card. 'I took my domestic problem into the match,' he confessed.

Rangers had been allocated 2,200 tickets for the Amsterdam Arena, but undeterred by warnings about Ajax's hooligan followers several thousand more fans had travelled to Holland and had a trouble-free time. As the day of the match progressed, Dam Square filled up and became a sea of red, white and blue, while some of the unique Amsterdam attractions enjoyed a welcome boost. Bemused locals were also treated to the sight of an impromptu Orange Walk, complete with flute band, through the streets around the square.

Amsterdam was Stewart Walker's first trip abroad following Rangers and it was an eye-opener:

> The bus journey was an event in itself and by the time we got to the hotel all I wanted to do was go to my bed, but surprise, surprise it was straight down to the red-light district. One of the highlights was a live sex show featuring two female dwarves and a *very* large black man. I left when one of our bus was dragged onto the stage. I never did find out what happened but he was very quiet the next day.
>
> We spent most of the next day 'relaxing' in one of the coffee shops until we were dragged out onto the street to see a flute-band march past. It was one of the most bizarre things I have ever seen. There seemed to be thousands of folk walking behind them and the funny thing was that there were all these Dutch people and foreign tourists joining in. I've never really got into the whole Orange thing but it was a brilliant sight.

But the defeat was yet another kick in the teeth for the travelling fans who sang their hearts out throughout the match. They got some unexpected sympathy from Dutch legend Johan Cruyff: 'I was completely overwhelmed by the reaction of the Scottish supporters,' he said in an interview. 'The noise they made, even when their team was down 3–1, was quite incredible. They must be the best anywhere. It must be very hard for them that Rangers have not delivered in Europe. Frankly they deserve a better team than the one they've got.'

The red card and bookings for Gough, Alex Cleland and Craig Moore meant Walter Smith would be without four players due to suspension for the return game at Ibrox, before he even considered any injuries. It was a shadow Rangers team, including young defenders Scott Wilson and Greg Shields, that took on Ajax but they were unlucky to lose 1–0. Both Wilson and Shields played well against class opponents and looked to have promising careers ahead of them. In the next match against Grasshoppers, Rangers finally managed to end their twelve-game winless run in the Champions League with a 2–1 victory. It was a personal triumph for Ally McCoist, whose two goals were his first in the group stages after fourteen appearances. Against Auxerre, in the final game, normal service was resumed as the Scots went down 2–1, the Rangers goal coming from Richard Gough in his thirty-sixth and last appearance in Europe for the club.

The strips worn by Rangers against Auxerre provided a piece of trivia for football anoraks. A French ban on alcohol advertising meant the usual McEwan's Lager logo was banned, so instead the strips carried the name of holiday firm Center Parcs, which was owned by the same firm. The tops have since become collectors' items – as have the one-off, red Adidas strips, which were specially produced for the opening match against Grasshoppers because of a colour clash.

For the second year in a row Rangers had finished bottom of their Champions League group with just three points. However, as the domestic season progressed the disappointment of another failed European campaign was slowly forgotten. Rangers were on their way to a record-equalling ninth title in a row and it was duly achieved on a spring evening at Tannadice. Fittingly, Brian Laudrup, probably the best Rangers player of that era, headed the goal that won the title and allowed bluenoses everywhere finally to silence the taunts of their rivals across the city.

Some felt that equalling the record would allow Rangers to look at the bigger picture, rather than concentrating so heavily on the domestic scene. Real progress could be made in Europe, or so the theory went. But of course nine-in-a-row was not enough for the Rangers fans, who were desperate for ten to beat Celtic's record. And the theory unravelled somewhat as Rangers plumbed new depths, knocked-out of not one, but two, European competitions before Christmas.

Yet more tinkering with the rules of the European Cup by UEFA meant each of the Continent's top-eight nations were granted two slots, one for their league champions and one for the runners-up. It took the competition even further away from its original principles and left countries like Scotland lower down the pecking order.

Rangers – who had spent £15 million in the summer of 1997 on new players – found themselves having to play two qualifying rounds to even get into the group stage. The first match was in the remote Faroe Islands, a nation whose entire population could fit inside Ibrox with 7,000 seats to spare. Ally McCoist and Gordon Durie both scored twice and there was a fifth goal from one of the new signings Marco Negri on his competitive debut. McCoist's two goals set a new Scottish scoring record of twenty goals in Europe, overtaking Willie Wallace of Celtic. He added another in the home leg as Rangers ran out 6–0 winners, but it was to be his last in Europe for the club after fifteen seasons.

Although their opponents in the next qualifier were of a much higher standard it was assumed that Rangers, with their multi-national, multi-million pound, team would have little difficulty in dealing with IFK Gothenburg. Not for the first time, such confidence was misplaced.

The Swedish port of Gothenburg was basking in unusually high temperatures soaring into the eighties as Rangers arrived for the first leg. The party was minus Danish international Erik Bo Andersen who made the trip on his own by ferry from his home in Jutland after a £1 million move to French club Nantes collapsed at the last minute.

Rangers were said to be on £24,000-a-man to beat the Swedes and reach the Champions League and a deal thrashed out between new captain Brian Laudrup and David Murray would have provided each player with £6,000 per win in the group stages. But with Laudrup missing due to chicken pox, on a stiflingly hot evening, any chance of progression to the group stages all but disappeared in yet another awful performance. After a first half in which they were in control, Rangers collapsed in the second half. Goals from Stefan Pettersson, Par Karlsson and Peter Eriksson gave Gothenburg an unexpected 3–0 victory and condemned Rangers to one of their worst European defeats of all time.

Slack defensive play was blamed for the goals, but in reality it was the poor performance of the Rangers midfield of Jonas Thern, Jorg Albertz and Paul Gascoigne that caused most of the problems. The trio visibly wilted in the heat as the second half wore on. Thern later blamed the lack of organisation in midfield, claiming the players did not know what they should be doing. Gothenburg coach Mats Jingblad observed that Rangers didn't look fit in midfield and he also expressed his surprise at their defensive approach.

In the Swedish media there was widespread rejoicing at the result, coupled with heavy criticism of Rangers. *Goteborg Posten* columnist Jan Hansson argued that the IFK players deserved credit as the team was a shadow of those that had achieved great things for the club in the past. 'The team has been ripped apart by foreign clubs and injuries and put together again with

the help of second-stringers and players with little or no international experience,' he wrote. Hansson was also critical of Gascoigne, writing, 'He seems
to have lost ten kilos in weight, but he also has lost his creativity and ability to break a predictable pattern.' He could not understand why Walter
Smith let the Englishman 'lumber throughout the game'. *Aftonbladet*, the
leading Swedish daily, called the win a 'miracle' and was scathing of Rangers'
highly paid stars. The paper said, 'Absolutely none of these professionals
justified their high salaries'. Stockholm-based *Expressen*, carried the headline 'Goodnight, Glasgow'.

Despite the tie being virtually a lost cause, more than 45,000 turned out
at Ibrox hoping for a miracle. Brian Laudrup had recovered from illness but
was left on the bench and he watched on as Charlie Miller gave Rangers a
glimmer of hope with a twenty-third minute goal. Just as Smith was preparing to bring on Laudrup for a final assault, Gothenburg got the killer away
goal and the tie was over.

There was more criticism for Smith after the game both at home and
abroad. Former Sweden international striker Ralf Edstrom, who was working as a radio commentator, felt Laudrup should have been on from the
beginning. 'Smith's decision was unbelievable,' he said. 'If Laudrup was fit
to play a part, he should have started the game.' Edstrom also criticised
Gascoigne for being 'too fired up' and the Swedish paper *Expressen* accused
him of elbowing Stefan Pettersson in the back.

It was yet another undignified episode for Rangers and, given the contrast
in spending power, there was no doubt that the 4–1 aggregate defeat ranked
alongside some of the worst the club had suffered in Europe, including the
loss to Gornik Zabrze in 1967 that cost Davie White his job. Despite the
discontent being expressed by fans, David Murray insisted that the manager
would not be sacked and would only leave when Smith himself decided the
time was right.

Smith immediately had the chance partially to remedy the situation,
thanks to the latest UEFA wheeze. Teams that failed in the final qualifying
round for the Champions League now dropped into the UEFA Cup and
Rangers were drawn against the decidedly average French team Strasbourg.
Once again, the Scots were found seriously wanting.

In the first leg in France, Smith took a huge gamble by leaving eleven-
goal top scorer Marco Negri on the bench in favour of Gordon Durie.
Third-choice goalkeeper Theo Snelders had to be played because Goram and
Antti Niemi were out. Young Italian midfielder Rino Gattuso – who would
later win the Champions League with AC Milan and the 2006 World Cup
with Italy – made his European debut. After a reasonably comfortable first

half, Strasbourg took the lead a minute before the break from the penalty spot after Joachim Bjorklund fouled Baticle in the area. In the second half, Rangers fought back and got the reward of an away goal, also from a penalty; Albertz, who had been fouled, converted the spot kick. Remarkably, there was a third penalty; Baticle scoring again after a theatrical dive won him the kick. Although it had been far from the best Rangers performance, a 2–1 defeat on foreign soil is not a bad result.

But, in the return, in front of 40,000 at Ibrox, Rangers endured another disastrous night and crashed out of the UEFA Cup to a team lying just a point off the foot of the French League. An early Gattuso goal put Rangers on course but the technically superior Strasbourg players soon cancelled it out with goals either side of half-time, the second coming from Celtic target David Zitelli. Realising there was little sign of a comeback, even against ten men, the Rangers fans began streaming out of Ibrox with ten minutes to go. Many of those who stayed booed the players off the pitch and dozens of furious fans staged a demonstration outside the main entrance.

Soon after the defeat Smith announced he would be standing down as manager at the end of the ill-fated campaign to win a tenth league title in a row. Despite domestic dominance, it was a sad fact that Rangers had performed poorly in Europe for most of his tenure. Apart from the glorious 1992/93 Champions League campaign, and one or two good results, it was a decidedly undistinguished record.

Rangers had entered the European Cup seven times under Smith, qualifying for the group stages on three occasions. They had played thirty-eight games in all, winning fourteen and losing fifteen, although half of the victories had come in the first two seasons. In the remaining five seasons, Rangers won just one game in the Champions League, a virtually meaningless match against Grasshoppers. The other seven wins came in qualifiers, including two against Faroese part-timers and one against Levski that wasn't enough to see them go through.

In his defence, Smith could rightly point to the restrictions he had operated under. The three-foreigner rule had limited his team selections and there was no doubt that the step-up in class from playing in the Scottish league every Saturday was a large one. But with the money and players at his disposal Rangers under-achieved on the European stage. Nothing should detract from the achievement of winning nine league titles in a row, but the failure in Europe is a matter of some regret.

22

1998: The Coming of Advocaat

It was clear that a dramatic change in culture would be needed if Rangers were ever to compete at the highest level in Europe. It was with that in mind that David Murray recruited Dick Advocaat from PSV Eindhoven, to become the first foreign manager in Rangers' history. He was given two main tasks: regaining the Premier League title that had been lost to an average Celtic team the season before; and achieving credibility in Europe. The Dutchman was given even more money than Walter Smith and he set about creating a new team capable of competing on two fronts.

Advocaat's first competitive match in charge of Rangers was against Irish minnows Shelbourne in the preliminary round of the UEFA Cup in July 1998 and it almost ended in abject failure. Fears that the match would be blighted by crowd trouble led the authorities to sanction a change of venue away from Dublin. The first leg was moved across the Irish Sea to Merseyside and Prenton Park, the home of Tranmere Rovers. Around five thousand Rangers fans travelled from all over Scotland, England and Northern Ireland for the game, outnumbering the Shelbourne support by at least five-to-one at their 'home' match.

The buses set off in the early hours of the morning and by midday the pubs around Prenton Park were packed. Craig Stewart was picked up near his home in the West End of Glasgow just after eight in the morning and the supporters club mini-bus he was travelling with arrived on Merseyside at lunchtime:

> I was amazed by the numbers who were already there. The pubs were all busy
> and it was obvious lots of drink was going to be consumed before kick-off.

The atmosphere was pretty good although it wasn't really like a normal away European trip. Normally we would congregate somewhere central like a town square on the day of the game and would make that a base. This was totally different. We were basically roaming around a residential area all day and drinking in local pubs. The landlords were delighted because there was plenty of money being spent, but I would imagine the local residents would have suffered a bit of disruption. Not that there was any trouble. All day, the only thing I saw was a guy shinning up the flagpole in an attempt to get at the Irish tricolour that was flying over the ground.

Many of the Rangers fans had gathered in the Mersey Clipper pub; it was yards from the ground and had been serving alcohol to fans all day, as Stewart explains:

We went to a few of the pubs in the surrounding area, then settled on the one next to the ground. Inside it was really claustrophobic because it was so busy and the ceilings seemed really low. There was lots of singing but the mood did seem to have changed. It was far more tense, but there was nothing to suggest what would follow. After a while we moved to the tables they had outside to get some fresh air. Next thing we knew the riot police had suddenly appeared from nowhere and everyone was piling out of the pub.

The police, brandishing shields and batons, formed a barricade blocking entry to the ground. Seconds later a few idiots threw bottles at the officers and this prompted an aggressive response, with some indiscriminate swinging of batons in the direction of anyone within reach. Several innocent fans suffered bloody head injuries and others received bruising to the legs and body. As the police lashed out, more bottles were hurled. The *Evening Times* the next night reported fans complaining of brutal tactics from the riot police, a unit that had a reputation on Merseyside for heavy-handedness. Colin Wood, of Renfrew, told the paper, 'They were shouting and screaming. It was terrifying.' It emerged that the police had moved in after pub staff reported a fight between two fans but the suspicion among those caught up in the trouble was that they had been waiting for an excuse.

The events outside soured the atmosphere and by the time the match got underway it was poisonous inside Prenton Park. With the Rangers fans at one end of the ground and the small number of Irish at the opposite end, there was never any danger they would clash, but that didn't stop the taunts being hurled.

The mood of the Rangers supporters wasn't improved by what was happening on the pitch. With almost an hour of the match played, Rangers were heading for their most humiliating defeat of all time. After seven minutes, Sergio Porrini headed into his own net then, shortly before half-time, goal-keeper Antti Niemi flapped at a corner and a Shelbourne forward doubled their lead. On fifty-eight minutes Morley scored a third for the Dubliners and it looked like a disaster was on the cards. Then came the fight back, prompted by the introduction of substitute Jonatan Johansson. Almost immediately after the third goal, Jorg Albertz scored from the penalty spot after a handball. Amato then pulled a second back, before Dutch midfielder Giovanni van Bronckhorst equalized. With eight minutes to go, Amato headed Rangers into the lead and Albertz added a fifth with another penalty. It was an incredible comeback and had transformed the mood of the crowd, easing any fears of more trouble.

On the way back to Glasgow, Craig Stewart's bus made an unscheduled detour to Blackpool. Considering it was now approaching midnight, and he was supposed to be at work in eight hours, the plan to visit a well-known Scottish pub in the resort did not sound like a good idea. He and a pal decided to make their own travel arrangements instead, and took a taxi home. 'The driver almost had a heart attack when we told him we were going to Glasgow!' he recalled.

Having survived the scare, the second leg was uneventful, with Rangers winning comfortably through two goals from the Finnish striker Johansson. Memories of the nightmare visit to Greece in 1992 were rekindled in the next qualifying round, when Rangers were drawn with PAOK Salonika. The last visit had been marred by a dreadful performance on the pitch and trouble off it, as Rangers fans came under attack from the home support. It proved to be almost a carbon copy of the previous trip, the only difference being the performance of the team.

In the first leg at Ibrox, Rangers had a comfortable 2–0 win, and looked confident throughout. The Greeks had been reduced to ten men just eight minutes into the game, after Triantafilos Maheridis was red-carded. He was booked in the second minute for a horrific tackle on Gordon Durie that left the striker with a broken ankle, then Danish referee Kim Milton Nielsen – who controversially dismissed David Beckham during the 1998 World Cup in France – gave him a second yellow four minutes later for dissent. Frankly, Maheridis should have been sent off for the original tackle and the second booking appeared to be a belated recognition of that.

Boosted by the numerical advantage Rangers went on to dominate the game, putting in the sort of performance that quite simply had been lacking in previous campaigns. In fifty-five minutes an Andrei Kanchelskis header, his first goal since being signed from Fiorentina for £5.5 million in the summer, broke the deadlock. Rod Wallace doubled the lead after sixty-nine minutes.

With PAOK's ground known as The Tomb and their supporters going under the nickname of the Black Death, there was little doubt what Rangers were going to come up against in Greece. If anything PAOK's fanatical thugs were even more notorious than those from Athens. They earned the club a two-year European ban for rioting during a match against Paris St Germain in 1992 and during a domestic fixture against AEK Athens, supporters hurled oranges loaded with razor blades at each other. Arsenal supporters were also beaten up and hit with missiles when they were knocked-out of the competition by PAOK in 1997.

Rangers had advised fans not to travel, although they knew it was inevitable that many would ignore the warnings and in the end a group of around one hundred made the trip. Ibrox chief executive Bob Brennan and security chief Laurence Macintyre sat alongside the Rangers supporters and, despite being surrounded by riot police for their own protection, endured a terrifying ninety minutes, with flares, bottles, coins and even a piece of fence raining down on them. There had also been trouble on the way to the stadium, with missiles being thrown at the Rangers team bus. Riot police and soldiers had to guard the players as they entered the ground and they had coins thrown at them as they warmed up.

Rangers' preparations had already been thrown into chaos the day before when they were grounded in Glasgow for eight hours, thanks to a faulty charter plane. Just as in 1992, the party did not reach their hotel until the early hours of the morning. But, despite the testing conditions, Rangers put in a mature performance in the searing heat and managed to keep the Greeks at bay, with former Auxerre goalkeeper Lionel Charbonnier playing especially well. The defensive partnership of Craig Moore and Lorenzo Amoruso also did a good job as Rangers held PAOK to a 0–0 draw and moved into the next round. It was a fine tactical performance in the sort of game that had proved so troublesome in previous seasons.

The first-round proper brought another difficult trip for Rangers, this time to Israel, to face Beitar Jerusalem. Rangers drew the first leg at the Teddy Kollek Memorial Stadium 1–1, Jorg Albertz scoring with an unstoppable twenty-five-yard shot. Beitar had taken the lead through a dubious penalty after Ofer Shitrit went to ground in the area, with Charbonnier insisting he didn't touch the player.

Ahead of the return match, Rino Gattuso predicted an 'easy' victory for Rangers, with goals aplenty. Such comments have a habit of backfiring, but when the Italy under-21 international opened the scoring after just twenty-one seconds, his prediction seemed to be coming true. A second goal by fellow countryman Sergio Porrini after twenty-four minutes gave Rangers a comfortable lead, but the Israelis, who had fasted ahead of the game because of Yom Kippur, pulled one back in the thirty-fourth minute. It needed two second-half goals from Johansson and Rod Wallace to steady the nerves but even then Rangers conceded a late goal when Shitrit won another penalty and Eli Ohana converted to make it 4–2 on the night and 5–3 on aggregate.

Having already negotiated three tricky ties, Rangers stepped up a level in the next round as they returned to Germany yet again to face Bayer Leverkusen. The city of Leverkusen is in the Rhine-Ruhr area, a heavily populated region that Rangers have visited an astonishing number of times. Other teams they have faced from the area over the years include Borussia Dortmund (four visits), Cologne (four), Borussia Moenchengladbach (two) and Fortuna Dusseldorf (one). Two visits to Eindhoven, just across the Dutch border, meant the area was almost a second home for the Scots.

But the familiarity of the surroundings would not make the task any easier. Rangers hadn't won an away leg in Germany for thirty-seven years. Leverkusen, backed by the pharmaceutical giant Bayer, had reached the quarter-final of the Champions League the previous season and were on an upward trajectory that would see them reach the final of the competition in 2002. The team featured players of the calibre of German internationals Jens Nowotny, Carsten Ramelow and Ulf Kirsten, the Brazilians Ze Roberto and Emerson and Croatian brothers Niko and Robert Kovac.

The team was led by flamboyant coach Christophe Daum, never a man short of a word or two before a big game. In the run-up to the first leg he focused on Rangers' 20-year-old midfielder Barry Ferguson, who was flourishing under Dick Advocaat after considering leaving the club when Walter Smith was in charge. Daum identified Ferguson as the danger man and valued him at an astonishing £15 million. In a pre-match press conference he described Ferguson as the 'perfect player'. Daum said, 'He can read games and is the playmaker out of defence. He is superb in possession of the ball and 95 per cent of his passes are good ones.' He may have been playing mind games, but there was no doubt that Ferguson was a key man for Rangers and he proved it in the 22,000 capacity Bay Arena.

A disciplined first-half performance ensured that Leverkusen were left frustrated as the break approached. Rangers began to create chances themselves and on the stroke of half-time deservedly took the lead, and sent the three-thousand-strong travelling support into ecstasy. Leverkusen had failed to clear a Rangers corner properly and Albertz won the ball in midfield, playing it back to Ferguson on the edge of the centre circle. The young Scot was facing his own goal with five red shirts around him, but he suddenly stopped and swivelled, leaving his opponents wrong-footed and out of the game. Ferguson then played a perfectly weighted pass through to Jonatan Johansson who laid it on for van Bronckhorst charging into the penalty area. The Dutchman slid in to slip the ball past the advancing goalkeeper from the right-hand corner of the six-yard box.

In the second half the Germans threw everything at Rangers in a bid to get an equalizer, but the defence, superbly marshalled by stand-in captain Colin Hendry, withstood the pressure. In the sixty-third minute as Bayer tried to launch another attack, van Bronckhorst brilliantly won a tackle in the middle of the pitch and released Rod Wallace down the right. His cross for Johansson was perfect and the Finnish striker swept the ball past goal-keeper Matysek and into the net.

Leverkusen had a goal disallowed for offside with twelve minutes to go and Hendry cleared a chance off the line in the closing minutes. But Leverkusen finally got a consolation in injury time when Reichenberger volleyed home a cross from Ze Roberto. It was disappointing to lose a goal so late, but to win 2–1 in Germany was beyond everyone's expectations. The jubilant fans remained in the stadium for half an hour after the final whistle and were even applauded by the Bayer players as they did their post-match warm-down.

Unfortunately, the Rangers supporters who couldn't make it to Leverkusen had to make do with radio coverage or scramble to find a German channel showing the game on satellite television, as the Scottish channels chose not to cover the match. Rangers were even thwarted in their attempts to broad-cast the match on big screens because they said the television companies took too long to decide if they were going to show a highlights package.

The build-up to the second leg was overshadowed by the continuing controversy over Rangers captain Lorenzo Amoruso. He had not had the best of starts to the season and it culminated in a calamitous first half against Dundee United on the weekend before the Leverkusen game. He was booed by a section of the Ibrox crowd after making a mistake that allowed United to score. In typical Amoruso style he scored the winner for Rangers with five minutes to go, but the doubts over his performances continued.

Dick Advocaat gave his full backing to the Italian and urged the Rangers supporters to do likewise as the team went in search of a place in the last sixteen of the UEFA Cup. With left back Arthur Numan back in the team after injury, Rangers' defence was at full strength and it had to be. Leverkusen dominated the first half and it needed brilliant goalkeeping from Charbonnier to keep Rangers level at half-time. In the second half, the Germans still looked the more threatening, until Johansson scored a brilliant breakaway goal in the fifty-sixth minute. Amoruso broke down a Leverkusen attack and his long clearance broke off a German defender to the Finn on the halfway line. He carried the ball to the edge of the 'D' where he was faced with two defenders and, as Rangers fans screamed for him to lay it off, he lashed an unstoppable shot high into the net.

Ten minutes later, Charbonnier injured himself after clattering into the post and had to be replaced by Niemi. There were plenty of nervous moments as Leverkusen scored an equalizer on the night through Kristen, with twelve minutes to go. From the sidelines, the injured Charbonnier repeatedly turned to the fans in the enclosure and urged them to keep up the support in the closing stages. It seemed to help as Rangers managed to hold on for a famous aggregate victory by the odd goal in five.

The result was an undoubted boost for the club and seemed to justify the massive outlay on players that David Murray had authorised in the summer. Rangers were not only playing superb passing football, but had also learned how to play against top European teams.

If the victory over Leverkusen was a yardstick of how far Rangers had come already under Advocaat then their next opponents, *Serie A* superstars Parma, would provide an even stiffer test. Carlo Ancelotti was in charge of a team that contained such stars as Gianluigi Buffon, Lilian Thuram, Roberto Sensini, Fabio Cannavaro, Dino Baggio, Juan Sebastian Veron, Mario Stanic, Enrico Chiesa and Hernan Crespo. It was a formidable line-up but if Rangers were to achieve anything in Europe they would need to be able to compete with that level of opponent.

On an exciting night at Ibrox, Rangers found themselves behind six minutes into the second half when Abel Balbo broke the deadlock. Parma had been the better team in the first half, but the goal drew Rangers out, and, roared on by a capacity crowd, the home team equalized through Rod Wallace. Rangers powered forward looking for a winner and the game ended in a spectacular climax when Gordon Durie somehow missed with a close-range header in injury time, before Parma raced up the other end and forced Niemi into a brilliant save. The match ended one apiece but Rangers had shown in the second half that they were a match for the Italians.

In the second leg at the rickety Ennio Tardini stadium Rangers sadly reverted to type, pulling off a typical Scottish European performance of glorious failure. The match was played in the afternoon for the benefit of Italian television and in the bright December sunshine Rangers started in dazzling fashion, Albertz driving home a spectacular goal from long-range after picking up on a slack pass from defence.

For twenty minutes it seemed that Rangers could pull off what would have been one of their best-ever results. But in injury time in the first half the self-destruct button was pressed for the first time. Sergio Porrini was sent off for a second yellow card after fouling Veron. He had been booked just two minutes earlier for tripping the same player. Two minutes after the restart, Parma exploited the gap where Porrini should have been and Balbo scored the equalizer. Rangers were still level but as they lost their shape, it was inevitable Parma would score again, and in the sixty-third minute Stefano Fiore put them into the lead. Any chances of a Rangers comeback were extinguished in a moment of madness from Lorenzo Amoruso, who inexplicably handled a Veron pass in the penalty area when there was little danger. Chiesa scored from the spot and Rangers were out.

The inevitable inquests focused on the role of the two Italians, with some fans suggesting that they had done their fellow countrymen a favour. The notion is ludicrous. Anyone with any idea of football and footballers would understand that Porrini and Amoruso would have loved nothing more than to return to their homeland and triumph. Even now Amoruso can't explain why he threw his hand out and gave away that penalty.

The disappointment of the defeat to Parma was softened by a tremendous domestic season that resulted in a glorious treble. German goalkeeper Stefan Klos, winger Neil McCann and USA international Claudio Reyna were brought in to boost the quality of the squad and all made telling contributions. Rangers were playing some of the best football their fans had ever seen and they went into the following season's Champions League qualifiers of 1999/2000 with great optimism.

Advocaat strengthened the squad further in the close season, bringing in Dutch forward Michael Mols from FC Utrecht, a player who could have become a Rangers legend if he had not suffered a serious injury months into his Ibrox career. Mols started in spectacular fashion, scoring a double in the away leg of the opening qualifier against Finnish champions FC Haka in what was their twentieth European Cup campaign.

Haka were comfortably disposed of 7–1 on aggregate, but there was shock when Rangers were drawn in the next qualifying round against the team that had conquered them just eight months earlier. Could Rangers rise to the occasion and overcome Parma to reach the Champions League after going so close the season before?

23

Parma, August 1999: Revenge is Sweet

In years gone by, it would have been a recipe for disaster. A Scottish football team locked away in a five-star hotel in a foreign land, with dozens of glamorous beauty-pageant contestants for company. Frankly, what Baxter and co would have made of it doesn't bear thinking about. But this was a different era. Under Dick Advocaat, Rangers were not your typical Scottish team. So, as the scantily clad competitors from the Miss Italia 1999 contest strolled past the players they barely received a second glance. Nothing it seemed could divert the squad's attention from the task at hand, namely conquering Parma and reaching the Champions League group stages.

At their luxury headquarters in the spa town of Salsomaggiore, around twenty miles from Parma, Advocaat was also oblivious to the presence of the beauty contest as he drew up his battle plans for the second leg of the qualifying tie. Beautiful football would not be part of his thinking. This was a night where winning ugly would take precedence over appearances. No Scottish team had knocked an Italian side out of Europe since Rangers had beaten Juventus twenty-one years earlier. On that occasion, the Scots had lost the first leg in Turin 1–0 and went through by winning the return 2–0. This time, the order was reversed. Rangers had already won the Ibrox leg 2–0 and a 1–0 defeat in Parma would be enough to see them through.

Just like the Juve team of 1978, Parma were formidable opponents, as Rangers knew only too well from their clash the season before. If anything, Parma were even stronger than they had been at their last meeting. Veron had left for Lazio, but it remained a multi-billion-lira squad of international superstars. New coach Alberto Malesani still had players like Buffon, Thuram, Baggio, Stanic and Crespo at his disposal but had added the French-Ivorian defender Saliou Lassissi and strikers Ariel Ortega, Marco di Vaio and Marcio Amoroso. The money lavished on the Parma squad made Advocaat seem positively frugal.

Having knocked Rangers out of the UEFA Cup the previous season, the Italians had gone on to win the competition. Amazingly it was their fourth European trophy in five years, yet in comparison with Rangers, the club had very little in the way of history or tradition. Parma had only risen to prominence in the late 1980s under the coach, Nevio Scala. He was able to bring in a number of foreign internationals with money supplied by the multinational dairy company Parmalat, the club's main sponsors and part-owners.

Scala led Parma to the Italian Cup in 1992, their first major honour, and the following season they went on to win the European Cup Winners Cup at the first attempt. Later in the year they added the Super Cup before collecting their first UEFA Cup two years later. During this golden period Parma signed a galaxy of stars, like Claudio Taffarel, Tomas Brolin, Faustino Asprilla, Gianfranco Zola, Fernando Couto, Hristo Stoichkov and Filippo Inzaghi. In 2004, a massive financial scandal enveloped Parmalat, leading inevitably to the proposed sale of the football club. The money dried up and they went from competing at the highest level in Europe to battling against relegation. In the summer of 2006 a buyer was still being sought.

However, that was all in the future. In 1999, Parma were at the height of their powers, one of the top clubs in Europe, but on 11 August – on the day of a total solar eclipse – they were destroyed at Ibrox. Inspired by a raucous crowd, Rangers had overwhelmed the Italians with a brand of passionate, high-tempo, skilful football that their opponents simply could not cope with. Long-suffering Rangers supporters, who had endured years of heartache in Europe, could hardly believe what they were watching. Before the match Dick Advocaat had urged the fans to act as a twelfth man and they responded in fine style, the fans and the players feeding off each other, to inspire brilliant performances from both. Players later told how they could barely hear each other speak even when they were standing just three yards away from their colleagues.

With the noise of the welcome still ringing in their ears, Rangers started strongly, missing a great chance in the opening minute. Van Bronckhorst chipped the ball to Rod Wallace who got in a shot despite pressure from Paolo Vanoli, but Buffon was able to save. The pressure continued and Parma were forced into committing fouls, Cannavaro getting a yellow card in the fifteenth minute for a crude challenge on Wallace. Eleven minutes later – ironically at a time when Parma were beginning to get back into the game – the same two players clashed again, with the same outcome: a booking for Cannavaro. The two yellow cards meant he had to walk, and Parma faced playing more than a third of the match with ten men.

Rangers were quick to take advantage and their goal came from the unlikeliest of sources. Australia international Tony Vidmar – only playing because first-choice left back Arthur Numan had been injured – took a pass from McCann down the left and, rather than cross, he cut inside and let fly. The ball took a deflection off the outstretched leg of Thuram and flew beyond Buffon and into the net. The goal set off a roar that shook the stadium to its foundations.

Into the second half and Rangers continued to press for another goal. Finally, in the seventy-fourth minute, it arrived through Claudio Reyna. Wallace got away from Torrisi down the right and crossed to McCann. The Scotland winger laid it back into the path of the American and he drove it low through a forest of legs into the net. As the ball hit the net, on the other side of the Atlantic, his father Miguel leapt to his feet at the supporters club in Kearney, New Jersey, where he was watching the game. His son had put in a man-of-the-match performance and later described it as the best night of his career.

It was a sign of the dominance Rangers had enjoyed that there was a little disappointment that they hadn't won even more convincingly in the first leg. However, on reflection, the team could be proud of their performance against one of the finest teams on the Continent. It was easily their best result in Europe since the 1992/93 season. After a decade of humiliations against the likes of Juventus, Ajax and Gothenburg, the supporters were finally being rewarded for their loyalty.

As with so many visiting teams, the unique Ibrox atmosphere made a huge impression on the Parma players. On signing for Rangers in 2003, Paolo Vanoli recalled the two European clashes he played in the stadium. 'I will never forget playing against this club in the UEFA Cup for Parma and then in the Champions League when they knocked us out,' he said. 'All I remember from then is the incredible atmosphere at Ibrox and I can't wait to play in front of those fans again.' Goalkeeper Buffon found himself the brunt of some good-natured abuse from the fans behind each goal:

> It was an incredible atmosphere but for some reason the fans seemed to pick on me. We all know about Scottish fans in Italy and they have a very friendly tradition so it was a shock for me to see them shouting at me in this way. But it was different from Italy as the people here are very bad and they say bad things. At Ibrox I think a lot of what was being shouted was just for fun.

Parma's general manager Salvatore Scaglia was also blown away by the noise. 'I have never before seen supporters like those,' he said. 'You could look all over Europe at some of the great stadiums but you won't find another atmosphere like that. The supporters helped Rangers win that match.'

The atmosphere overwhelmed even the Rangers players. As Michael Mols said, 'Every player dreams of one day playing in this kind of atmosphere and in these kind of games.' It was obvious as he walked out to the strains of Tina Turner's 'Simply the Best' that Mols was in awe of the experience. 'I love that song and I love the atmosphere it creates in our stadium, it's very special,' he said afterwards. During the pre-match line-up Mols could also be seen clenching his fists and looking around, revelling in the spectacle. Claudio Reyna was also quick to pay tribute to the contribution made by the fans. 'They gave me goose bumps even when I was in the tunnel, and I can only think they must have put Parma off their stride. I've never known fans to get so involved in a game. They lived every kick of the ball, every minute of the action.'

However, as Dick Advocaat was quick to point out, it was only half-time and Rangers still had to travel to the north of Italy. Even with a two-goal advantage, the players would have to dig deep to keep the Italians at bay. When the teams were announced for the second leg, the results of Advocaat's plotting in Salsomaggiore were revealed. He had gone for a 3-5-2 formation with Sergio Porrini being moved into the middle alongside Amoruso and Moore, and Vidmar and Darius Adamczuk deployed as wingbacks. In reality, as the game panned out, and Parma launched wave after wave of attack, Rangers were playing with at least five at the back most of the time.

On a hot, sticky night – with the mercury still over 70 degrees Fahrenheit and humidity running at 36 per cent at the 9.00 p.m. kick-off – Rangers had to rely on dogged defending and no small measure of luck to book their place in the Champions League. But somehow they did it. At the end the players threw their sweat-soaked blue jerseys to the Rangers fans. It was said the Italians had imposed a beer ban, but something fuelled the party that had been raging from the moment the first of the five thousand Rangers supporters arrived in the medieval city.

The fans had taken up three areas of the Ennio Tardini stadium and out-sang the twenty thousand or so *Parmensi* for most of the match. By the end they were as exhausted as the players but that didn't stop them continuing the party into the night. Hundreds were still cheering on their heroes at Parma airport as the Rangers party boarded their flight home.

From as early as the sixth minute it was clear that Rangers were going to have a difficult night. Vanoli shot over the bar from close range, then, nine minutes later, Charbonnier, replacing the injured Stefan Klos, leapt across the goal to claw away an Ortega free kick. Before half-time di Vaio and Fuser had two clear-cut chances each and it wasn't until the fortieth minute that Rangers managed to break out of defence for the first time and put together an attack, Van Bronckhorst's effort being cleared by Lassissi.

A reinvigorated Rangers team appeared in the second half and, three minutes after the break, Wallace forced Buffon into an excellent save with a powerful downward header. Then, first-leg goal hero Tony Vidmar came close in the fifty-ninth minute with a drive that rebounded off the post. Parma continued to press but the sting had gone out of their attack. Then, with twenty-two minutes remaining, a free kick was touched to Walem twenty yards out. Charbonnier stopped his shot but he fumbled it and the ball crept in at the near post. For the remainder of the match, Parma bombarded the Rangers goal, with Stanic, Walem and Ortega all guilty of spurning good chances. But somehow there were no further breaches and the whistle finally blew to signal the end.

After the shambles of the previous season's defeat against Parma the result brought a huge outpouring of emotion from the players. It was especially sweet for Porrini and Amoruso, who had both been heavily criticised after the defeat the year before. Parma coach Malesani had also been quoted in the Italian papers criticising the Rangers defence, and to make matters worse Amoruso had been the victim of obscene chanting from the Parma fans. So it was understandable that the Rangers captain savoured the moment.

The travelling fans were also delirious. After the suffering the disappointment of the Ajax defeat, Stewart Walker was on his second European trip:

To be honest the trip itself wasn't as good as Amsterdam, for obvious reasons, but I have to say the result made up for it. I've spoken to lot of people who say the match is the least important thing when they go abroad with Rangers, and I can see their point, especially when you are getting humped by teams from Sweden or whatever. But it makes the trip so much better when you can go home in a good mood after seeing your team actually beat one of the best teams in the world. It was great to see the players come over at the end and actually celebrate with you instead of them clapping you just for coming along and singing. For some reason, I remember the look on Michael Mols's face. It was brilliant.

The Italian media rounded on Parma coach Alberto Malesani the next morning. Sports newspaper *Gazzetta dello Sport* stated: 'There was effort and energy but Malesani could not find the way to make them worried.'

Corriere della Sera declared: 'Parma, the team that cost billions, have failed.'

For Rangers, the result was a signal to the rest of Europe that they were no longer the pushovers they had been for most of the 1990s. For the first time, they could go into the group stage with confidence. While nobody predicted that they would win the competition, within Ibrox there was a belief that they should not be afraid of anyone.

24

Michael Mols's Darkest Night

Rangers went into the 1999 Champions League group phase with the sort of confidence not seen since the early 1960s. Having disposed of Parma, there was a genuine belief that they could compete with anyone. Rugged Italian right-back Sergio Porrini had lifted the European Cup with Juventus three years earlier and even he had been bitten by the bug. 'We are now close to teams like Manchester United, Arsenal and AC Milan,' he argued. 'After beating Parma we have no reason to be scared of anyone.' The fact that no-one thought he had lost the plot told how far Rangers had come.

The draw brought Rangers up against three teams they had faced in momentous European clashes in the past: Bayern Munich, Valencia and PSV Eindhoven. It was a tough group but, on the basis of the Parma result, one from which the Ibrox club expected to qualify.

The opening Group F encounter was against Valencia at the Mestalla. Rangers fans had been reliably informed that Valencia were the Aberdeen of Spain, so it came as something of a shock to discover that they were actually quite good. Three days ahead of their clash, Dick Advocaat flew to southern Spain and saw Valencia perform lamentably in a 2–0 home defeat to Alaves. Earlier in the day, Rangers had overwhelmed a lacklustre and bottom-of-the-league Aberdeen side at Ibrox and the Scottish newspapers were quick to draw parallels. One report carried the headline, 'We are the Aberdeen of Spain' and stated confidently, 'If this is the best Valencia can offer, expect them to be the whipping boys of this Euro group.'

But those who thought a Valencia team that included the French defender Jocelyn Angloma – who had played for Marseille in the Champions League at Ibrox seven years earlier – veteran Italian Amedeo Carboni, the strike pair of Kily Gonzalez and Claudio Lopez and midfield general Gaizka Mendieta would be a pushover were deluding themselves.

Rangers were totally overrun by the Spaniards, and could have lost by four or five goals. They managed to survive until the fifty-sixth minute when Charbonnier and Craig Moore got into a tangle trying to deal with a cross. The goalkeeper palmed the ball out but it came back off the Australian defender and rolled into the net. Five minutes later Rangers had a narrow escape when a shot bounced off the goalkeeper into the path of Lopez, who knocked it home, only to see the goal ruled out for offside. But it was only a matter of time before Valencia got their second, Kily Gonzalez splitting the Rangers defence with a one-two with Mendieta before blasting a shot past Charbonnier.

There was a chilling moment when Lorenzo Amoruso suddenly collapsed as if shot by a sniper. The captain lay unconscious for thirty seconds as teammates and Rangers medics tried to revive him. He eventually came round and, amazingly, was able to continue following treatment for a head injury. Rangers managed to keep Valencia at bay for the rest of the match but it was a less than convincing performance that brought back bad memories of previous away days.

The 2–0 defeat upset everyone in the Rangers camp. Charbonnier was so angry at being blamed for the first goal that he stormed into a press conference at Ibrox later in the week and demanded an immediate meeting with Advocaat. When the coach pointed out that he was busy, the goalkeeper responded, 'It's more important than talking to journalists.' Rangers captain Amoruso admitted the players were annoyed at their performance. 'Maybe we thought it was going to be easy to beat them because of the problems that Valencia were having at home,' he admitted.

The visit of Bayern Munich to Ibrox a week later promised little in the way of respite. The Germans had lost out in the final of the previous season's competition against Manchester United, having been seconds away from victory when Alex Ferguson's team somehow produced two goals from nowhere. Rangers and Bayern had plenty of history, having previously faced each other on seven occasions. The Germans had the advantage, winning four of the matches to Rangers' one. The other two were drawn.

Bayern went into the match with their 20-year-old fourth-choice goalkeeper because of injuries to Oliver Kahn and his two understudies. Stefan Wessels normally turned out for Bayern's amateur team in front of crowds of two hundred, but he was now faced with the prospect of having to cope with 50,000 screaming Rangers fans.

If the noise generated by the crowd as the teams came out had frightened the youngster he didn't show it. In fact he later admitted the din had helped him stay calm, although his mother was less impressed. Wessels said, 'It was incredible to play in such an important match in such an atmosphere. When the game started, my nervousness was simply blown away.' Frau Wessels, who was attending her first match, did not appreciate the fans' efforts to unsettle her son. 'I can't believe that these people could be so hostile towards my boy,' the schoolteacher told reporters. 'They did not stop whistling and shouting at him but he had done nothing to them. I don't know how he managed to concentrate on playing football when people were being so horrible to him.'

Advocaat had dropped Neil McCann, Tony Vidmar and Gabriel Amato from the team that had played in Valencia and recalled Jorg Albertz, Arthur Numan and Jonatan Johansson. All three were heavily involved as Rangers threw off the disappointment of the previous week's shambles and set about unsettling the Germans. The midfield snapped and harried their opponents and didn't give them a moment to settle, and the German defenders struggled to cope with the pace and movement of Mols and Johansson up front. Rangers' whirlwind start inspired the crowd to even greater noise levels and at times it was hard to hear yourself think.

Wessels made a brilliant one-handed save from Johansson at his near post. But a Rangers goal was inevitable and it came from Jorg Albertz, a trademark left-foot blast. He ran off to celebrate, jabbing his thumbs at the name on the back of his top, presumably a message to his countrymen watching at home.

Rangers should have scored more and, as they ran out of steam towards the end, how they rued those misses. With just seconds left, Bayern won a dubious free kick on the right. Michael Tarnat's shot took a wicked deflection off Santa Cruz and the ball flew into the net. Ibrox was stunned, and the Rangers players devastated, but as the dust settled they realised just how well they had done against one of the Continent's top teams. Bayern were delighted to escape with a point. President Franz Beckenbauer – a veteran of three classic ties between the clubs as a player – was full of praise for Rangers and the atmosphere inside Ibrox. 'If a team can come through that they can come through anything,' he said afterwards. 'I remember how tough it was for visiting teams when I was a player, and it's no different nowadays. It's full of passion and the fans make it so difficult so we have to be happy with the draw.'

Rangers had every reason to think that they should have taken all three points. They could point to the fact that Bayern had conned the referee into giving them a free kick in the closing minutes and they could moan about the bad luck they suffered when the resulting shot deflected past

Charbonnier. But had they taken even half their chances, especially in the first half, the dodgy decisions would have been irrelevant.

The next game was an emotional return to Eindhoven for Dick Advocaat. Rangers had won a famous victory at PSV's Philips stadium in 1978 and they needed to repeat the feat twenty-one years later to stay in contention in Group F. Rangers were allocated just 1,300 tickets for the match but demand was huge, with an estimated 2,000 travelling without tickets.

Leading the line for PSV was highly rated striker Ruud van Nistelrooy, who revealed before the match that he had been the subject of a failed bid by Dick Advocaat to join Rangers. At the other end of the pitch for the Dutch side was controversial goalkeeper Ronald Waterreus, who had fallen out spectacularly with coach Eric Gerets after a newspaper article in which he branded his boss crazy for dropping him. Ironically, Waterreus was to find himself in a similar position seven years later when, as a Rangers player, he gave an interview to a Dutch magazine in which he was less than complimentary about his teammates and manager.

Surprisingly Albertz was dropped to the bench, despite his goal against Bayern. He was understandably disappointed, especially as his parents and brother were watching from the stands. Advocaat had never taken to Albertz and the assumption was that he considered him to be lazy. Unfortunately for the coach, Albertz kept on scoring and he became difficult to drop to the bench without causing controversy, especially as he was a fans' favourite.

In Eindhoven, the German was given an unexpectedly early chance to shine, when he replaced the injured Claudio Reyna after twenty-four minutes. Both teams played well and there were chances at both ends but the game looked as if it was heading for a goalless draw. Then, in the eighty-fourth minute, the breakthrough came, and it was no surprise that it was Albertz who delivered the killer blow. He started the move off with a superb pass out of defence towards Mols on the right. The Dutchman battled with Heintze on the touchline and managed to get in a cross that was only half-cleared. The ball spun in the air and Albertz, who had continued his run forward, reacted first to volley it past Waterreus, securing Rangers a vital win. The goal sent the Rangers fans wild and, as Albertz celebrated in front of them, there was no hiding his emotion.

With Valencia and Bayern drawing the same night, Rangers were back in the running and a victory over PSV in the return match in Glasgow would put them in the driving seat for qualification. If Albertz thought his match-winning performance in Holland had guaranteed him a starting berth at Ibrox he was mistaken. Advocaat handed a surprise recall to Derek McInnes, who a month earlier was being lined up for a move to Sheffield United. If Albertz was looking for further confirmation that Advocaat did not consider him a key player then surely this was it.

In fairness to the manager this time his decision was tactical. McInnes was deployed in a holding role in front of central defenders Amoruso and Moore. His task was to snuff out the threat from the PSV strikers van Nistelrooy and Luc Nilis and he performed admirably. Rangers delivered one of their best European performances, destroying PSV with a display of passing and controlled aggression that should be the model for every Scottish club in Europe.

It took Rangers a while to make the breakthrough and, after a typically raucous opening, by the time they scored the crowd had gone quiet. That all changed when Amoruso powered a header past goalkeeper Ivica Kralj after an excellent van Bronckhorst corner. Rod Wallace was having a difficult night up front, missing a string of good chances that, on another night, could have been costly. But luckily for him, his strike partner Michael Mols came to the rescue. Seven minutes before the break he converted a cross from Neil McCann with a back-post header. Mols had started the move, by first winning the ball in his own half then releasing McCann on the wing.

Shortly before half-time, PSV pulled a goal back through a van Nistelrooy penalty, after Moore fouled the striker. But any hope the Dutch had of recovering the situation in the second half were quickly dashed. In fifty-five minutes, van Bronckhorst struck a powerful free kick that Kralj failed to hold. Wallace pounced quickly and tangled with the goalkeeper in a bid to force it over the line. As the PSV defence stood static, McCann raced in to finish. Minutes from time, Michael Mols added his own second and Rangers' fourth. He raced onto a long pass from Porrini and, as he burst through on Kralj, stopped the ball before blasting it beyond the keeper.

The celebrations went on long into the night. It was the biggest victory Rangers had enjoyed over a team from a 'major' country since 1969 when they beat Athletic Bilbao by the same 4–1 scoreline and the fact that it had been achieved against the manager's old team made it all the sweeter. For the Dutch players in the Rangers team it proved a point to those in their homeland who criticised them for going to the Scottish league. Arthur Numan in particular had been the subject of derision for leaving PSV for Rangers. In Holland the result was greeted with the sort of headlines Rangers had suffered after past Euro disasters. The biggest selling newspaper, *De Telegraaf*, headlined its match report 'Murder at Ibrox!' while *De Volkskrant* described PSV as being from a 'Mickey Mouse' league. It was the sort of jibe Rangers had suffered for so long and it made a pleasant change to see others endure the same treatment.

Valencia and Bayern drew again, so the result actually pushed Rangers to the top of Group F. One win from the last two games would put them through to the next round. It was almost within touching distance, but caution was required. Valencia were the next visitors to Ibrox and they had already proved their quality. The ludicrous 'Aberdeen of Spain' tag had long since been shaken off and they came to Ibrox expecting a result.

McInnes kept his place as Advocaat persevered with the system that had brought so much success against PSV. But this time it did not work. Valencia were superb. They were stronger and faster than Rangers, who were pedestrian by comparison. Gaizka Mendieta in particular was brilliant, dominating the midfield and putting in a performance that many consider to be one of the best ever seen from an opponent at Ibrox.

The Valencia captain almost opened the scoring in the twenty-first minute when he headed wide from a Claudio Lopez cross, then thirteen minutes later he did score, volleying an unstoppable shot past Klos after a good pass from Carboni. Just before half-time Claudio Lopez added a second and Rangers were beaten. A Craig Moore header after sixty minutes gave a flicker of hope but despite pressure from the home team, an equalizer never looked likely.

The result meant Rangers needed at least a point from the Olympic stadium against Bayern to qualify. Despite the performance against the Bavarians earlier in the group stage, no-one was in any doubt that it would be an incredibly difficult task. Yet confidence was high among the Rangers supporters, who travelled in huge numbers.

German media and police estimated that there were 16,000 bluenoses inside the Olympic stadium, the biggest travelling support the city has seen for a European game. It was also the highest number to follow Rangers in Europe since the Cup Winners Cup final of 1972. The huge bank of Rangers fans behind the goal was a tremendous sight, especially with the spectacular display of red-white-and-blue flags laid out on the running track. During the day, the Rangers fans had mingled happily with the Germans in the city's *bier* halls and in the marquee behind the stadium.

In the run-up to the match, Bayern lived up to their FC Hollywood nickname as two of their most senior players, Lothar Matthaus and Markus Babbel, defied club orders and refused to take part in a press conference. Meanwhile goalkeeper Oliver Kahn was attempting to win back fitness after the neck injury that kept him out of the Ibrox clash in September. He underwent intensive treatment that involved pain-killing injections, massage therapy and a bizarre Italian treatment called Fango, which involves mineral-rich mud being smeared over the injury and covered with bandages. It seemed to do the trick as he made the line-up, which turned out to be bad news for Rangers for more than one reason.

Had Kahn not passed his late fitness test, the career of Michael Mols would certainly have turned out differently. With fourteen goals in his short Rangers career the Dutchman was a fans favourite. But it wasn't just his scoring record that made him so popular. Mols possessed an amazing ability to turn defenders inside out; a talent that made him mesmerising to watch. Coupled with electric pace, brilliant ball control and clinical finishing ability, it made him the complete forward. He had the potential to be an all-time great and what made it all the more remarkable was that before he signed from FC Utrecht very few Rangers supporters had heard of him.

That November night in Munich could have been Mols's greatest hour. Instead it was his darkest. He had played so well in the first half-hour of that match that it seemed incvitable he was going to lead Rangers into the next phase of the Champions League single-handedly. The Bayern defenders were finding his movement impossible to cope with. On one memorable run down the right, Mols twisted and turned and left a trail of defenders in his wake, before teeing up a shot for van Bronckhorst, who blazed over. Rangers recovered from their shaky start in style and, in the twenty-fifth minute, Mols headed a van Bronckhorst cross against the post.

But just three minutes later his world came crashing down. Kahn rushed out of his penalty area to knock the ball away from the incoming Rod Wallace. He continued to chase after the ball as it broke out to the touch-line. Mols was also pursuing it, but he pulled up when he realised Kahn was going to get there a split-second ahead of him. The pair collided on the line and as Mols landed he tried to avoid falling on the keeper. Unfortunately, in his attempts to protect his opponent from injury he landed awkwardly and twisted his knee. At first, as Mols received treatment, it seemed to be a minor knock. But it quickly became apparent that he would not be able to continue and, as he was helped down the tunnel by Rangers officials, there was concern about long-term damage. The player knew right away that there was a chance that he had suffered a bad injury. 'I felt something was wrong because immediately I had a strange feeling inside my knee' he recalled later.

Everyone's worst fears were realised when scans revealed that he had suffered serious ligament damage and would miss the rest of the campaign at the very least. It was a major blow to Rangers, and especially cruel to Mols, whose early-season form had been devastating. Although he eventually returned to the team in 2000/01, and contributed to future triumphs, Mols never again scaled the heights.

A few minutes after Mols went off Rangers suffered another blow when Bayern were awarded a soft penalty, the referee adjudging van Bronckhorst to have fouled Mehmet Scholl in the penalty area. If there was contact it was minimal and Scholl went down easily, but the kick was given and Thomas Strunz scored, although Klos almost stopped it. Having lost a goal, and their main attacking threat, Rangers could have given up, but they continued to pile forward and, but for the woodwork, inspired goalkeeping from Kahn and a poor decision by the referee would have got the point they needed to go through.

Four minutes after Bayern's goal Kahn made a brilliant save, turning a close-range shot from Rod Wallace onto the bar. Rangers continued to attack, but found themselves thwarted by a keeper in inspired form. Even when they managed to beat Kahn, Rangers couldn't get the equalizer; a twenty-five-yard shot from van Bronckhorst rebounded off the post. Chances fell for Wallace and Johansson, and there was a good shout for a penalty rejected by Portuguese referee Vitor Pereira, but the equalizer just wouldn't come. As proud as he was of his players, Advocaat said later, 'I would rather play badly and get through.'

A sign of the times was the reaction of chairman David Murray to the Mols injury. Rather than relying on the players already on the books – like Wallace, Johansson, Gabriel Amato and Kanchelskis – his first reaction was to buy a replacement striker. Murray was quoted as saying, 'If the manager says to me we have to buy a new player to win the championship then we'll bring the purchase forward.'

A third-place finish in Group F meant Rangers dropped into the UEFA Cup third round. Group winners Valencia went on to reach that season's Champions League final where they lost out to Real Madrid, and were runners-up again the following year. Not bad for 'whipping boys'.

In the UEFA Cup, the Ibrox club were given a money-spinning draw against old foes Borussia Dortmund. It may not have been the Champions League, but Rangers sold the television rights for the Ibrox leg to German broadcasters for £2.5 million. Borussia, who had also failed to get through the Champions League, still had many of the players who had won the European Cup two years earlier and were immediately installed as favourites. Rangers also went into the game in the midst of a goalkeeping crisis. Former Dortmund keeper Stefan Klos and Lionel Charbonnier were both injured, and third choice Antti Niemi had been loaned to Charlton Athletic. The only other goalkeeper available was teenager Mark Brown and Advocaat was granted permission by UEFA to bring in Everton reserve Thomas Myhre on loan. Nevertheless, Rangers took the lead in the eighteenth minute when

Dortmund captain Jurgen Kohler tried to divert an Amato cross back to Jens Lehmann in goal, and instead sliced it into his own net.

The second goal came just before half-time and was one of the best European goals ever scored at Ibrox. The move started deep in the Rangers half with Craig Moore and saw a string of passes involving all bar one of the outfield players. The ball was worked down the right then switched to the left as they probed for an opening. As the attack moved closer to the Dortmund goal, the interchange of passes became more intricate. Finally, after eighteen passes, Arthur Numan slid the ball into the penalty area for Jorg Albertz. Just as it looked like he was about to unleash a shot, he played a reverse pass into the path of Rod Wallace who curled it past Lehmann. The move consisted of twenty passes and some wonderful vision and movement off the ball. It was arguably the high-point of the Advocaat era, which had seen Rangers adopt a style of play that no Scottish team before or since could have matched.

There was no scoring in a scrappy second half but Rangers travelled to Germany expecting their two-goal lead would see them through. But, as so often in the past, the Scottish champions came up short when it really mattered. Nigerian international Viktor Ikpeba scored in the first half for Dortmund but, despite territorial domination, the Germans never looked likely to score a second. Then, with the game in injury time, Lehmann went forward for a corner and remained there for the next two minutes even when the attack broke down. Rather than letting the clock run down by playing for time, Rangers naively tried to send the ball forward. Borussia regained possession and launched it into the Rangers penalty area. Lehmann swung at the ball and completely miskicked, but it fell to Fredi Bobic who fired home the equalizer.

In extra time, Neil McCann had a glorious chance to settle the tie, but after an excellent cross from Vidmar he managed to bundle the ball wide when the goal was gaping. There were no goals in extra time, so, for the first time since the Sporting Lisbon shoot-out that shouldn't have been, Rangers were involved in a penalty shoot-out in Europe. Van Bronckhorst, Numan and Reyna all tamely missed their kicks, and, although Thomas Myhre saved one, the Germans converted their other three to go through.

The aftermath was dominated by a controversy over racist comments made by Amoruso towards Ikpeba. Television pictures captured the Rangers captain calling the Nigerian a 'black bastard' during a flashpoint in the game. The evidence was clear-cut but Amoruso hardly helped his case when he claimed that he only ever swore in Italian. The Scottish press roundly condemned the Italian, although in Germany the incident barely registered. Ikpeba himself told a German radio station that he had 'no problems' with Amoruso and Dortmund ruled out making a complaint to UEFA. But in Scotland the controversy raged for days, leading Amoruso – who later acknowledged making the comment – to write in his autobiography *LA Confidential*: 'The only people it seemed I had really upset were those in the Scottish press and I reached the conclusion that they were working to another agenda.'

Despite the excellent performances against Parma, PSV and Bayern, Rangers were out of Europe before Christmas yet again. It was now seven years since they had enjoyed a run that stretched beyond the festive season; a sad state of affairs. The following season would see yet another attempt and, as Dick Advocaat's team had won the Scottish Premier League at a canter, they would be taking part in the Champions League qualifiers again.

During the summer of 2001 Advocaat spent more than £10 million in a bid to add even more quality to the squad. The two most notable arrivals were defenders Fernando Ricksen and Bert Konterman, both Netherlands internationals. Both were put straight into the team but they failed to settle and Rangers looked a shadow of the team that had stormed to five out of the last six domestic trophies. Martin O'Neill had taken over as Celtic manager, and a 6–2 defeat at Parkhead suggested that the wheels were beginning to come off the Advocaat wagon just months after tens of thousands of Rangers fans turned Hampden into a sea of orange at the Scottish Cup final in tribute to their Dutch boss.

Dutch superstar Ronald de Boer was signed from Barcelona after the Celtic defeat and he would have a major impact in Europe. For once, qualification for the Champions League had been straightforward. A 4–1 aggregate victory over Zalgiris Kaunas of Lithuania was followed by two impressive 3–0 wins over the Danish champions, Herfolge. The reward was a Champions League group in which Rangers would face Monaco, Turkish giants Galatasaray and Sturm Graz of Austria. It was a relatively easy group and one from which Rangers should have qualified, especially after an excellent start.

Inspired by a virtuoso performance from Ronald de Boer, Rangers crushed Sturm Graz at Ibrox in the opener. The 5–0 win was arguably the club's best Champions League performance, although the quality of the opposition was questionable. Nevertheless Rangers put on a great display for the capacity crowd. Michael Mols opened the scoring in the ninth minute with a side-footed volley after a cutback from de Boer. The former Barcelona man scored the second himself, prodding home a cross from another summer signing, Allan Johnston. Albertz added a third before half-time with a swerving shot that would have been called a daisy-cutter in days gone by, then van Bronckhorst scored almost a carbon copy in the seventieth minute. The fifth goal was an exquisite chip from the edge of the penalty area by Billy Dodds.

The second game was in Monaco, where Rangers fans made up at least half the 11,000 crowd inside the Stade Louis II (the venue in which Jim Baxter had put on such a dazzling performance almost forty years before). In another tactical gamble, Advocaat played Turkish midfielder Tugay as sweeper and it proved to be a shrewd move. In eight minutes, Rangers were a goal up, through a long-range shot from van Bronckhorst and for the next eighty-two minutes they defended manfully against the Monaco onslaught, especially in the second half. Despite the introduction by Monaco of a certain Dado Prso, Rangers held on for a famous victory and gave themselves a great chance of progressing.

A week later, Rangers travelled to Istanbul, knowing that a win at the Ali Sami Yen stadium would virtually guarantee a place in the next round. Fears of crowd trouble in the Turkish city – where two Leeds United supporters had been stabbed to death the previous season – came to nothing but Rangers endured a torrid time on the field. A twenty-minute spell after half-time saw Galatasaray score three times, including one from former Rangers target Jardel, and a late rally from the Scottish champions wasn't enough to prevent defeat. Goals from Andrei Kanchelskis and a thunderous free-kick from van Bronckhorst gave the score a more respectable look but the points went to the Turks, who now led the group.

In the return at a rain-lashed Ibrox, Rangers had to field a makeshift team due to injury and suspensions and despite a brave second-half performance they were unable to break down the Galatasaray defence. With Craig Moore injured and Amoruso suspended, Advocaat had gone for a frightening-looking central-defence partnership of Bert Konterman and Sergio Porrini. Van Bronckhorst, Allan Johnston, Numan, Wallace, Mols and Ricksen were also out and Barry Ferguson was named captain for the first time.

The Turks, with Gheorghe Hagi back, had the better of the first half but after the break Rangers dominated and only the efforts of Brazilian goalkeeper Taffarel kept them at bay. The goalless draw still left Rangers in a strong position and a victory in the next game away to Sturm Graz would guarantee qualification. Unfortunately, Rangers' season was now in turmoil. Days before the Graz game, Advocaat launched a stinging attack on his players, following a defeat to St Johnstone. Morale among the squad was at rock-bottom and it later emerged that there were deep divisions between the players. In the Arnold Schwarzenegger stadium Rangers slumped to a 2–0 defeat to a team they had thrashed just weeks earlier.

Giovanni van Bronckhorst, who had scored three goals during the Champions League campaign, was rushed back from injury but was clearly unfit. Danish goalkeeper Jesper Christiansen made his debut in the absence of Stefan Klos. With Rangers a goal behind and chasing the game, forgotten striker Marco Negri was introduced in the closing stages. Rangers dominated possession but had no cutting edge, and it wasn't a surprise when Graz added a second goal with virtually the last kick of the ball.

To add to Rangers' woes, Arthur Numan was sent off for two yellow cards. The second was debatable but the first was harsh in the extreme. Having gone off for treatment, the referee appeared to signal for the Dutchman to come back onto the pitch. But when he re-entered the field and intercepted a pass, he was immediately shown a yellow card. Despite protests the Spanish referee Antonio Lopez Nieto refused to budge and was insistent he had been waving to tell Numan *not* to come on. The UEFA appeals board clearly disagreed and revoked Numan's yellow card, meaning he was no longer suspended for the crucial final game against Monaco.

Prior to Rangers' first European Cup tie in 1956, their French opponents Nice had to take a train to Glasgow because of weather-related flight problems. Forty-four years later, there was almost a repeat. Torrential rain and high winds in the south of France delayed Monaco's flight by several hours as Nice airport was closed. The team returned to the Stade Louis II for a training session as preparations were made for a long-distance rail trip. Eventually the weather cleared and Monaco were finally able to fly into Glasgow moments before the twenty-four-hour UEFA deadline passed.

The scenario was straightforward. If Rangers beat Monaco they would go through to the next round, and they got off to the perfect start when Kenny Miller scored early on. Monaco equalized before half-time but Michael Mols shot Rangers back into the lead in the second half. As the match wound to its conclusion, it seemed Rangers had done enough. Then, in the closing stages, Amoruso gave the ball away in the Rangers half. Marco Simone was allowed to run unchallenged through the Rangers defence and shot past Christiansen, who made a poor attempt at a save. Amoruso took most of the flak for the goal, although the blame surely should have been spread throughout the team. A draw in the other match between Galatasaray and Graz put Rangers into third place and the UEFA Cup. After such a tremendous start to the campaign it was another failure. For all the money spent, and for all the good work against the likes of Parma, Rangers were no further forward in Europe than they had been under Walter Smith.

The UEFA Cup tie against Germans Kaiserslautern was no better. Jorg

Albertz scored his twelfth European goal to give Rangers a 1–0 first-leg victory at Ibrox, but in the return at the Fritz Walter stadium they suffered a crushing 3–0 defeat and crashed out before Christmas yet again.

The domestic season had been an absolute disaster, with Rangers finishing an unacceptable fifteen points behind Celtic. But their efforts in Europe over the last three years had improved Scotland's co-efficient to the extent that the league runners-up as well as the winners would now take part in the Champions League qualifiers. After three years of limited progress, it was time for Advocaat's Rangers to step up a level.

25

Simply Out of Their Depth

The collapse of communism and the break-up of Eastern Europe in the early nineties created a headache for European football's bureaucrats. The creation of so many new countries meant an influx of members, and the authorities had to find a way of accommodating them. As a result, new qualifying rounds were created for both the Champions League and the UEFA Cup and these were filled with exotically named clubs from these infant nations.

Unfortunately, the general standard of football in Scotland meant that teams from this country often found themselves competing in these far-flung corners of Europe before the domestic season had started. The Republic of Slovenia, formerly part of Yugoslavia, was one such developing nation, having gained independence in 1991. NK Maribor had quickly become the most successful club, winning seven titles in a row and qualifying for the Champions League in 1999 at the expense of Lyon. So when Rangers drew them in the first qualifying round of the 2001/02 season, progression was by no means a foregone conclusion. A 3–0 victory was gained in Slovenia on 25 July, with a double from Tore Andre Flo and one from Christian Nerlinger, a German midfielder brought in to replace the departed Jorg Albertz. Former Argentina World Cup star Claudio Caniggia scored twice in the second leg in a 3–1 win to secure a place in the final qualifier.

Rangers were drawn against Turkish champions Fenerbahce and their chances weren't helped by a foolish sending-off for Michael Mols, who clearly raised a hand to an opponent during the first leg at Ibrox. The match ended goalless and Rangers went to Istanbul knowing that a score draw would take them through. They went two goals behind, but Fernando

Ricksen brought fresh hope when he scored from long-range. The Italian referee Pierluigi Collina made a number of dubious decisions during the match, including the free kick that led to Fenerbahce's first goal. He also denied Rangers a very good claim for a penalty when they were chasing the equalizer that would have taken them into the group stages. In his autobiography, Lorenzo Amoruso claimed Collina, probably the world's most famous referee, had done a lap of honour *before* the game, which is bizarre to say the least. Regardless of the referee's decisions, Rangers had enough chances in the second half to go through but they failed to find the net and had to make do with a place in the UEFA Cup instead.

The first round of Europe's second tournament saw Rangers at the centre of a diplomatic row that could have seen them thrown out of the competition and banned from Europe. The draw paired the Scots with Anzhi Makhachkala from the Russian republic of Dagestan. Apart from the fact that their name was a Scrabble player's dream, the most notable thing about the club was that they were based in one of the most dangerous areas of Europe. Hours after the draw, Glasgow's *Evening Times* told how the city of Makhachkala – like Vladikavkaz, where Rangers had played five years before – was only a few miles from the war zone of Chechnya. The conflict had escalated in recent years, but Chechen rebels also had a foothold in Dagestan and Westerners were often the target for kidnappings in Makhachkala. Terrorist attacks were also a regular occurrence and the Foreign Office's guidance was that British citizens should not travel to the area.

The situation sparked a remarkable piece of brinkmanship by Rangers chairman David Murray. He took an early decision that the club would not travel to Dagestan and refused to budge, even at the risk of being expelled from the tournament and facing a lengthy ban. Days before they were due to travel, Rangers cancelled their flight despite the repeated insistence of UEFA that the game must go ahead.

On the morning of 11 September 2001, two days before the match was due to be played, UEFA issued their final decision that Rangers would have to play the first leg in Makhachkala. Five hours later, came the horrific terrorist attacks on the World Trade Center. The timing was entirely coincidental, but as the world reeled from the shock of the atrocities in the United States, it seemed remarkable that UEFA continued to insist that Rangers travel to an area plagued by its own terrorist outrages. An appeal by Rangers to the Court of Arbitration for Sport in Lausanne failed, leaving the club on the verge of being kicked-out of Europe.

However, they got a last-minute reprieve when UEFA cancelled all European matches in the wake of the World Trade Center attacks. The governing body insisted the match would eventually still take place in Dagestan but a week later they finally saw sense. Increased levels of violence in Chechnya prompted UEFA to announce that the game would now be played as a one-off tie in Warsaw. Inevitably, Anzhi were furious but the decision vindicated Murray's uncompromising position. Had UEFA refused to budge, the consequences for the club would have been far-reaching. A European ban would have cost Rangers millions in lost revenue.

The game – when it eventually went ahead at the ground of Legia Warsaw in Poland – was uninspired and Rangers struggled to break down the Russians. The only goal of the match came five minutes from the end when Bert Konterman's long-range shot took a deflection. In typical Konterman style, he said afterwards, 'There was not a lot of sunshine for us in football land.' The victory came on Dick Advocaat's fifty-fourth birthday and Konterman revealed, 'We congratulated him beforehand and we had a nice cream cake.'

The next round saw Rangers up against Russian opposition again, but this time the destination was Moscow to face old adversaries Dynamo. The tie not only brought back memories of the famous clashes between the clubs in 1945 and 1972 but also rekindled memories of the last time Rangers had gone to Russia in the summer of 1962. The three-match trip was the first time any British team had toured the USSR and the Scots returned as conquering heroes. Rangers beat Lokomotiv Moscow 3–1 in the capital, and then defeated Dynamo Tblisi in what is now Georgia. Then it was on to the Ukraine where they drew with Kiev. The tour received a great deal of media coverage in Scotland and thousands of fans swarmed onto the runway at Renfrew airport to meet the team as it returned in triumph. The tour was also the making of a certain John Greig, then a teenager, who rose to prominence in the absence of Jim Baxter and went on to serve the club for another sixteen years as a player.

Rangers had never lost a competitive match to a club from Russia and they had a comfortable victory over Dynamo. A 3–1 first-leg win at Ibrox may have left some fans feeling nervous, but they achieved an excellent 4–1 win in Moscow to get through to the next round, where they would face Paris St Germain.

The star of the French team was the sublimely skilful Brazilian forward Ronaldinho. He would go on to be the star of the 2002 World Cup and developed into the world's greatest player. The team also contained the talents of Frederic Dehu and Nicolas Anelka but it was Spanish teenager Mikel Arteta, on loan from Barcelona, who caught the eye, particularly in the first leg at Ibrox. His impressive performance persuaded Rangers to pay more than £6 million for him in the summer. He was the last big-money signing Rangers would make before the board finally faced financial reality.

In the first leg at Ibrox on 22 November 2001 Rangers had the better of the first half but failed to turn their domination into goals, PSG goalkeeper Lionel Letizi (signed by Rangers manager Paul Le Guen in the summer of 2006) making a string of good saves. The Parisians came back into the game in the second half and could have won the match but for Stefan Klos. Rangers played the last ten minutes with ten men after Fernando Ricksen was sent off. He had been booked for a bad tackle on Leroy, and received his red for a petulant push on a PSG player as he tried to collect the ball for a throw-in. The match ended goalless and both teams were confident of going through.

Between ten and twelve thousand Rangers fans made the trip to Paris for the second leg on 6 December but a French air-traffic-control-strike posed travel difficulties for some of the supporters. Gary King jetted out from Glasgow on a one-day trip, but the plans to fly straight into Paris had to be changed at the last minute:

> Because of the strike we flew to Ostend and then got a bus to Paris. We were dropped off at the stadium, and went to the Eiffel Tower to have a red-white-and-blue party, which was great. After that, we went to a pub near the stadium. It was supposed to be in the 'safe' area according to the handouts we were provided with by the club, but we were confronted by several hardcore French fans. It ended up with riot police thinking we were starting something and throwing tear gas into the pub. After this, we got to the stadium, but there were no turnstile operators to let us in, so we climbed over the turnstiles in hordes to get into the Gers end.

Inside the ground many Rangers fans were interspersed with the French supporters in the 32,000 crowd but there was no sign of trouble. Rangers had last played in the Parc des Princes in a European Cup play-off against Nice in 1956 and forty-five years later they enjoyed a degree of revenge for their defeat, by beating their French opponents on penalties.

It had been another tense night and neither team was able to make the breakthrough in the ninety minutes. A Ronaldinho corner hit the crossbar, but it was the only significant contribution from the Brazilian. The match went to extra time and penalties looked a certainty. Then, with two minutes left, PSG goalie Letizi pulled down Claudio Caniggia in the area and a penalty was awarded. Ronald de Boer took responsibility and promptly blasted it over the bar. The Rangers fans were stunned and were convinced they were about to witness another glorious failure. But for once, it was the Scots who came through. Despite misses from Konterman and Caniggia, the shoot-out went to sudden death. Rangers captain Barry Ferguson stepped up and slotted his home before his PSG counterpart Mauricio Pochettino missed the vital kick.

Gary King recalled, 'The match was good, with the exception of de Boer missing a penalty. That match probably helped Barry Ferguson grow as a player because he coolly slotted home his penalty. We had a gruelling trip back to Ostend for the return flight to Glasgow, and didn't get home until around seven in the morning, and I had to go to work for nine!'

The victory sparked huge celebrations. In a rare show of emotion, Dick Advocaat raced onto the pitch at the end and celebrated with his players. No-one realised it then, but it was to be his last major triumph as a Rangers manager, because five days after the victory he moved into a role as director of football and was replaced as manager by Alex McLeish. It was a surprising choice and one that split the support. McLeish was recruited from Hibs, where he had enjoyed some success the previous season. He quickly re-established a sense of unity among a squad riven by factionalism and although the league was out of reach when he took over he made progress in the domestic cups and had the chance to win a place in the UEFA Cup quarter-final.

Ironically, it was Dutch opposition Rangers would face in the last sixteen, in the shape of Feyenoord of Rotterdam. The first leg at Ibrox, on 21 February 2002, was marred by violence from Feyenoord's notorious hooligan element, who attempted to storm through the segregation and attack Rangers supporters. The area of the Govan stand that they attempted to get into contained many elderly supporters and a large number of terrified children, who were left in tears. Thankfully the police managed to restore order before the trouble got out of hand but it was a worrying incident. The match itself was less incident packed, Feyenoord taking the lead before Barry Ferguson equalized from the penalty spot with ten minutes to go.

In the second leg at Feyenoord's De Kuip stadium it was yet another case of what might have been. Rangers took the lead through Neil McCann and were well in control until a devastating period just before half-time. Former Celtic striker Pierre Van Hooijdonk was renowned for his prowess with a dead ball, so it was vital that Rangers didn't give him any opportunities round the penalty area. Unfortunately, Feyenoord were well-versed in conning referees into doing just that and twice they won free kicks on the edge of the box. On both occasions Van Hooijdonk curled almost identical shots into the net, although some questions had to be asked about the positioning of Stefan Klos. Feyenoord scored again in the second half, but Barry Ferguson converted another penalty eight minutes later to set up a grandstand finish.

Neil McCann was then sent off for talking back to the referee and Rangers missed a number of chances. Feyenoord eventually went all the way to the final, beating Borussia Dortmund in their own stadium to lift the trophy. Many felt Rangers could, and should, have beaten Feyenoord, as they were the better team on the night. Some fans still believe Dick Advocaat may have been able to provide that vital edge in his homeland that could have taken Rangers through, maybe even to win the tournament.

The following season's UEFA Cup, of 2002/03, provided Rangers with one of their most inglorious European defeats against the unknown Czechs, Viktoria Zizkov. In the first leg in the Czech Republic, Rangers were poor and conceded two goals, but even though they had played badly they could have come back with a better result. Barry Ferguson missed a first-half penalty and Shota Arveladze had a late goal disallowed. The second leg at Ibrox was an astonishing match and even now it's hard to believe that Rangers didn't go through. Ronald De Boer scored twice to take the game into extra time and had things turned out differently the match would have been remembered as one of his best for the club.

Rangers' bombardment of the Zizkov goal continued and Neil McCann looked to have secured the win when he scored in the ninety-seventh minute. Then, out of nothing, Zizkov scored a crucial away goal, Licfa capitalising on poor marking. Rangers threw everything at Zizkov but were unable to find the net. Goalkeeper Pavel Kucera was inspired, making unbelievable save after unbelievable save. At one point the referee appeared to give Rangers a penalty before changing his mind. In a last, desperate throw of the dice Stefan Klos went forward and almost scored, but, inevitably, his header was brilliantly saved by his opposite number. Rangers were out on away goals, but in reality the tie had been lost in the first leg. It was an inauspicious start for Alex McLeish in his first full season as manager, especially as Celtic would go all the way to the final of the 2003 UEFA Cup in Seville, where they lost to Porto.

If Europe had been a disaster, McLeish enjoyed a better time of things domestically, winning a glorious treble. The league was clinched in a dramatic, last-day shoot-out, Rangers beating Dunfermline 6–1 while Celtic could only manage a 4–1 win over Kilmarnock, although in fairness it should have been secured much earlier. The title triumph put Rangers into the following season's Champions League qualifiers, in which they faced a tricky tie against Danish champions FC Copenhagen. A 1–1 draw at Ibrox meant Rangers faced an uphill battle in the Danish capital. However, a Mikel Arteta penalty gave them the lead in the Parken stadium. The Danes equalized in the second half but with four minutes to go Shota Arveladze scored a wonderful winner, hooking a Nerlinger cross over his shoulder and into the net.

Growing speculation that captain Barry Ferguson was leaving to join Blackburn Rovers in the English Premiership overshadowed the result. The controversial £6.5 million move was soon confirmed. It meant he missed out on a mouth-watering Champions League group featuring yet another 'Battle of Britain', this time with the biggest of them all, Manchester United. German side Vfb Stuttgart and Panathinaikos of Greece were the other teams in the group. Stuttgart were a talented young team and riding high in the *Bundesliga* when they faced Rangers at Ibrox in the opening match. They had gone five matches without conceding a goal and the omens were not good for Rangers when an early strike by Kevin Kuranyi put the Germans in control. But with less than twenty minutes to go the match sprung into life. Christian Nerlinger scored an equalizer in the seventy-third minute that sent the home fans wild with delight, and five minutes later Peter Lovenkrands burst through to score the winner. Lovenkrands scored several vital goals both in Europe and domestically before leaving for Schalke in the summer of 2006, but he was a frustrating player. A glaring miss in the last minute of the Stuttgart game summed him up. With an open goal gaping he somehow managed to hit the crossbar from just a few yards. The victory was as welcome as it had seemed unexpected and got Rangers off to a great start.

The second match was against Panathinaikos in Greece. Fernando Ricksen missed the game as he was recovering from a bad head injury he suffered in the Stuttgart match. Nevertheless, he still found himself making the headlines: as club officials relaxed in the sun by the pool at the team hotel in Athens, Ricksen took it upon himself to throw chairman John McClelland into the water. Unfortunately the prank backfired as McClelland could barely swim and the player had to jump in and help him out of the pool. McClelland reportedly lost his Cartier watch, a digital camera and his mobile phone but insisted he was not upset by the Dutchman's japes. He told the *Daily Record*: 'There was nothing sinister about it. It was just good fun and he and I sat and watched the Panathinaikos game together the following evening and were laughing our heads off about it.'

On the pitch, Rangers scored an early goal through the Brazilian Emerson and looked in control, but they sat too deep and were punished by conceding an equalizer in the closing minutes. Before the match a 1–1 draw would have seemed a good result in a hostile atmosphere, but, in retrospect, Rangers felt they should have won the game. That match was the start of a dreadful spell in which close-season signings Emerson, Nuno Capucho and

Paolo Vanoli were subjected to trenchant criticism and the first doubts about Alex McLeish's tenure were aired.

The much-hyped double-header with Manchester United came next but few Rangers fans approached the games with anything other than trepidation. United were the richest club in the world and possessed players like Roy Keane, Ruud Van Nistelrooy and Cristiano Ronaldo; Rangers were in dire financial straits and a team very much in transition. Alex McLeish's squad was barely good enough for the SPL and these matches put that in stark relief.

A major police operation was launched for the first game in Glasgow but it failed to prevent trouble in the vicinity of Ibrox from a group of United hooligans known as The Men in Black (so named because they dressed from head to toe in black). Estimates of the numbers involved range from 20 to 200, but it was probably closer to the former. Their reign of terror amounted to running down Paisley Road West and punching or kicking any Rangers fans they encountered, including men with their wives and children. The United fans inside Ibrox were a credit to their club though, and gave their team plenty of backing throughout the match. The atmosphere was fevered, with a card display creating a 'Blue Sea of Ibrox' when the teams emerged. It coincided with the reintroduction of an old song of that name as part of the fans' repertoire.

The din from the Rangers fans was deafening, but it was killed stone-dead in the opening minutes when the unlikely figure of Phil Neville opened the scoring. Rangers recovered from the shock to play well and almost scored through a spectacular diving header from Vanoli. Lovenkrands was deployed on the right and he was Rangers' most dangerous player. But the goal didn't come and Sir Alex Ferguson departed from the home of his former club with the three points.

If Rangers had been unlucky in the first game, then they were totally outplayed at Old Trafford and were lucky to escape with only a 3–0 defeat. Diego Forlan opened the scoring in the sixth minute with a brilliant volley. For the rest of the match the Ibrox men were chasing shadows and for Rangers supporters it was a sad sight. It was hard to imagine any other Rangers team in history going down with such a lack of fight, even against a team of United's quality. Two goals from Van Nistelrooy, whose threat had been so effectively dealt with when he played for PSV against Rangers four years earlier, completed the scoring.

Defeat in Germany against Stuttgart on 26 November 2003 would almost certainly rule out qualifying for the next stage. Despite the poor showing in Manchester, around seven thousand Rangers fans made the trip with the team and on the day of the game most of them gathered in the main square, known as the *Schlossplatz*. As usual the beer was flowing but it was a good-natured day with fans of both teams mixing freely. The match coincided with the start of Stuttgart's Christmas market and the thousands of Rangers fans shared the *Schlossplatz* with a children's funfair, a somewhat surreal sight. The good humour continued on the underground trains to the Gottlieb-Daimler stadium as the two sets of supporters happily travelled together. However, when the Rangers fans got to the ground they faced chaotic scenes.

The away allocation for the ground was only 3,000 and as a result many Scots had bought black-market tickets for the home section or simply turned up without tickets. But when they got to the ground, anyone who was obviously a Rangers fan was directed to the away section, no matter where their ticket was for, or whether they even had one at all. Ignoring all protests, riot police corralled the Rangers fans into a narrow, fenced-off lane that was unlit and slippery underfoot, and eventually led to a security checkpoint.

Scott Buchanan had a ticket for the Stuttgart end but was forced into the Rangers section by police. He recalled:

> A ticket checkpoint was set up outside the ground but most people were allowed to pass through without any actual checks being done. Some showed tickets for other sections of the ground and others just waved blank pieces of paper. Some just walked through unchallenged. I had paid £70 for my ticket and it's still sitting at home completely intact. We then had to cross a rickety, temporary bridge that crossed a fence surrounding the outside of the stadium. You genuinely felt that this could collapse at any time. It was covered in leaves and was really slippy and it created a bottleneck. Serious crushing could have happened if there had been any sort of panic. Inside the Rangers section there was literally no room to move. There were at least 5,000 inside there, probably more, and you were forced to stand in passageways and on stairways. No-one could have sat down even if they wanted to, and if Rangers had scored there could have been a tragedy. I would always have thought Germany would have been the strictest place for crowd safety but this was a shambles. A disaster waiting to happen.

On the pitch, Rangers lost an uninspiring game 1–0 and were knocked out of the Champions League. All that remained was the prospect of a place in the UEFA Cup, but even that proved beyond their means when they lost 3–1 to a less-than-impressive Panathinaikos team at Ibrox. Michael Mols had opened the scoring with a good header in the first half and even when the Greeks equalized there seemed little danger that Rangers wouldn't get the required point. But, in the second half, Basinas scored with a spectacular thirty-five-yard shot after the defence parted and a third was added in the closing minutes. It was a dreadful night and the fans were quick to vent their spleen. Rangers had proved to be little more than average during their campaign and apart from the first two matches it had been painful viewing.

The rest of the season was just as dire. Rangers finished nineteen points behind Celtic in the league, scoring twenty-nine fewer goals in the process, lost a League Cup semi-final on penalties to Hibs and were knocked out of the Scottish Cup in the fifth round by Celtic. The only consolation was that the rest of the SPL were even worse; Rangers managed to finish second and enter the Champions League qualifiers for season 2004/05.

The draw sent Rangers back to Russia again, and reunited them with opponents from their first Champions League campaign in 1992, CSKA Moscow. It was not the draw that Alex McLeish wanted. The Soviet era had long-since gone, and big money was being spent at Russian clubs. CSKA, the former army club, were no longer just a team hand-picked from the local regiments. The Brazilian forward Vagner Love had cost them more than £6 million and there were top-class players from all over Eastern Europe in their team, notably Jiri Jarosik of the Czech Republic and the Croatia international, Ivica Olic.

In the first leg in Moscow, Alex McLeish sprung a surprise by playing new signing Dado Prso on the left, rather than through the middle. He also recalled Maurice Ross at right back, a player who had seemed to have little future at the club. Rangers got off to the worst possible start as defensive slackness allowed Love to head past Rangers captain Stefan Klos from close-range in just four minutes. CSKA continued to cause problems for Rangers and would have considered themselves unlucky not to add to their lead. As the first half progressed, Rangers gradually came back into things and shortly before half-time managed to get an equalizer through another new signing, Nacho Novo. But a minute into the second half, Rangers were caught out again. Jarosik was able to breeze past two weak challenges before shooting past Klos.

Rangers managed to prevent any further breaches of their defence and their away goal gave them every chance of progressing. However, they would have to do so without Alex Rae. The veteran midfielder, signed from Wolves in the summer, was suspended for five games by UEFA following an incident towards the end of the match, his European debut. With the ball free and a mêlée of players surrounding it, CSKA's Moldovan international Serghei Dadu took a kick in the head from Rae. Slow-motion replays made for painful viewing as the Scot's boot did make contact; however, it was by no means clear-cut that he had kicked out deliberately at his grounded opponent, as was alleged.

The ball was free and Rae was perfectly entitled to put in a challenge. He said afterwards: 'The ball was actually there and he put his head down between my foot and the ball. It looked worse than it was, without a doubt.' Dutch referee Jan Wegereef, who was well-placed, agreed, as he took no action at the time and made no mention of the incident in his report. But after days of saturation media coverage in Scotland, UEFA suddenly announced they 'had been made aware' of the incident and would be assessing television pictures, which were quickly made available. Subsequently Rae received the astonishing five-match ban that was upheld after an appeal.

With Rae missing, McLeish gambled on the fitness of £1 million summer signing Dragan Mladenovic, who was recovering from a hamstring injury. An even bigger gamble was the recall for Craig Moore. The Australian had been stripped of the club captaincy and put on the transfer list after insisting on turning out as an overage player at the Olympics instead of playing for his club in the early part of the season. The fans were stunned that Moore had been brought back in to play alongside France international Jean Alain Boumsong. Apart from anything else he hadn't been the same player since the departure of Lorenzo Amoruso, but his defiance of the manager and the club was seen as a calculated snub and one that should have seen him banished for good. The fact that he was at fault when CSKA scored the goal that knocked Rangers out only added to the anger.

Seconds before half-time, Nacho Novo thought he had put the home side in front when he shrugged off the challenge of a defender and fired a superb shot into the net from the edge of the penalty area. But as the celebrations began it became apparent that referee Wolfgang Stark had blown for a foul on the Spaniard. Had he waited a few seconds before going for his whistle, Novo's 'goal' would have stood.

In the second half, CSKA got the goal that silenced the 49,000 crowd. Jarosik got away from Moore in the penalty area and squared for Love, who prodded it home from close-range despite the best efforts of Boumsong. As the tie drifted away, McLeish threw defender Marvin Andrews on as a centre forward for the last few minutes. The move smacked of desperation although it almost paid off. First he set up a goal for fellow substitute Steven Thompson in the eighty-seventh minute, and then had a glorious chance to level the tie in the last minute, but shot wide. CSKA went through to the group stages 3–2 on aggregate, and although they failed to qualify, they dropped into the UEFA Cup and went on to lift the trophy.

After being beaten by the Russians, Rangers also went into the UEFA Cup. Because the competition had by now lost much of its allure, the European governing body introduced a group stage for the first time. It guaranteed more games and, of course, more money, although it remained a pale imitation of the Champions League. It was still vital that Rangers took part, so victory in the qualifying round against Portuguese club Maritimo was essential.

Rangers were lucky to escape from the holiday island of Madeira with only a 1–0 defeat after a dreadful first-leg performance. It was Alex McLeish's fifteenth European match with Rangers and he had never seen his team keep a clean-sheet. The return at Ibrox was a dour encounter, with Dado Prso scoring the equalizer in the seventieth minute. With no more goals, the match went to extra time and then penalties. The French left back Gregory Vignal, on loan from Liverpool, emerged as the unlikely hero in the shoot-out. Maritimo, who were apparently unsettled by the racket from the Ibrox crowd during their kicks, missed two while Shota Arveladze was the only Rangers player to fail. It came down to Vignal, and he stepped up to score the winning penalty. The victory sparked scenes of celebration that some thought excessive, but they were probably inspired by relief. Defeat would have been disastrous for Rangers and could easily have cost Alex McLeish his job. Rangers had already dropped seven points in their opening seven league games, including a defeat to Celtic in the first Old Firm match of the season. But the victory over Maritimo gave new impetus to a season that would eventually end in glory, in the most dramatic fashion imaginable.

Rangers were top seeds in their group and were drawn with Auxerre, Dutch club AZ Alkmaar, Grazer AK from Austria and the Poles Amica Wronki. The teams played each other once, and had two games at home and two away, with the top three qualifying. Rangers' opening match on 21 October 2004 saw them travel to Wronki in Poland. The local team was sponsored by the white-goods company, Amica, and the firm dominated the small town.

The travelling Rangers fans based themselves at the Polonez hotel in the neighbouring city of Poznan and the local newspaper *Gazeta* reported how some – between the 'singing, cheering and drinking beer' – visited the Poznan Citadel, a graveyard for pilots killed during wartime air-raids on Poland. As well as Britons, the cemetery is also the final resting place for pilots from Canada, Australia, New Zealand, Greece, Czechoslovakia, Lithuania, South Africa and Jamaica. It also contains the graves of prisoners from the war camp in Zagan, who were captured and shot in 1944 during an escape bid. The events were immortalised in the classic Steve McQueen film, *The Great Escape*. The newspaper reported a Rangers supporter called Allan saying on his arrival at the airport, 'We want to go there, because we are Rangers fans. And Rangers fans are patriots.'

Gazeta also told the story of one of the men buried in the Commonwealth cemetery at the citadel. RAF pilot sergeant John Macintosh, a Scot, was flying a Lancaster bomber that took part in a bombing raid on the Baltic Sea coast between Denmark and Poland on the night of 28 April 1943. Out of 207 British planes, the Germans managed to shoot down twenty-two, including the Lancaster that sergeant Macintosh was flying. Three men died instantly, while the other four crew members parachuted to safety. Sergeant Macintosh was buried with his friend, an air gunner by the name of M. Savage. The inscription on the gravestone reads: 'In loving memory of our dear son Johnny. Fondly remembered. Dad, mum and family.'

The small band of Rangers supporters in the 3,000 crowd enjoyed one of their best away performances in Europe for several years and their biggest win since the victory over Sturm Graz in September 2000. Goals from Lovenkrands, Novo, Ricksen, Arveladze and Thompson gave Rangers an emphatic victory against a team that had threatened sporadically in the first half but were overwhelmed after the break.

A 3–0 victory over Grazer at Ibrox in the second game made Rangers odds-on favourites to go through. The Austrians had the best of the first half, thwarting Rangers' laboured attempts at attack and causing plenty of problems of their own. Stefan Klos had to make a good save in the thirty-fourth minute to stop Grazer taking the lead. Alex McLeish changed the tactics in the second half, pushing young French-Tunisian Hamed Namouchi from midfield into an attacking role alongside Dado Prso. The move had a positive effect and in the fifty-eighth minute he was involved as Rangers broke the deadlock. He was barged off the ball thirty yards out and, from the resulting free kick by Fernando Ricksen, Novo scored at the back post. Four minutes from the end, another Ricksen free kick was nodded down by Prso to Namouchi; his shot was cleared off the line but fell to Shota Arveladze who tapped in from close-range. Namouchi capped a good performance by shooting home after a fine run and cross from the right wing by Novo.

Next Rangers travelled to Holland – on 3 December 2004 – to face AZ Alkmaar. Coached by former Ajax boss Co Adriaanse, AZ were flying high in the Dutch league and brought an end to Rangers' sixteen-match unbeaten run in all competitions. Danny Landzaat got the only goal of the game in the seventh-minute but the Dutch team's speed and mobility caused Rangers plenty of problems.

Significantly, Newcastle United manager Graeme Souness and his assistant Dean Saunders watched the match. They had travelled to monitor the performance of France central defender Boumsong. The 24-year-old had only been signed in the summer on a Bosman from Auxerre, but almost from the day of his arrival he was being linked with a big-money move away. He had been Rangers' best player in the opening half of the season and supporters were alarmed at the prospect of him leaving.

On the morning of the final group match, coincidentally against his old club Auxerre, it emerged that Souness had lodged an £8 million bid for Boumsong. This news seemed to unsettle the player and he put in an atrocious performance. He was not alone. Rangers only needed to draw to go through, but were awful on the night. Their performance was not helped by a team selection that left the 49,000 crowd scratching their heads. In an attempt to outwit the veteran French coach Guy Roux, Fernando Ricksen was moved to right back from midfield, where he had been outstanding all season. Zurab Khizanishvili, who had been playing well at full back, was moved into a holding-midfield role. Ricksen was uncomfortable in the defensive role while Khizanishvili was out of his depth against Auxerre's Bonavenuture Kalou. Namouchi and Bob Malcolm were preferred in midfield to Alex Rae, who was left on the bench on his return from suspension.

Auxerre took the lead in the ninth minute after a slick move that stemmed from a botched Rangers corner. Kanga Akale made off on a speedy run down the right and, as the Rangers defence desperately tried to get back, he played it inside to Mwaruwari. His cross found Kalou and from the six-yard line he shot against the crossbar, before converting the rebound. Rangers tried to get back into it and had numerous chances, but were always at risk of being caught on the break. At half-time, McLeish switched Ricksen and Khizanishvili but before the Georgian had a chance to settle back into his more familiar role he made a mistake that led to a second and decisive Auxerre goal. Moments after the restart, his weak headed clearance went straight to Akale who played it into Kalou. The Ivory Coast international beat Boumsong with ease and shot past Klos. As news that Grazer had gone 2–0 up against Alkmaar spread around Ibrox, the mood in the stands darkened even further. There were no more goals in either match and Rangers were out, Grazer joining Auxerre and Alkmaar in the next round.

The end of the match was greeted by boos. The fans had seen their team fail to progress from an almost unassailable position. It was yet another blot on Alex McLeish's European record. For the second season in a row Rangers had lost a European game at Ibrox that they only needed to draw in order to progress. Even more galling for the fans was the fact that this wasn't even the Champions League. Rangers had been the top seeds, yet contrived to finish fourth in a five-team group that was far from top quality. The bottom line was that Rangers were simply out of their depth, even in the shallow end of European football.

26

2006: Making History

In the parochial world of the average Old Firm supporter, winning is usually everything and second is nothing. Beating your rival, and gaining the all-important bragging rights for the next twelve months, is the only thing that matters. But where does Europe fit into that? Most Rangers fans would accept that success in European football means more to the outside world than domestic triumphs in Scotland. But how many fans would sacrifice a league championship win for a European trophy? Would second place in the league be acceptable if it was accompanied by a run to the Champions League semi-final? Can a losing UEFA Cup-final appearance compensate for a season without trophies?

It is an almost impossible choice to make, but, over the years, Rangers have demonstrated how difficult it is to enjoy success on two fronts in the same season. Almost all their best European campaigns have come in seasons when they have failed domestically. In 1967, Scot Symon's team reached the final of the European Cup Winners Cup but won nothing at home. The 1972 Cup Winners Cup victory coincided with third place in the league, an early exit from the League Cup and a semi-final defeat in the Scottish Cup. Rangers finished a distant third in the Premier League in 1987/88 when Dynamo Kiev were defeated on the way to the European Cup quarter-final. The first European run beyond Christmas for nine years came in 2001/02, when Rangers finished eighteen points behind Celtic in the league.

And then there was season 2005/06. A season in which Rangers finished outside the top two in the league for the first time in eighteen years, were knocked out of both cup competitions early and suffered the longest run without a victory in the club's history. Yet it was also the season that Rangers went further in the Champions League than any other Scottish club had managed since its reorganisation in the mid 1990s.

Players who struggled against the likes of Aberdeen, Motherwell and Livingston were transformed when they turned out against Inter Milan, Porto and Villarreal. A defence that leaked six goals in two games at Ibrox against Hibernian was able to keep Diego Forlan at bay in the Champions League. A midfield overrun at times by Clyde did not look out of place alongside Villarreal's Juan Roman Riquelme, one of the best players in the world. And a strike force that struggled to penetrate the defence of Dundee United scored three times against Porto, Champions League winners two years earlier. Even the manager was transformed. After being embarrassed by the tactics of Falkirk coach John Hughes, Alex McLeish outmanoeuvred the wily Co Adriaanse of Porto.

Rangers had gone into the final qualifying round of the Champions League as Scottish champions after a dramatic title win on the final day of the last season. Going into the final games on 22 May 2005, Rangers knew that their only chance of winning the league was to beat Hibernian in Edinburgh and for Celtic to fail to overcome Motherwell at Fir Park. With minutes remaining, it looked like Celtic had done enough. Rangers were ahead but Celtic were leading 1–0 at Motherwell. Suddenly the Rangers supporters at Easter Road erupted. News had filtered through that Terry Butcher's Motherwell had scored. Then, unbelievably, they got a second goal. Seconds later both games were over and Rangers were the champions for the fifty-first time in the most dramatic circumstances imaginable.

After a summer of celebrations, the Rangers fans could look forward to another assault on the Champions League. Anorthosis Famagusta, the Cypriot champions, were the opposition in the qualifying round after they beat Trabzonspor of Turkey in the previous round. The SPL's fixtures computer did Rangers no favours. The first leg in Cyprus on 9 August was sandwiched between gruelling trips north to Inverness Caledonian Thistle and Aberdeen. 'Only in Scotland I feel that could happen,' said an exasperated Alex McLeish. But, regardless of the fixture list, as Dado Prso pointed out, if Rangers couldn't beat Famagusta then they did not deserve to be in the Champions League.

During the summer, McLeish had plundered the French market to strengthen his squad. Defender Jose-Karl Pierre-Fanfan was signed from Paris St Germain along with Marseille midfielder Brahim Hemdani. Ian Murray was snapped up from Hibs on a Bosman but attempts to keep Greek central defender Sotirios Kyrgiakos, who had signed on a short-term deal the previous January, collapsed over terms. Instead, McLeish turned back to France and brought in the Monaco defender Julien Rodriguez, who had been a team-mate of Dado Prso when Monaco had played Rangers in the Champions

League five years earlier. He jumped at the chance of coming to Glasgow after experiencing the Ibrox atmosphere.

Rodriguez was thrown straight in at the deep-end, making his debut in the first leg against Famagusta in Nicosia. The Rangers players were reputedly on a bonus of £45,000 per man to reach the Champions League proper, a payout of almost £1 million for the squad. It was an indication of just how vital progression to the lucrative group stage was. After several seasons of downsizing, Rangers' financial position was far healthier than it had been in the aftermath of Dick Advocaat's profligate era. But there was no doubt that the funds generated by the Champions League were still hugely important.

Playing Rodriguez from the start was not McLeish's only gamble in Cyprus. Marvin Andrews – who had been informed in the middle of the previous season that he urgently required surgery for knee-ligament damage – partnered the Frenchman in the centre of defence. He had refused to go under the knife, preferring to put his faith in God to repair his injury, and continued to play an important part in the league-winning campaign. Doubts remained over his fitness, though, not to mention his ability to play at the highest level. Fanfan was deployed in an unfamiliar role at right back and there was a return to the team for Michael Ball at left back. After starting the season at full back, Fernando Ricksen was moved into midfield, where he had played so well the previous season.

Although the defence occasionally looked unconvincing, the decision to put Ricksen in a more forward role paid off. He put in a man-of-the-match performance and was involved in both goals as Rangers secured an impressive 2–1 first-leg win. The Anorthosis player-manager was Georgian Temuri Ketsbaia, who previously played for Newcastle United and Dundee, and his team included former international teammate Georgi Kinkladze. The Cypriots caused some problems for Rangers in the first half, with Andrews in particular looking vulnerable. But as the game wore on Rangers looked stronger and in sixty-five minutes took the lead. Prso got to the goal-line and sent in a dangerous cross from the right that was met by an acrobatic volley from Ricksen. The goalkeeper pulled off a tremendous save but could only palm it out to Novo who reacted quickly to stab home his first goal of the season. Five minutes later Prso and Ricksen were involved again, as Rangers doubled their lead. The Croatian international produced a clever reverse pass that released Ricksen in the penalty area. He spun before prodding the ball under the onrushing goalkeeper. An error by Rodriguez moments later allowed Frousos to score and give the Cypriots some hope, but Rangers were in a strong position for the second leg.

Days before the return at Ibrox, Famagusta were struck by tragedy when a Helios Airways flight from Larnaca airport in Cyprus crashed just outside Athens, killing 115 passengers and 6 crew. On board were several well-known supporters of the club, as well as four members of captain Nikos Nikolaou's family. A perfectly observed one-minute silence took place before the match.

Ketsbaia was roundly booed by the home fans whenever he touched the ball thanks to his pre-match suggestions that Rangers were cheats because they had more money to spend than his club. However, despite the barracking, the 37-year-old caused problems for Rangers in the opening stages and after several optimistic long-range efforts sailed over the bar he eventually found his range with a thirty-yard drive that crashed off the post. Ian Murray was deployed to man-mark the Georgian and the veteran quickly became a marginal figure. In the thirty-ninth minute Thomas Buffel calmed Rangers nerves with a fine left-foot finish after build-up play from Ricksen and Novo. In the fifty-eighth minute, Prso ended the game as a contest with a solo run that left two defenders floundering before curling a shot past goalkeeper Georgallides.

For the seventh time, Rangers were in the sectional stages of the Champions League. The draw put them in Group H with Inter Milan, Porto and Artmedia Bratislava of Slovakia. The Italians and Portuguese were the clear favourites to go through but the presence of Artmedia was the more interesting story. The tiny Slovakian side had caused a major upset in the first qualifying round when they sensationally defeated Celtic 5–0 in the first leg in Bratislava. The Scots were embarrassingly knocked out of Europe before the season had even begun, with a 4–0 victory at Parkhead in the return proving too little too late.

In the opening group match on 13 September 2005 Rangers played host to Co Adriaanse's Porto. A spectacular red-white-and-blue card display welcomed the teams onto the pitch and set the scene for a classic. Porto looked impressive in patches during the game but an excellent performance from Barry Ferguson helped Rangers to a famous victory. Twice the Ibrox side took the lead through Peter Lovenkrands and Dado Prso, only to see Porto equalize. Then, with the match drifting towards a 2–2 draw, Rangers won a free-kick forty yards out. It was taken short to Ferguson who launched the ball into the penalty area and Kyrgiakos rose to flick it into the net.

A trip to the San Siro to face Internazionale would normally be a daunting task. As Rangers discovered when they travelled to Milan in 1984, the combination of *Serie A* superstars and a hostile crowd can be a potent mixture. So when the 80,000 screaming fans are removed from the equation, it can only be of benefit to the visiting team. UEFA had imposed a four-match spectator ban on Inter following trouble at the Champions League semi-final against city rivals AC Milan the season before. Unfortunately, it meant Rangers fans were also prevented from attending, although that didn't stop several from doing their best to beat the ban.

In the end, seven hundred people including club officials, sponsors and press witnessed the match. Given Rangers domestic woes, there were many who feared what Inter might do to them, even in an empty stadium. As it turned out, Rangers put in a battling performance in the surreal atmosphere and were unlucky to lose the game by a goal to nil. It could have been so different; after just two minutes, Inter had the ball in the back of the net through Nigerian striker Obafemi Martins but it was ruled offside. Later in the first half, a perfect cross from Buffel found Peter Lovenkrands six yards from goal. He looked certain to score but somehow blasted it over. Inter also missed a penalty, although justice was done as television replays showed that Ronald Waterreus had played the ball rather than the player when Martins fell in the box.

Inter made the breakthrough from a free kick two minutes after the restart. Pizarro's effort from just outside the box took a wicked deflection off Esteban Cambiasso and landed in the back of the net. Late in the game, Rangers threw caution to the wind in the search for an equalizer but they couldn't make the breakthrough. A 1–0 defeat was no embarrassment, though, and it gave Rangers confidence for the remaining matches.

There was shock news from the other match. Artmedia, who had been two goals down in Oporto, had fought back to win 3–2.

Suddenly Group H was wide open and Rangers needed a positive result when they played host to Artmedia in the next match. Rangers had a succession of chances, but a combination of good goalkeeping and poor finishing denied them the lead their play deserved. First Dado Prso then the young Argentinian, Federico Nieto, had good opportunities in the first half but had their shots saved well by Juraj Cobej. The goalkeeper pulled off another good save when Hamed Namouchi broke through one-on-one and five minutes before half-time he denied Sotirios Kyrgiakos. After the break Cobej continued his inspired form, saving from Olivier Bernard, and for all their pressure Rangers couldn't break Artmedia down. The match ended goalless and Rangers' hopes of becoming the first Scottish club to make it into the knockout stages suffered a serious blow, especially when news came through that Porto had beaten Inter 2–0.

The return match on 1 November took place at the Tehelne Pole stadium. The game had been moved from Artmedia's ground to the larger stadium but Rangers fans still found themselves in conditions that would have been considered unacceptable in Scotland in the 1950s. A lack of turnstiles meant lengthy delays to get in and, with no obvious stewarding, the scenes outside the ground were chaotic. Police in riot gear stood by menacingly on the lookout for any troublemakers and when none were forthcoming, they occasionally lashed out with their batons at random. Just as in Stuttgart three years earlier, the Rangers section was dangerously overcrowded because the authorities were herding away fans into that area whether they had a valid ticket or not. It seemed that the lessons of Stuttgart had not been learned and it beggars belief that in the modern era, when UEFA insists that competing clubs must meet stringent standards for the media, advertisers and their own delegates, no such criteria are in force to ensure the safety of supporters.

On the pitch, Rangers took the lead within three minutes. Brahim Hemdani's free-kick was headed on by Kyrgiakos, who set up Dado Prso for a close-range header. But in a whirlwind opening, Artmedia were back on level terms within five minutes. Balazs Borbely scrambled the ball home from close range after a mêlée in the Rangers penalty area. Rangers were on top for the rest of the half and they got their just reward when Steven Thompson powered home a header from a Dado Prso cross a minute before the break. In the second half, Artmedia were more dangerous and Jan Kozak scored another equalizer with half an hour to go. The match finished at 2–2, leaving both teams level on five points in second place behind Inter. 'Three points would have given us a marvellous chance to progress but we still have a great opportunity,' said Alex McLeish, afterwards. 'The players know what they are capable of doing and they have shown that tonight.'

A 2–1 defeat for Porto in Milan left them languishing at the bottom of the group and the Portuguese champions desperately needed to win against Rangers to keep in contention. Having lost four points in their double-header with Artmedia it was important for Rangers to get at least a point in the Estadio do Dragao on 23 November. The Scottish champions had gone into the game in fourth place in the SPL, fifteen points behind leaders Celtic. The league was already out of reach and the pressure on Alex McLeish was becoming intense. David Murray had set a deadline for him to turn the club's fortunes around: he would be assessed at the beginning of December and it seemed that only a dramatic improvement in results would save him from the sack.

On the night, Rangers got the result they had set out for against Porto, but it was by no means a pretty performance. With the ineffectual Francis Jeffers playing as a lone striker, Rangers barely ventured out of their own half for an hour, opting instead to soak up the Porto attacks. It was only after Porto broke the deadlock in the sixtieth minute, when Lisandro Lopez headed home a cross from Jose Bosingwa, that Rangers emerged from their shell. Steven Thompson was immediately brought on and was shortly followed by teenage striker Ross McCormack and winger Chris Burke.

The introduction of the three Scots changed Rangers' fortunes and with seven minutes to go they got an unexpected equalizer. A cross from Fernando Ricksen on the right seemed to be overhit, but Burke refused to give up and managed to head it back across goal. McCormack was the first to react and he side-footed the ball past Vitor Baia, becoming the first Scot to score for Rangers in the Champions League group stage since Kenny Miller five years earlier. Later McCormack insisted he was keeping his feet on the ground amid the adulation: 'I don't want to get too carried away because if you do that your career could be over before it starts.' The youngster must have been wondering if his words were coming back to haunt him after he was shipped out on loan the following January. Three months after his Champions League heroics he was fighting it out for Doncaster Rovers in England's League One, the equivalent of the old third division.

The equalizer stunned Porto, but Rangers still had to hang on in the closing minutes. Only a superb double save from Ronald Waterreus as the game drew to a close kept them level. But the point was invaluable and meant Rangers held their fate in their own hands. Captain Barry Ferguson summed up the Rangers approach afterwards. 'There wasn't much football played but we came to frustrate them because they are a very good side. It wasn't a great display, but the effort was unbelievable.'

It now all came down to the final match-day on 6 December. Four years to the day after the last time they clinched European football after Christmas, the stage was set for a night of drama at Ibrox. Victory for Rangers would guarantee them a place in the knockout stages, while a draw would be enough as long as Artmedia didn't win their home match against Porto. Even a defeat would take Rangers through if Artmedia and Porto drew. It was widely expected that the Inter match would be Alex McLeish's last in charge as domestic results had not improved since Murray's ultimatum in November.

The Blue Order, a fans' group based in the Broomloan stand, raised funds from supporters to provide another card display for the match. It featured a massive Union flag in the Govan stand and two saltires at either end. The resulting display was even more spectacular than the one before the Porto game and provided an inspirational backdrop as the teams emerged from the tunnel. The Union flag even gained the fans a world record for the biggest-ever human national flag, beating a record set in the United Arab Emirates.

Rangers were in all blue, reminiscent of their historic European nights against Bayern and Juventus in the seventies, and started the match positively. They had a good opportunity early on when Chris Burke broke clear on the right and sent in a dangerous cross to the back post. Hamed Namouchi managed to get a head to it but Marco Andreolli blocked his effort. The Austrian referee turned down a penalty appeal from Rangers but it was Inter who broke the deadlock with their first serious pressure. A long-range shot from Adriano was deflected wide for a corner. The first in-swinger from Sinisa Mihailovic was punched behind by Waterreus but the second attempt found the head of Adriano who headed in off the post despite the attentions of Andrews.

Those Rangers fans who had watched their team fall at the final hurdle so many times before could have been forgiven for thinking they were about to see a repeat performance, but eight minutes later the Scots were level. A brilliant pass from Thomas Buffel inside the Rangers half released Peter Lovenkrands through the middle. He ran half the length of the pitch before finishing low past goalkeeper Francesco Toldo.

The second half was a tense affair both on the pitch and in the stands. With no goals in the other match, Rangers could afford to play for a draw but at any moment that could change. In the eighty-seventh minute Inter's Cristiano Zanetti was sent off for a second yellow card. From the resulting free kick, Bob Malcolm whipped in a superb cross only to see an unchallenged Namouchi head wide from close range. Even though a draw may not have been enough, the last few minutes were played out at walking pace with Rangers terrified that Inter would break and score. The final whistle was greeted with half-hearted cheers as the match in Bratislava was still going on. When that game finally ended goalless the Rangers players and fans could begin their celebrations.

Rangers were into the last sixteen of the Champions League, the furthest they had been since 1993. It was also the first time any Scottish team, including the national side, had qualified from the group stages of an international competition. Despite the achievement, with Rangers struggling in fifth place in the league, most commentators expected Alex McLeish either to be sacked or to stand down after the match. But, not for the first time, David Murray shocked everyone by announcing that McLeish would be staying on to lead the team in the knockout stages. It was a brave decision in some ways. McLeish had been a dead man walking for weeks and most chairmen would have taken the easy option of sacking him. On the other hand, cynics suggested that the only reason McLeish was still in a job was because Murray couldn't find a suitable replacement. Rumours were already circulating in Glasgow that the French coach, Paul Le Guen, had been lined up to take over.

The draw for the last sixteen paired Rangers with Villarreal of Spain's *La Liga*. The club, nicknamed *El Submarino Amarillo* (The Yellow Submarine), hail from the small town of Vila-real, which was best known for the production of ceramic tiles until the rise to prominence of the local football club at the end of the 1990s. Formed in 1923, Villarreal spent their first seventy years in the relative obscurity of Spain's regional leagues before winning promotion to the national second division. Six years later they competed in the *Primera* league for the first time. Progress was steady if unspectacular, but, in the summer of 2003, they won their first European trophy, beating Heerenven in the final of the Intertoto Cup. That allowed them to play in the UEFA Cup, in which they reached the semi-final, beating Celtic in the last eight. The following season they repeated their Intertoto feat and this time reached the last eight of the UEFA Cup, losing to Rangers' conquerors AZ Alkmaar. The same year, Villarreal achieved their best league position ever, finishing third in *La Liga* behind Barcelona and Real Madrid to qualify for the Champions League for the first time.

With star names like Juan Roman Riquelme, Diego Forlan, Juan Pablo Sorin and Alessio Tacchinardi, Villarreal beat Everton 4–2 on aggregate in the qualifying round. In the group stage, they were drawn with Manchester United, Portuguese champions Benfica and French club Lille. Against expectations they qualified by topping the group with two wins and four draws, including two goalless matches with United.

Twelve days before the crucial last-sixteen tie, it was announced that McLeish would be leaving Rangers at the end of the season after four-and-a-half years in charge. His domestic record of seven trophies, including two league titles, stood up to scrutiny but most Rangers fans felt he had reached the end of his shelf-life. McLeish himself admitted his time had come. By now Rangers were twenty-one points behind Celtic and struggling to qualify for the UEFA Cup, let alone the Champions League. Paul Le Guen was now the firm favourite to take over. In the run-up to the Villarreal match, Le Guen, working as a summariser for French television channel Canal Plus, warned the Spaniards they faced a difficult task against the Glasgow side:

It is true from a technical point of view that this Rangers side is perhaps not as good as Villarreal at the moment.But Rangers have other, vital qualities at their disposal. There is a reason that they have got this far and it is thanks to those very qualities; commitment, a never-say-die attitude and a hungry approach to such challenges.

Villarreal arrived in Scotland for the first leg on 22 February 2006 antici-
pating a tough battle to overcome both the Rangers players and their
'twelfth man' – the Ibrox crowd. Midfielder Josico scored in a 1–1 draw
against Celtic in the UEFA Cup two years earlier and he said, 'Those Celtic
supporters made a big difference and we are worried the Rangers fans will
do the same. That is our big worry; we have to beat their support before we
can beat them.' Teammate Roger added: 'If we can cope with the long balls
and the passion of Ibrox then we can get a result.'

Rangers had secured a much-needed victory over Hibernian on the
weekend before that first leg but McLeish decided to change a winning team.
Champions League specialist Peter Lovenkrands was picked ahead of Kris
Boyd, while Belgian playmaker Thomas Buffel was surprisingly relegated to
the bench in favour of fans' scapegoat Hamed Namouchi. Any tactical plan
Alex McLeish had, though, would have been discarded in the eighth minute
thanks to an inexplicable blunder by Dado Prso. As a cross came in from
the right, the Croat threw his hand in the air and punched the ball away.
French referee Eric Poulat immediately pointed to the spot and Riquelme,
who was back in the team after several weeks out through injury, converted
the penalty. Soon after, the Spaniards thought they had doubled their lead
but Gonzalo's effort was ruled offside.

But Rangers gradually battled their way back into the game and they were
rewarded in twenty-three minutes. Chris Burke burst through the middle
towards the Villarreal penalty area. A defender knocked the ball away from
him but it went straight into the path of Lovenkrands. From the edge of the
penalty area, the Dane struck a powerful, curling shot first time into the top
corner. Ten minutes later, with Rangers on top, Ibrox was stunned again as
Villarreal took the lead through Diego Forlan. The Uruguay international had
been standing well in front of the Rangers defence when Riquelme played
in the original pass, but by the time he received the ball from Gonzalo he
was onside and, under the new offside rules, the goal was allowed to stand.

After the break, Rangers threw everything into attack but it wasn't until
Buffel was brought on with twenty minutes to go that they looked like
equalizing. He was involved in the goal when it came, although it was a
blunder by Villarreal's Juan Manuel Pena that put Rangers level with eight
minutes to go. Buffel's cross from the left was acrobatically deflected into
his own net by the Bolivian defender. A 2–2 draw gave Rangers a slim hope
of progressing but a goal in Spain was essential and they would have to get
it without Prso, who completed a personal nightmare by receiving a needless yellow card in the last minute.

The second leg two weeks later saw a massive travelling support, estimated at between ten and fifteen thousand, head for the Costa Blanca. Unfortunately, Villarreal had only given Rangers 3,000 tickets for the 23,000 capacity El Madrigal stadium. After the crushing at Bratislava, Rangers had fears that the influx of fans without tickets would cause major problems. A lack of organisation and heavy-handed policing created a powder-keg situation in the narrow street outside the ground. As police batons were wielded, some supporters responded by throwing missiles, and, in the mêlée, a window in the Villarreal team bus was cracked. Rangers security chief Lawrence Macintyre later blamed the flashpoint on the local authorities. 'The infrastructure for a match of this magnitude was not good enough,' he said. 'There were no serious injuries but people were traumatised. If the stewarding and policing had been right it would have been great.' Police said they were happy with the behaviour of the travelling fans. Superintendent Tim Love, who was in Spain for Strathclyde Police, played down the incident outside El Madrigal and noted that local police had 'no issues with it'. Earlier, Spanish riot police were accused of attacking British tourists and Rangers fans in the resort of Benidorm. Eight people were arrested in the incident and several Rangers fans were injured.

Apart from overcrowding in the Rangers section, inside El Madrigal there was no trouble at all. Thousands of Rangers fans had bought tickets from Spaniards and mixed happily with home supporters in all sections of the ground. They provided noisy backing for their heroes, who realised a goal was essential. Burke and Namouchi both had early long-range efforts before Buffel forced Sebastian Viera into a save. In twelve minutes the fans were in dreamland, as Peter Lovenkrands opened the scoring. The Dane started the move with a pass out to Buffel who played it into the path of Barry Ferguson. As Viera raced off his line the captain cut the ball back to Lovenkrands, who shot home from twelve yards.

At half-time Villarreal made two changes, Guillermo Franco and Hector Font replacing Jose Mari and Javi Venta and four minutes after the restart the move paid off when Villarreal got an equalizer through Rodolfo Arruabarrena. Kris Boyd was brought on in sixty-three minutes and had Rangers' best chance of the second half. A cross from Burke fell to him yards from the Villarreal goal but he failed to make a connection. The chance was gone and with it went Rangers' hopes of reaching the last eight. There was considerable disappointment at being eliminated on away goals but there was no doubt that reaching the last sixteen was a genuine achievement, especially for a team that was performing so badly at home.

Days later, it emerged that UEFA had launched an investigation into the incident outside the ground, but even more alarmingly for Rangers, Europe's governing body also announced they were looking into claims of 'discriminatory chants' at both legs of the Villarreal tie. The chant in question was 'The Billy Boys', a song sung by Rangers supporters for decades, and containing the line 'Up to our knees in Fenian blood.' The argument by those who defend the song is that 'Fenian' is a word Irish republicans use to describe themselves. Opponents insist it has developed into an abusive term for Roman Catholics. On 12 April, UEFA indicated that this was an issue outwith its remit and therefore took a decision that Rangers fans were not guilty. The singing of the song had to be considered in the context of 'Scotland's social and historical background', UEFA reasoned. A statement read:

> After studying the evidence at hand as well as the statement of Rangers FC, the Control & Disciplinary Body conceded that supporters have been singing the song 'Billy Boys' for years during national and international matches without either the Scottish football or governmental authorities being able to intervene. The result is that this song is now tolerated.

Bizarrely, UEFA's own inspector, the Austrian Gerhard Kapl, then challenged the verdict by the disciplinary committee. He was the official who compiled the evidence during Rangers' matches against Villarreal, and had recommended a £25,000 fine and the closure of a stand at Ibrox. His appeal was partially upheld and Rangers were fined £13,000. Even more worryingly, the club was warned that chants would henceforth be closely scrutinised and a directive effectively banning the singing of 'The Billy Boys' was issued by UEFA.

Opinion is divided among the Rangers support over the song but one thing is clear; if it continues to be sung, particularly in European matches, Rangers will face more stringent punishment. It does raise some questions that so far UEFA have failed to answer. Who defines what is discriminatory or offensive? Will Celtic supporters be punished for their pro-IRA repertoire? Will Aberdeen fans be punished for their obscene chants about the Ibrox disaster? Will Liverpool supporters be taken to task for taunting Manchester United about the Munich air crash? Furthermore, according to *The Herald*, some members of the disciplinary-and-control body that cleared Rangers were concerned about taking action following an anonymous complaint. They were worried that UEFA could face a deluge of complaints from rival supporters with an agenda. Interestingly, a UEFA spokesman insisted the body 'had not disguised' that the investigation was prompted by an anonymous complaint.

The affair cast a shadow over an exciting European campaign and the implications will no doubt be far-reaching. However, with Paul Le Guen installed as coach, it is to be hoped that the focus will shift back to events on the park. The Frenchman was one of the most sought-after young coaches in Europe and having taken Lyon to three consecutive French league titles and a quarter-final of the Champions League, Rangers fans will be hoping he can restore their domestic dominance and build on the European credibility gained in Alex McLeish's final season.

27

The Future

For European Cup pioneers like Eric Caldow and Harold Davis, football has changed out of all recognition since they played their first matches against Continental opposition fifty years ago. Today's big-money Champions League bears little relation to the competition they proudly took part in all those years ago. But the more things change, the more they stay the same. Five decades on, and Rangers are still suffering brave defeats on foreign soil. Managers and players are still complaining about the number of matches they have to play and commentators are still issuing doom-laden dispatches about the state of Scottish football. Capacity crowds still flock to Ibrox for big European nights and the atmosphere under the floodlights is still as special and unique as ever.

But there is no doubt that Rangers have underachieved in Europe over the years. Reaching just three finals in forty-five attempts has to be considered a poor return for a club of Rangers' standing. The fact that the last final appearance was more than thirty years ago underlines the fact. The lack of success has not been for the want of trying, though. The amount of money spent chasing the dream of a European trophy in the 1990s under Walter Smith and Dick Advocaat put the club in severe financial difficulty and ironically made the likelihood of future success even more unlikely.

It is difficult to identify the reason for the underachievement. There is no doubt that the desire has always been there. From the very outset, the Rangers players, management and directors have always made it very clear that they craved success in Europe but, for one reason or another, successive generations have fallen short. Bad luck played its part; in their first decade Rangers were unfortunate to be drawn against quality teams from Europe's big five of France, Italy, Spain, West Germany and England. Had the hand of fate dealt them more favourable draws, especially in the early rounds, perhaps they would have done better.

There is no doubt, though, that Rangers were ill-prepared for taking on more tactically astute opponents from overseas. There was a naivety, perhaps even arrogance, in the approach to those early games. But even in the first match against Nice it was obvious that their traditional Scottish style was rapidly becoming outdated. As defender Harold Davis put it: 'Our tactics were a bit behind the times; we were plodding a wee bit.' Arguably their biggest downfall was the lack of guile and craft in attack. The cavalry charge upfield may have worked in the domestic game, but such a tactic was rarely successful in Europe. As long ago as 1964, Ralph Brand identified the nature of the problem: 'It is one of the most difficult situations in football to find yourself suddenly faced with a wall of defenders who simply will not venture upfield and leave you the tiniest chink to get through,' he argued. 'It has been our inability to beat this kind of defence which has led to our failure in the European Cup.'

As well as lacking the subtlety to break down packed defences, the gung-ho approach also left Rangers open to the sucker punch. The last fifty years have seen Rangers consistently concede crucial goals on the counter-attack, suggesting they failed to learn the lessons of the past.

A critical assessment of Rangers' performances in Europe over the last fifty years would conclude that there have been maybe five seasons that are worthy of praise. In addition to the 1972 Cup Winners Cup victory, seasons 1960/61 and 1966/67 could be considered a success, as Rangers reached the final of the same competition. In 1978/79, John Greig's team knocked out two of the finest outfits in Europe before losing narrowly to the West German champions, while the Champions League run of 1992/93 was the equivalent of reaching the semi-final, a remarkable achievement in the modern era. Reaching the last sixteen in 2006 should not be underestimated, but it should not be forgotten that clubs like PSV, Monaco, Porto, Villarreal and Lyon have all gone further in recent seasons.

There have been several humiliations along the way too. Normally, reaching the semi-final of the European Cup would be considered an achievement to savour but the 12–3 aggregate defeat by Eintracht Frankfurt in 1960 soured that experience. A 6–0 loss to Real Madrid was an embarrassment, as were the comprehensive home-and-away defeats to Gornik Zabrze at the end of the decade. The 1970s saw Rangers well beaten by teams like FC Zurich and Twente Enschede while the eighties were scarred by heavy losses to Cologne, Dukla Prague and Bayern Munich. Sparta Prague, Levski Sofia,

AEK Athens and Strasbourg all inflicted crushing defeats in the nineties while the Champions League campaigns of 1995 and 1996 were abject failures. Under Alex McLeish, unknown Czechs Viktoria Zizkov knocked Rangers out of the UEFA Cup, while home defeats to Panathinaikos (Champions League 2003) and Auxerre (UEFA Cup 2005) dumped them out of Europe before Christmas.

Perhaps it is not as bad as it seems, though. An unofficial European club table compiled for the respected football-statistics website **www.rsssf.com** places Rangers in thirteenth position in the all-time ranking for European tournaments up until the end of the 2005/06 season. Barcelona and Real Madrid are at the top of the table and most of the teams above Rangers are from Europe's elite. Celtic are four places behind their Glasgow rivals.

And regardless of the results, the Rangers fans have been privileged to see some of the world's greatest players. The list is too long to name them all, but how about this for an all-time eleven:

1. Sepp Maier: Bayern Munich/Germany
2. Lilian Thuram: Parma/France
3. Antonio Cabrini: Juventus/Italy
4. Franz Beckenbauer: Bayern Munich/Germany
5. Franco Baresi: Inter Milan/Italy
6. Billy Bremner: Leeds United/Scotland
7. Ronaldinho: Paris St Germain/Brazil
8. Johan Cruyff: Ajax/Holland
9. Gerd Muller: Bayern Munich/Germany
10. Alfredo Di Stefano: Real Madrid/Spain
11. Ferenc Puskas: Real Madrid/Hungary

The substitutes wouldn't be too bad either. Dino Zoff: Juventus/ Italy; Karl-Heinze Rummenigge: Inter Milan/Germany; Alessandro Del Piero: Juventus/Italy; Didier Deschamps: Juventus/Marseille/ France; Gaizka Mendieta: Valencia/Spain; Kurt Hamrin: Fiorentina/ Sweden; Eric Cantona: Leeds United/France

These days it almost seems that the players on the pitch are the least important part of the European football experience. At the start of every campaign, there is a huge amount of focus on the monetary benefits a good European run can bring and conversely the financial implications of an early exit.

The money generated by the Champions League when it was introduced in the early nineties increased the pressure to succeed. Ironically, Rangers were key players in the formation of the new group format, attracted to the guarantee of six money-spinning matches and the elimination of the unpredictability of knockout competition. Unfortunately, Rangers have found themselves victims of the new format. With the threat of a breakaway super league always hanging over UEFA, the clubs in Europe's most powerful nations were in the position of being able to demand changes in the competition to preserve their own interests.

The G14 group of clubs, featuring giants of the game like AC Milan, Juventus, Real Madrid, Manchester United and Bayern Munich, are the true powerbrokers in European football and it is no coincidence that every winner of the European Champions Cup since 1992 has been a member of this grouping. Even Porto and Ajax, the last winners from 'smaller' countries, are members. Not since Red Star Belgrade lifted the trophy in 1991 has there been a winner from outside the traditional power base. These facts highlight the difficulty teams like Rangers face when they enter the Champions League. Clubs from the big countries already pocket far more cash from domestic television deals, so are at an immediate advantage when they compete in the Champions League. This means they are all the more likely to progress in the competition, in turn boosting their finances yet further. The more the cycle repeats, the less likely it is that clubs from mid-ranking countries like Scotland, Belgium, Turkey and Greece can compete.

It seems unlikely that this situation will change in the foreseeable future. A restructuring of the European Cup to provide a level-playing field is never going to happen, as the G14 clubs will not allow anything to interfere with their ability to raise the maximum amount of money. In fact the big clubs want more games inserted into the Champions League group stages to ensure they maximise their earnings on the off chance that they lose. The G14 wants the rewards without the messiness of having to actually win. It seems the antithesis of the spirit that saw the competition created more than fifty years ago. This is no meritocracy: Liverpool have not won the English domestic championship since 1990; Inter Milan last won *Serie* A in 1989; Paris Saint Germain have won one league title in twenty years; Bayer Leverkusen have never won the *Bundesliga*. For all their talk of promoting sport, UEFA have shown no desire to challenge this self-preservation society, and in fact have gone out of their way to placate its members.

Equally, UEFA are vehemently opposed to the sort of cross-border initiatives that could give Rangers and Celtic access to the television money their Continental rivals enjoy and at least give them the chance to compete on something approaching a level playing field. The Old Firm have been warned off their attempts to join both the Premiership in England and a proposed Atlantic League (which would have featured teams from Scotland, Holland, Belgium and Portugal).

The best hope of European glory for teams outwith the G14 now lies with the UEFA Cup. Winners in the last ten years have included Sevilla, CSKA Moscow, Valencia, Galatasaray and Schalke 04, none of whom come from the top rank of European clubs. Celtic, Alaves and Casino Salzburg have shown in recent years that it is possible for teams with limited resources to reach the final of that competition. But such is the emphasis on the Champions League that the UEFA Cup is very much the second-best option. The fact is that few people outside their own support would be able to name the winners of the competition in any given year, let alone the runners-up.

While David Murray has attempted to play down hopes that Rangers could one day win another European trophy, the dream lives on for the fans. Paul Le Guen declared at his first press conference in June 2006 that his priority was to win the league in his first season. But there is no doubt that European success will have been high on the agenda when he was being courted by David Murray and supporters will be hoping that he can replicate the success he enjoyed with Lyon in the Champions League.

For all the disappointments that have come their way over the last fifty years, there seems to be an insatiable appetite for European football among the Rangers supporters. Ibrox continues to sell out for every match, regardless of the opposition, and hundreds of thousands have followed Rangers all over the Continent. From the most obscure outposts of the former Soviet Union, to Newcastle, just a few miles over the English border, wherever Rangers have played, fans have gone with them. Even when they went to Dublin. No matter whether Rangers ever manage to lift another European trophy, it seems certain they will continue to Follow On.

Appendix

1956/57 EUROPEAN CUP

FIRST ROUND

24 Oct 56	Rangers 2 OGC Nice 1
14 Nov 56	OGC Nice 2 Rangers 1 (agg 3–3)
28 Nov 56	Play-off (Paris) Rangers 1 OGC Nice 3

1957/58 EUROPEAN CUP

FIRST ROUND

4 Sep 57	Rangers 3 St Etienne 1
25 Sep 57	St Etienne 2 Rangers 1 (agg 4–3)

SECOND ROUND

27 Nov 57	Rangers 1 AC Milan 4
11 Dec 57	AC Milan 2 Rangers 0 (agg 1–6)

1959/60 EUROPEAN CUP

PRELIM ROUND

16 Sep 59	Rangers 5 Anderlecht 2
23 Sep 59	Anderlecht 0 Rangers 2 (agg 7–2)

FIRST ROUND

11 Nov 59	Rangers 4 Red Star Bratislava 3
18 Nov 59	Red Star Bratislava 1 Rangers 1 (agg 5–4)

SECOND ROUND

9 Mar 60	Sparta Rotterdam 2 Rangers 3
16 Mar 60	Rangers 0 Sparta Rotterdam 1 (agg 3–3)
30 Mar 60	Play-off (Highbury) Rangers 3 Sparta Rotterdam 2

SEMI-FINAL

13 Apr 60	Eintracht Frankfurt 6 Rangers 1
5 May 1960	Rangers 3 Eintracht Frankfurt 6 (agg 4–12)

1960/61 EUROPEAN CUP WINNERS CUP

QUALIFYING ROUND
28 Sep 60   Rangers 4 Ferencvaros 2
12 Oct 60   Ferencvaros 2 Rangers 1 (agg 5–4)

QUARTER-FINAL
15 Nov 60   Borussia Moenchengladbach 0 Rangers 3
30 Nov 60   Rangers 8 Borussia Moenchengladbach 0 (agg 11–0)

SEMI-FINAL
29 Mar 61   Rangers 2 Wolverhampton Wanderers 0
19 Apr 61   Wolverhampton Wanderers 1 Rangers 1 (agg 3–1)

FINAL
17 May 61   Rangers 0 Fiorentina 2
27 May 61   Fiorentina 2 Rangers 1 (agg 1–4)

1961/62 EUROPEAN CUP

PRELIMINARY ROUND
5 Sep 61   Monaco 2 Rangers 3
12 Sep 61   Rangers 3 Monaco 2 (agg 6–4)

FIRST ROUND
15 Nov 61   ASK Vorwaerts 1 Rangers 2
23 Nov 61   (Played in Malmo, Sweden) Rangers 4 ASK Vorwaerts 1
               (agg 6–2)

QUARTER-FINAL
7 Feb 62   Standard Liege 4 Rangers 1
14 Feb 62   Rangers 2 Standard Liege 0 (agg 3–4)

1962/63 EUROPEAN CUP WINNERS CUP

FIRST ROUND
5 Sep 62   Rangers 4 Sevilla 0
26 Sep 62   Sevilla 2 Rangers 0 (agg 4–2)

SECOND ROUND

31 Oct 62   Tottenham Hotspur 5 Rangers 2

11 Dec 62   Rangers 2 Tottenham Hotspur 3 (agg 4–8)

1963/64 EUROPEAN CUP

25 Sep 63   Rangers 0 Real Madrid 1

9 Oct 63   Real Madrid 6 Rangers 0 (agg 0–7)

1964/65 EUROPEAN CUP

FIRST ROUND

2 Sep 64   Rangers 3 Red Star Belgrade 1

9 Sep 64   Red Star Belgrade 4 Rangers 2 (agg 5–5)

4 Nov 64   Play-off (Highbury)Rangers 3 Red Star Belgrade 1

SECOND ROUND

18 Nov 64   Rangers 1 Rapid Vienna 0

8 Dec 64   Rapid Vienna 0 Rangers 2 (agg 3–0)

QUARTER-FINAL

17 Feb 65   Internazionale 3 Rangers 1

3 Mar 65   Rangers 1 Internazionale 0   (agg 2–3)

1966/67 EUROPEAN CUP WINNERS CUP

FIRST ROUND

27 Sep 66   Glentoran 1 Rangers 1

5 Oct 66   Rangers 4 Glentoran 0 (agg 5–1)

SECOND ROUND

23 Nov 66   Rangers 2 Borussia Dortmund 1

6 Dec 66   Borussia Dortmund 0 Rangers 0 (agg 2–1)

QUARTER-FINAL

1 Mar 67   Rangers 2 Real Zaragoza 0

22 Mar 67   Real Zaragoza 2 Rangers 0 (aet)
               (agg 2–2 Rangers win on toss of coin)

SEMI-FINAL

19 April 67   Slavia Sofia 0 Rangers 1

3 May 67   Rangers 1 Slavia Sofia 0 (agg 2–0)

FINAL (Nuremberg)

31 May 67   Rangers 0 Bayern Munich 1(aet)

1967/68 INTER CITIES FAIRS CUP

FIRST ROUND

20 Sep 67   Dynamo Dresden 1 Rangers 1

4 Oct 67   Rangers 2 Dynamo Dresden 1 (agg 3–2)

SECOND ROUND

8 Nov 67   Rangers 3 Cologne 0

28 Nov 67   Cologne 3 Rangers 1 (aet) (agg 4–3)

QUARTER-FINAL (Rangers got a bye in the third round)

26 Mar 68   Rangers 0 Leeds 0

9 April 68   Leeds 2 Rangers 0 (agg 0–2)

1968/69 INTER CITIES FAIRS CUP

FIRST ROUND

18 Sep 68   Rangers 2 Vojvodina 0

2 Oct 68   Vojvodina 1 Rangers 0 (agg 2–1)

SECOND ROUND

30 Oct 68   Rangers 6 Dundalk 1

13 Nov 68   Dundalk 0 Rangers 3 (agg 9–1)

THIRD ROUND

15 Jan 69   DWS Amsterdam 0 Rangers 2

22 Jan 69   Rangers 2 DWS Amsterdam 1 (agg 4–1)

QUARTER-FINAL

19 Mar 69   Rangers 4 Athletic Bilbao 1

2 Apr 69   Athletic Bilbao 2 Rangers 0 (agg 4–3)

SEMI-FINAL

14 May 69	Rangers 0 Newcastle United 0
21 May 69	Newcastle United 2 Rangers 0 (agg 0–2)

1969/70 EUROPEAN CUP WINNERS CUP

FIRST ROUND

17 Sep 69	Rangers 2 Steaua Bucharest 0
1 Oct 69	Steaua Bucharest 0 Rangers 0 (agg 2–0)

SECOND ROUND

12 Nov 69	Gornik Zabrze 3 Rangers 1
26 Nov 69	Rangers 1 Gornik Zabrze 3 (agg 2–6)

1970/71 INTER CITIES FAIRS CUP

FIRST ROUND

16 Sep 70	Bayern Munich 1 Rangers 0
30 Sep 70	Rangers 1 Bayern Munich 1 (agg 1–2)

1971/72 EUROPEAN CUP WINNERS CUP

FIRST ROUND

15 Sep 71	Rennes 1 Rangers 1
28 Sep 71	Rangers 1 Rennes 0 (agg 2–1)

SECOND ROUND

20 Oct 71	Rangers 3 Sporting Lisbon 2
3 Nov 71	Sporting Lisbon 4 Rangers 3 (aet) (agg 6–6, Rangers win on away goals)

QUARTER-FINAL

8 Mar 72	Torino 1 Rangers 1
22 Mar 72	Rangers 1 Torino 0 (agg 2–1)

SEMI-FINAL

5 Apr 72	Bayern Munich 1 Rangers 1
19 Apr 72	Rangers 2 Bayern 0 (agg 3–1)

FINAL (Barcelona)

24 May 72   Rangers 3 Dynamo Moscow 2

1973/74 EUROPEAN CUP WINNERS CUP

FIRST ROUND

19 Sep 73   Ankaragucu 0 Rangers 2

3 Oct 73   Rangers 4 Ankaragucu 0   (agg 6–0)

SECOND ROUND

24 Oct 73   Borussia Moenchengladbach 3 Rangers 0

7 Nov 73   Rangers 3 Borussia Moenchengladbach 2   (agg 3–5)

1975/76 EUROPEAN CUP

FIRST ROUND

17 Sep 75   Rangers 4 Bohemians 1

1 Oct 75   Bohemians 1 Rangers 1   (agg 5–2)

SECOND ROUND

22 Oct 75   St Etienne 2 Rangers 0

5 Nov 75   Rangers 1 St Etienne 2   (agg 1–4)

1976/77 EUROPEAN CUP

FIRST ROUND

15 Sep 76   Rangers 1 FC Zurich 1

29 Sep 76   FC Zurich 1 Rangers 0   (agg 1–2)

1977/78 EUROPEAN CUP WINNERS CUP

PRELIM ROUND

17 Aug 77   Rangers 1 Young Boys Berne 0

31 Aug 77   Young Boys Berne 2 Rangers 2   (agg 3–2)

FIRST ROUND

14 Sep 77   Rangers 0 Twente Enschede 0

28 Sep 77   Twente Enschede 3 Rangers 0   (agg 0–3)

1978/79 EUROPEAN CUP

FIRST ROUND
13 Sep 78   Juventus 1 Rangers 0
27 Sep 78   Rangers 2 Juventus 0   (agg 2–1)

SECOND ROUND
18 Oct 78   Rangers 0 PSV Eindhoven 0
1 Nov 78   PSV Eindhoven 2 Rangers 3   (agg 3–2)

QUARTER-FINAL
6 Mar 79   Cologne 1 Rangers 0
21 Mar 79   Rangers 1 Cologne 1   (agg 1–2)

1979/80 EUROPEAN CUP WINNERS CUP

PRELIM ROUND
21 Aug 79   Rangers 1 Lillestrom 0
5 Sep 79   Lillestrom 0 Rangers 2   (agg 3–0)

FIRST ROUND
19 Sep 79   Rangers 2 Fortuna Dusseldorf 1
3 Oct 79   Fortuna Dusseldorf 0 Rangers 0   (agg 2–1)

SECOND ROUND
24 Oct 79   Valencia 1 Rangers 1
7 Nov 79   Rangers 1 Valencia 3 (agg 2–4)

1981/82 EUROPEAN CUP WINNERS CUP

FIRST ROUND
16 Sep 81   Dukla Prague 3 Rangers 0
30 Sep 81   Rangers 2 Dukla Prague 1   (agg 2–4)

1982/83 UEFA CUP

FIRST ROUND
15 Sep 82   Borussia Dortmund 0 Rangers 0
29 Sep 82   Rangers 2 Borussia Dortmund 0   (agg 2–0)

SECOND ROUND
20 Oct 82   Rangers 2 Cologne 1
3 Nov 82   Cologne 5 Rangers 0   (agg 2–6)

1983/84 EUROPEAN CUP WINNERS CUP

FIRST ROUND
14 Sep 83   Valetta 0 Rangers 8
28 Sep 83   Rangers 10 Valetta 0   (agg 18–0)

SECOND ROUND
19 Oct 83   Rangers 2 Porto 1
2 Nov 83   Porto 1 Rangers 0
                 (agg 2–2, Porto win on away goals)

1984/85 UEFA CUP

FIRST ROUND
18 Sep 84   Bohemians 3 Rangers 2
3 Oct 84   Rangers 2 Bohemians 0   (agg 4–3)

SECOND ROUND
24 Oct 84   Internazionale 3 Rangers 0
7 Nov 84   Rangers 3 Internazionale 1   (agg 3–4)

1985/86 UEFA CUP

FIRST ROUND
18 Sep 85   Rangers 1 Club Atletico Osasuna 0
2 Oct 85   Club Atletico Osasuna 2 Rangers 0   (agg 1–2)

1986/87 UEFA CUP

FIRST ROUND
17 Sep 86   Rangers 4 Ilves Tampere 0
1 Oct 86   Ilves Tampere 2 Rangers 0   (agg 4–2)

SECOND ROUND

23 Oct 86	Rangers 2 Boavista 1
4 Nov 86	Boavista 0 Rangers 1 (agg 3–1)

THIRD ROUND

26 Nov 86	Rangers 1 Borussia Moenchengladbach 1
10 Dec 86	Borussia Moenchengladbach 0 Rangers 0
	(agg 1–1, Borussia win on away goals)

1987/88 EUROPEAN CUP

FIRST ROUND

16 Sep 87	Dynamo Kiev 1 Rangers 0
30 Sep 87	Rangers 2 Dynamo Kiev 0 (agg 2–1)

SECOND ROUND

21 Oct 87	Rangers 3 Gornik Zabrze 1
4 Nov 87	Gornik Zabrze 1 Rangers 1 (agg 4–2)

QUARTER-FINAL

2 Mar 88	Steaua Bucharest 2 Rangers 0
16 Mar 88	Rangers 2 Steaua Bucharest 1
	(agg 2–3)

1988/89 UEFA CUP

FIRST ROUND

7 Sep 88	Rangers 1 Katowice 0
5 Oct 88	Katowice 2 Rangers 4 (agg 5–2)

SECOND ROUND

26 Oct 88	Cologne 2 Rangers 0
9 Nov 88	Rangers 1 Cologne 1 (agg 1–3)

1989/90 EUROPEAN CUP

FIRST ROUND

13 Sep 89	Rangers 1 Bayern Munich 3
27 Sep 89	Bayern Munich 0 Rangers 0 (agg 1–3)

1990/91 EUROPEAN CUP

FIRST ROUND

18 Sep 90	Valetta 0 Rangers 4
2 Oct 90	Rangers 6 Valetta 0 (agg 10–0)

SECOND ROUND

24 Oct 90	Red Star Belgrade 3 Rangers 0
7 Nov 90	Rangers 1 Red Star Belgrade 1 (agg 1–4)

1991/92 EUROPEAN CUP

FIRST ROUND

18 Sep 91	Sparta Prague 1 Rangers 0
2 Oct 91	Rangers 2 Sparta Prague 1 (aet)
	(agg 2–2, Sparta win on away goals)

1992/93 CHAMPIONS LEAGUE

FIRST QUAL ROUND

16 Sep 92	Rangers 2 Lyngby 0
30 Sep 92	Lyngby 0 Rangers 1 (agg 3–0)

SECOND QUAL ROUND

21 Oct 92	Rangers 2 Leeds United 1
4 Nov 92	Leeds United 1 Rangers 2 (agg 4–2)

GROUP A

25 Nov 92	Rangers 2 Marseille 2
9 Dec 92	CSKA Moscow 0 Rangers 1
	(played in Bochum, Germany)
3 Mar 93	Club Brugge 1 Rangers 1
17 Mar 93	Rangers 2 Club Brugge 1
7 Apr 93	Marseille 1 Rangers 1
21 Apr 93	Rangers 0 CSKA Moscow 0

	P	W	D	L	F	A	Pts
Marseille	6	3	3	0	14	4	9
Rangers	6	2	4	0	7	5	8
Club Brugge	6	2	1	3	5	8	5
CSKA Moscow	6	0	2	4	2	11	2

1993/94 CHAMPIONS LEAGUE

QUAL ROUND

15 Sep 93   Rangers 3 Levski Sofia 2
29 Sep 93   Levski Sofia 2 Rangers 1
               (agg 4–4, Levski win on away goals)

1994/95 CHAMPIONS LEAGUE

QUAL ROUND

10 Aug 94   AEK Athens 2 Rangers 0
24 Aug 94   Rangers 0 AEK Athens 1   (agg 0–3)

1995/96 CHAMPIONS LEAGUE

QUAL ROUND

9 Aug 95   Rangers 1 Anorthosis Famagusta 0
23 Aug 95   Anorthosis Famagusta 0 Rangers 0   (agg 1–0)

GROUP C

13 Sep 95   Steaua Bucharest 1 Rangers 0
27 Sep 95   Rangers 2 Borussia Dortmund 2
18 Oct 95   Juventus 4 Rangers 1
1 Nov 95   Rangers 0 Juventus 4
22 Nov 95   Rangers 1 Steaua Bucharest 1
6 Dec 95   Borussia Dortmund 2 Rangers 2

	P	W	D	L	F	A	Pts
Juventus	6	4	1	1	15	4	13
Borussia Dortmund	6	2	3	1	8	8	9
Steaua Bucharest	6	1	3	2	2	5	6
Rangers	6	0	3	3	6	14	3

1996/97 CHAMPIONS LEAGUE

QUAL ROUND
7 Aug 96   Rangers 3 Alania Vladikavkaz 1
21 Aug 96   Alania Vladikavkaz 2 Rangers 7 (agg 10–3)

GROUP A
11 Sep 96   Grasshoppers Zurich 3 Rangers 0
25 Sep 96   Rangers 1 Auxerre 2
16 Oct 96   Ajax 4 Rangers 1
30 Oct 96   Rangers 0 Ajax 1
20 Nov 96   Rangers 2 Grasshoppers Zurich 1
4 Dec 96   Auxerre 2 Rangers 1

	P	W	D	L	F	A	Pts
Auxerre	6	4	0	2	8	7	12
Ajax	6	4	0	2	8	4	12
Grasshoppers Zurich	6	3	0	3	8	5	9
Rangers	6	1	0	5	5	13	3

1997/98 CHAMPIONS LEAGUE

FIRST QUAL ROUND
23 Jul 97   Gotu 0 Rangers 5
30 Jul 97   Rangers 6 Gotu 0 (agg 11–0)

SECOND QUAL ROUND
13 Aug 97   IFK Gothenburg 3 Rangers 0
27 Aug 97   Rangers 1 IFK Gothenburg 1 (agg 1–4)

UEFA CUP

FIRST ROUND
16 Sep 97   Strasbourg 2 Rangers 1
30 Sep 97   Rangers 1 Strasbourg 2   (agg 2–4)

1998/99 UEFA CUP

FIRST QUAL ROUND
22 Jul 98   Shelbourne 3 Rangers 5 (played at Prenton Park, Tranmere)
29 Jul 98   Rangers 2 Shelbourne 0   (agg 7–3)

SECOND QUAL ROUND
11 Aug 98   Rangers 2 PAOK Salonika 0
25 Aug 98   PAOK Salonika 0 Rangers 0   (agg 2–0)

FIRST ROUND
15 Sep 98   Beitar Jerusalem 1 Rangers 1
1 Oct 98   Rangers 4 Beitar Jerusalem 2   (agg 5–3)

SECOND ROUND
22 Oct 98   Bayer Leverkusen 1 Rangers 2
5 Nov 98   Rangers 1 Bayer Leverkusen 1   (agg 3–2)

THIRD ROUND
24 Nov 98   Rangers 1 Parma 1
8 Dec 98   Parma 3 Rangers 1   (agg 2–4)

1999/00 CHAMPIONS LEAGUE

SECOND QUAL ROUND
28 Jul 99   Haka 1 Rangers 4
4 Aug 99   Rangers 3 Haka 0   (agg 7–1)

THIRD QUAL ROUND
11 Aug 99   Rangers 2 Parma 0
25 Aug 99   Parma 1 Rangers 0   (agg 2–1)

GROUP F

15 Sep 99	Valencia 2 Rangers 0
21 Sep 99	Rangers 1 Bayern Munich 1
28 Sep 99	PSV Eindhoven 0 Rangers 1
20 Oct 99	Rangers 4 PSV Eindhoven 1
26 Oct 99	Rangers 1 Valencia 2
3 Nov 99	Bayern Munich 1 Rangers 0

	P	W	D	L	F	A	Pts
Valencia	6	3	3	0	8	4	12
Bayern Munich	6	2	3	1	7	6	9
Rangers	6	2	1	3	7	7	7
PSV Eindhoven	6	1	1	4	5	10	4

UEFA CUP

THIRD ROUND

25 Nov 99	Rangers 2 Borussia Dortmund 0
7 Dec 99	Borussia Dortmund 2 Rangers 0 (aet)
	(agg 2–2, Dortmund win on penalties)

2000/01 CHAMPIONS LEAGUE

SECOND QUAL ROUND

| 26 Jul 00 | Rangers 4 Zalgiris Kaunas 1 |
| 2 Aug 00 | Zalgiris Kaunas 0 Rangers 0   (agg 4–1) |

THIRD QUAL ROUND

| 9 Aug 00 | Herfolge 0 Rangers 3 |
| 23 Aug 00 | Rangers 3 Herfolge 0   (agg 6–0) |

GROUP D

12 Sep 00	Rangers 5 Sturm Graz 0
20 Sep 00	Monaco 0 Rangers 1
27 Sep 00	Galatasaray 3 Rangers 2
17 Oct 00	Rangers 0 Galatasaray 0
25 Oct 00	Sturm Graz 2 Rangers 0
7 Nov 00	Rangers 2 Monaco 2

	P	W	D	L	F	A	Pts
Sturm Graz	6	3	1	2	9	12	10
Galatasaray	6	2	2	2	10	13	8
Rangers	6	2	2	2	10	7	8
AS Monaco	6	2	1	3	13	10	7

UEFA CUP

THIRD ROUND

30 Nov 00   Rangers 1 Kaiserslautern 0

7 Dec 00   Kaiserslautern 3 Rangers 0   (agg 1–3)

2001/02 CHAMPIONS LEAGUE

SECOND QUAL ROUND

25 Jul 01   NK Maribor 0 Rangers 3

1 Aug 01   Rangers 3 NK Maribor 1   (agg 6–1)

THIRD QUAL ROUND

8 Aug 01   Rangers 0 Fenerbahce 0

22 Aug 01   Fenerbahce 2 Rangers 1   (agg 1–2)

UEFA CUP

FIRST ROUND

27 Sep 01   (at Warsaw in Poland)

               Anzhi Makhachkala 0 Rangers 1   (one-off tie)

SECOND ROUND

18 Oct 01   Rangers 3 Dynamo Moscow 1

1 Nov 01   Dynamo Moscow 1 Rangers 4   (agg 7–2)

THIRD ROUND

22 Nov 01   Rangers 0 Paris St Germain 0

6 Dec 01   Paris St Germain 0 Rangers 0 (aet)
               (agg 0–0, Rangers win on penalties)

FOURTH ROUND

21 Feb 02   Rangers 1 Feyenoord 1

28 Feb 02   Feyenoord 3 Rangers 2   (agg 3–4)

2002/03 UEFA CUP

FIRST ROUND

17 Sep 02   Viktoria Zizkov 2 Rangers 0

3 Oct 02   Rangers 3 Viktoria Zizkov 1   (aet)
                 (agg 3–3, Viktoria win on away goals)

2003/04 CHAMPIONS LEAGUE

THIRD QUAL ROUND

13 Aug 03   Rangers 1 FC Copenhagen 1

27 Aug 03   FC Copenhagen 1 Rangers 2   (agg 3–2)

GROUP E

16 Sep 03   Rangers 2 Vfb Stuttgart 1

1 Oct 03   Panathinaikos 1 Rangers 1

22 Oct 03   Rangers 0 Manchester United 1

4 Nov 03   Manchester United 3 Rangers 0

26 Nov 03   Vfb Stuttgart 1 Rangers 0

9 Dec 03   Rangers 1 Panathinaikos 3

	P	W	D	L	F	A	Pts
Manchester United	6	5	0	1	13	2	15
VfB Stuttgart	6	4	0	2	9	6	12
Panathinaikos	6	1	1	4	5	13	4
Rangers	6	1	1	4	4	10	4

2004/05 CHAMPIONS LEAGUE

THIRD QUAL ROUND

10 Aug 04   CSKA Moscow 2 Rangers 1

25 Aug 04   Rangers 1 CSKA Moscow 1   (agg 2–3)

UEFA CUP

FIRST ROUND

16 Sep 04	Maritimo 1 Rangers 0
30 Sep 04	Rangers 1 Maritimo 0 (aet)
	(agg 1–1, Rangers win on penalties)

GROUP F

21 Oct 04	Amica Wronki 0 Rangers 5
25 Nov 04	Rangers 3 Grazer AK 0
2 Dec 04	AZ Alkmaar 1 Rangers 0
15 Dec 04	Rangers 0 Auxerre 2

	P	W	D	L	F	A	Pts
AZ Alkmaar	4	3	0	1	6	3	9
Auxerre	4	2	1	1	7	3	7
Grazer AK	4	2	1	1	5	4	7
Rangers	4	2	0	2	8	3	6
Amica Wronki	4	0	0	4	3	16	0

2005/06 CHAMPIONS LEAGUE

THIRD QUAL ROUND

| 9 Aug 05 | Anorthosis Famagusta 1 Rangers 2 |
| 24 Aug 05 | Rangers 2 Anorthosis Famagusta 0 (agg 4–1) |

GROUP H

13 Sep 05	Rangers 3 Porto 2
28 Sep 05	Internazionale 1 Rangers 0
19 Oct 05	Rangers 0 Artmedia Bratislava 0
1 Nov 05	Artmedia Bratislava 2 Rangers 2
23 Nov 05	Porto 1 Rangers 1
6 Dec 05	Rangers 1 Internazionale 1

	P	W	D	L	F	A	Pts
Internazionale	6	4	1	1	9	4	13
Rangers	6	1	4	1	7	7	7
Artmedia Bratislava	6	1	3	2	5	9	6
FC Porto	6	1	2	3	8	9	5

SECOND ROUND

22 Feb 06	Rangers 2 Villarreal 2
7 Mar 06	Villarreal 1 Rangers 1
	(agg 3–3, Villarreal win on away goals)

Overall Record in European Competition

Pld	W	D	L	F	A	Pts
258	115	57	86	412	323	404

Average scored: 1.59
Average conceded: 1.25

Home games

Pld	W	D	L	F	A	Pts
126	77	30	18	256	117	261

Average scored: 2.03
Average conceded: 0.93

Away games

Pld	W	D	L	F	A	Pts
126	34	27	64	145	197	129

Average scored: 1.15
Average conceded: 1.56

Games at Neutral Stadiums

Pld	W	D	L	F	A	Pts
6	4	0	2	11	9	12

Most-Played Opponents

	P	W	D	L
Bayern Munich	9	1	4	4
Borussia Dortmund	8	3	4	1
Cologne	8	2	2	4
Borussia Moenchengladbach	6	3	2	1
Internazionale	6	2	1	3
Steaua Bucharest	6	2	2	2
Red Star Belgrade	5	2	1	2

Record by Country

	P	W	D	L
Germany (total)	**45**	**16**	**15**	**14**
- Germany (unified)	12	4	4	4
- West Germany	29	9	10	10
- East Germany	4	3	1	0
France	22	6	6	10
Italy	20	5	3	12
Holland	16	7	3	6
Spain	16	4	3	9
England	12	4	2	6
USSR/Russia/CIS (total)	**12**	**8**	**2**	**2**
- USSR	3	2	0	1
- Russia	7	5	1	1
- CIS	2	1	1	0
Portugal	10	6	1	3
Czech Republic/Czechoslovakia	8	4	1	3
Republic of Ireland	8	6	1	1
Poland	7	4	1	2
Yugoslavia	7	3	0	4
Belgium	6	4	1	1
Denmark	6	5	1	0
Greece	6	1	2	3
Romania	6	2	2	2
Switzerland	6	2	2	2
Turkey	6	2	2	2
Austria	5	4	0	1
Bulgaria	4	3	0	1
Cyprus	4	3	1	0

	P	W	D	L
Finland	4	3	0	1
Malta	4	4	0	0
Faroe Islands	2	2	0	0
Hungary	2	1	0	1
Israel	2	1	1	0
Lithuania	2	1	1	0
Northern Ireland	2	1	1	0
Norway	2	2	0	0
Slovakia	2	0	2	0
Slovenia	2	2	0	0
Sweden	2	0	1	1

Record home victories

10–0 Valetta. 1983/84, European Cup Winners Cup
8–0 Borussia Moenchengladbach. 1960/61, European Cup Winners Cup

Record away victory

8–0 Valetta. 1983/84, European Cup Winners Cup

Record aggregate victories

18–0 Valetta. 1983/84, European Cup Winners Cup
11–0 Borussia Moenchengladbach. 1960/61, European Cup Winners Cup
11–0 GI Gotu. 1997/98, European Cup

Record home defeat (goals)

3–6 Eintracht Frankfurt. 1959/60, European Cup

Record home defeat (margin)

0–4 Juventus. 1994/95, Champions League

Record away defeat

0–6 Real Madrid. 1963/64, European Cup

Record aggregate defeat

4–12 Eintracht Frankfurt. 1959/60, European Cup

Leading Appearances in European Competitions

	Total	Start	Subs	Goals
Greig	62	62	0	7
Ferguson, B	56	55	1	3
McCoist	54	44	10	21
Jardine	50	48	2	2
Henderson, W	46	44	2	10
Klos	45	45	0	0
McKinnon, R	45	45	0	1
McCloy	41	41	0	0
Moore	41	40	1	1
Albertz	41	30	11	12
Amoruso	40	40	0	4
Johnston, W	40	40	0	8
Ferguson, Ian	39	32	7	3
Durrant	39	29	10	8
Ricksen	38	38	0	3
Cooper	38	35	3	1
Wilson, D	37	37	0	10
Gough	36	36	0	4
Jackson	36	36	0	1
MacDonald, A	36	35	1	8
Mols	36	28	8	7
Caldow	35	35	0	3
Smith, D	34	29	5	3
Johnstone, D	33	29	4	9
Goram	31	31	0	0
Millar	31	31	0	12
Numan	31	31	0	0
Ritchie	30	30	0	0
Shearer	30	30	0	0
Baxter	29	29	0	3
McPherson	29	29	0	7

Leading European Scorers

	Goals	Apps
McCoist	21	54
Albertz	12	41
Millar	12	31
Brand	12	24
Scott	11	28
Henderson, W	10	46
Wilson, D	10	37
Stein	10	25
Johnstone, D	9	33
Johnston, W	8	40
Durrant	8	39
MacDonald, A	8	36
Lovenkrands	8	31
Johansson	8	17
Greig	7	62
Mols	7	36
McPherson	7	29
Wallace	7	26
McMillan	7	22
Hateley	6	17
Forrest	6	11
Ferguson, A	6	9
Van Bronckhorst	5	28
Durie	5	25
De Boer, R	5	18
Baird	5	16
McDonald, J	5	9
Johnston, M	5	6